ces *for the*
Us! ®

...confused by computers? Do you find
...re overloaded with technical details
...d family always call you to
...en the For Dummies®
...lishing, Inc. is for you.

...who know they
...e unique vocabulary of
...earted approach,
...el computer novices'
...se books are a perfect

...oncise, nontechnical,
...morous."

...A., Elburn, Illinois

can sleep at night."
— *Robin F., British Columbia, Canada*

**Already, millions of satisfied readers agree. They have
made For Dummies books the #1 introductory level
computer book series and have written asking for more.
So, if you're looking for the most fun and easy way to
learn about computers, look to For Dummies books to
give you a helping hand.**

Wiley Publishing, Inc.

5/09

Dreamweaver® 4

FOR

DUMMIES®

Dreamweaver® 4 FOR DUMMIES®

by Janine Warner and Paul Vachier

Wiley Publishing, Inc.

Dreamweaver® 4 For Dummies®

Published by
Wiley Publishing, Inc.
909 Third Avenue
New York, NY 10022
www.wiley.com

Copyright © 2001 Wiley Publishing, Inc., Indianapolis, Indiana

Published simultaneously in Canada

For general information on our other products and services or to obtain technical support, please contact our Customer Care Department within the U.S. at 800-762-2974, outside the U.S. at 317-572-3993, or fax 317-572-4002.

Wiley also publishes its books in a variety of electronic formats. Some content that appears in print may not be available in electronic books.

Library of Congress Control Number: 00-110906

ISBN: 0-7645-0801-6

Manufactured in the United States of America

10 9 8 7 6 5 4

1O/RV/QZ/QS/IN

Dedication

I dedicate this book to all those who have kept the faith and are still coura-
geous enough to find creative ways to use this new media to transform the
world. — Janine Warner

About the Authors

Janine Warner is the Director of Latin American Operations for ZDNet (a CNET Networks company), where she manages a team of journalists, producers, and translators who develop technology content in Spanish and Portuguese.

A frequent speaker at events in the United States and abroad, Warner is the author of several books on Web design, including *Dreamweaver 4 For Dummies* and *eBusiness Web Strategies*, both published by IDG Books Worldwide, Inc. She is also a founding board member of the Miami Internet Alliance and a member of the board of Women in Technology International (WITI). In addition, she is a part-time faculty member at the University of Miami, where she teaches an evening course in the Communications Department.

In 1998, Janine became Online Managing Editor of *The Miami Herald,* and a year later was promoted to Director of Operations. During that time, she managed the team that produces all of *The Miami Herald* Web sites, including `Herald.com`, `Elherald.com`, and `Miami.com`. After leading the corporate separation in Miami to create `KnightRidder.com`, she became Director of Spanish Business Development and reviewed and negotiated partnership deals with a wide range of organizations, including Telefonica, La Opinion, and The Miami Internet Alliance.

From 1994 to 1998, Warner ran her own business, Visiontec Communications, a Web design company that worked on such diverse projects as the corporate intranet for Levi Strauss & Co., an extranet sales site for AirTouch International, e-commerce solutions for many small- and medium-sized businesses, and media sites for *Publish Magazine* and the Pulitzer prize–winning newspaper *The Point Reyes Light*.

An award-winning former reporter, Warner earned a degree in journalism and Spanish from the University of Massachusetts, Amherst, and worked for several years in Northern California as a reporter and editor. She speaks fluent Spanish.

E-mail: `editor@janinewarner.com`

Paul Vachier is a freelance artist, author, and Web developer based in Santa Fe, New Mexico. Originally working in print media, Paul made the transition to Web publishing in 1995 and has since worked for companies such as Salon, Levis, Symantec, GoLive Systems, Samsung, Hewlett Packard, @Home, Adobe and Macromedia. He has also taught classes in Web development at The Academy of Art College in San Francisco and the Multimedia Studies Program of San Francisco State University. In addition to coauthoring two editions of *Dreamweaver For Dummies* (IDG Books), he has also coauthored two other books relating to the Web and graphics, *Plug N Play JavaScript* (New Riders Publishing) and *Debabelizer: The Authorized Edition* (Hayden Books).

Paul earned his BA in Anthropology and History from Montclair State University and later did graduate work at the University of California, Los Angeles, before discovering computers. Nowadays he spends time "humanizing" the Web through a vibrant online community based in San Francisco called "NoEnd," which he helped found. While not sitting at the computer, he likes to hit the ski slopes of northern New Mexico and grow exotic cactus plants in his high desert home.

You can visit his Web site at `www.transmitmedia.com`.

Acknowledgments

With every book it gets harder to write my acknowledgments. It's not easy to come up with new and inventive ways to thank all of my parents or the growing list of other supportive people in my life who make it possible for me to write books in my spare time. But everyone listed here deserves credit for the fact that I actually finished another revision of this book, so here goes.

I believe that the first people I should thank are those who contribute directly to the writing and production of each book, for without them, there would be no acknowledgements page. So, I have to first thank my fabulous coauthor, Paul Vachier, who managed to buy a house, move across the country, and still write great chapters on deadline. Paul and I evenly split the work on this version of *Dreamweaver For Dummies,* and I can't imagine ever revising it again without him.

Next, I must thank my wonderful editorial team. Andrea Boucher, who is raising a small child (which is at least the equivalent of two full-time jobs) and still found the time to be a gracious and conscientious editor. Tom Heine, my new acquisitions editor also deserves credit for being able to hit the deck running when he stepped into Mike Roney's big shoes. And to all the rest of the IDG staff, especially the talented team who put together the CD for this book — you rock!

Second only to the editorial team, I must thank my wonderful parents. My talented mother, Malinda McCain, who is the best copy editor on the planet and has contributed to many of my other books, but was not able to participate in this project. Her wonderful partner Janice, who always makes me laugh and has inspired me to teach my first college course this Spring. My fabulous father, who is quite technically savvy himself and still finds time to plant trees in the orchard he has growing in his 80-acre back yard. Thanks, too, to my wonderful stepmother, Helen, who is one of the best cooks I've ever known and provides another reason to look forward to Christmas every year.

Other members of my family include my brother Brian, who has finally found his way to California, and my brother Kevin and sister-in-law Stephanie, who are raising the most beautiful baby in the world. Warm wishes to Uncle Tom and Aunt Mindy (www.crittur.com), and to John, Gail, Ian, and especially Kate. Thanks also to all of the "Davids," too numerous to mention, and our wonderful Grandma McCain who always makes us feel so welcome at the lake. Thanks also to my aunt Margaret, whose brilliant career has always inspired me, and whose guidance has helped shape my life.

I always like to thank my journalism professors from the University of Massachusetts, Amherst, Norm Sims, Howard Ziff, Karen List, and Matty Blaise, for teaching me the fundamentals of good journalism and encouraging to me to write and write and write.

Now I get to my friends, and brace yourselves because I have many wonderful friends. Thanks to all my California friends who continue to support me, even from afar. My dearest Ken doll (www.kenmilburn.com), who is so talented he can write two books at once and still create such beautiful artwork that I want to hang it in my new house. Thanks to Adriene for so many things over the years, including Ken's nickname. A hearty thanks to David Mitchell (www.ptreyeslight.com), one of the most important mentors of my life and a dear and special friend, and thanks to Kare Anderson (www.sayitbetter.com) for cross-consulting, both personally and professionally. I still miss our long walks in Northern California. To Terry and Yolanda: May your lives and marriage continue to be happy and healthy. To Bob (Bobbins) Coward (www.brainsville.com) for finding new ways to share his knowledge of computers with the world, and to Victor Reyes for always being there when I need someone to talk to in Spanish or English.

To my long-lost Boston friends, Cathy, Linda, David, Gail, Brian, Robbie, and so many others — I'll never forget how much I enjoyed dancing with you.

A fresh thanks to all my Miami friends, especially the KR.com crew members: Karla Haynes, Kim Marcille, Anabel Llopis, Adela Morales, Bert Franquiz, Gina Cardenas, Sofia Perrino, Claudia Gabarain, Teresa Frontado, Jeordan Legon, Humberto Franquiz, and so many others. Thanks to Francisco for always being so great to work with — all the best in your new endeavor. Thanks to Adriana Pena (www.cnet.com), for making me think so much about what's next in my life and for learning to SCUBA so we can go diving together. Thanks to Shari Whitkoff for making me laugh, even when she's cleaning my teeth, and to Oleg for all his great massages. Thanks to the boards of WITI and the Miami Internet Alliance for all they are doing to promote South Florida as the Internet Hub of the Americas and a place that is truly fabulous to work in. And, finally, a very special thanks to Fareed Al Mashat (www.mashat.com) for helping me appreciate that there is more to life than working all the time, and to Yuki for always being there when I need her. — Janine Warner

Publisher's Acknowledgments

We're proud of this book; please send us your comments through our online registration form located at www.dummies.com/register/.

Some of the people who helped bring this book to market include the following:

Acquisitions, Editorial, and Media Development

Project Editor: Andrea C. Boucher

(*Previous Edition: Jodi Jensen*)

Acquisitions Editor: Tom Heine

Technical Editor: Yolanda Burrell

Permissions Editor: Carmen Krikorian

Media Development Coordinator: Marisa Pearman

Freelance Editorial Manager: Constance Carlisle

Media Development Manager: Laura Carpenter

Media Development Supervisor: Richard Graves

Editorial Assistants: Amanda Foxworth, Jean Rogers

Production

Project Coordinator: Maridee Ennis

Layout and Graphics: Jackie Bennett, Brian Torwelle, Julie Trippetti, Jeremey Unger

Proofreaders: Laura Albert, David Faust, Sossity R. Smith

Indexer: York Production Services, Inc.

General and Administrative

Wiley Technology Publishing Group: Richard Swadley, Vice President and Executive Group Publisher; Bob Ipsen, Vice President and Group Publisher; Joseph Wikert, Vice President and Publisher; Barry Pruett, Vice President and Publisher; Mary Bednarek, Editorial Director; Mary C. Corder, Editorial Director; Andy Cummings, Editorial Director

Wiley Manufacturing: Carol Tobin, Director of Manufacturing

Wiley Marketing: John Helmus, Assistant Vice President, Director of Marketing

Wiley Composition Services: Gerry Fahey, Vice President, Production Services; Debbie Stailey, Director of Composition Services

Contents at a Glance

Cartoons at a Glance

By Rich Tennant

"Sometimes I feel behind the times. I asked my 11-year-old to build a Web site for my business, and he said he would, only after he finishes the one he's building for his ant farm."

page 9

"I have to say I'm really impressed with the interactivity on this car-wash Web site."

page 163

"Just how accurately should my Web site reflect my place of business?"

page 89

"Maybe it would help our Web site if we showed our products in action."

page 231

"Sales on the Web site are down. I figure the servers chi is blocked, so we're fudgin' around, the feng shui in the computer room, and if that doesn't work, Ronnie's got a chant that should do it."

page 349

"Give him air! Give him air! He'll be okay. He's just been exposed to some raw HTML code. It must have accidently flashed across his screen from the server."

page 327

Cartoon Information:
Fax: 978-546-7747
E-Mail: richtennant@the5thwave.com
World Wide Web: www.the5thwave.com

Table of Contents

Introduction

*I*f you're working on a Web site, you probably don't have time to wade through another thick book while you're racing against a tight deadline. Neither do any other Web designers I know. That's why I wrote this book — to serve as a quick reference. It's also why I choose Dreamweaver for all of my Web design work. Dreamweaver enables you to work faster and more efficiently. And *Dreamweaver 4 For Dummies* helps you get the most out of this comprehensive Web design program by making it easy and fast to find the answers you need.

Macromedia Dreamweaver has clearly emerged as the top Web design program on the market for anyone serious about Web design work. Its ease of use and high-end features make it an ideal choice for professional Web designers, as well as for those new to the Internet. And the new features in Version 4 make it better than ever!

I've been reviewing Web design programs since the first ones hit the market in 1994, and I can assure you that Dreamweaver is the best one I've ever worked with. But don't take my word for it — Dreamweaver has already won a slew of awards, including Best of Show at Internet World, the prestigious five-mouse rating from *MacWorld*, and best Web program of the year from *PC Magazine*.

The best Dreamweaver features include its clean HTML code and sophisticated support for the latest HTML options (such as Dynamic HTML and Cascading Style Sheets). Dreamweaver 4 includes new features for high-end Web designers as well; including a state-of-the-art integrated text editor and a JavaScript debugger. Macromedia has integrated two dedicated HTML text editors — BBEdit, the most popular HTML editor for the Macintosh, and HomeSite, the powerful text editor for Windows — with the easy-to-use WYSIWYG (What You See Is What You Get) design environment of Dreamweaver. So switching back and forth between Dreamweaver and a text editor is a breeze, and you also have a best-of-both-worlds solution if you're a developer who still likes to work with raw HTML code at least part of the time.

If you've never written HTML before, don't be intimidated by these fancy features. The Dreamweaver graphical design environment uses sophisticated palettes and windows to enable beginners to create high-end Web sites that include such features as animations, interactive forms, and even e-commerce solutions, even if you don't know HTML.

My coauthor, Paul Vachier, is also an experienced Web designer who still appreciates what it was like to be new to the Web. His creative contributions make this an even stronger book and serve to beef up the more technical sections for those who want to get into the really cool stuff. Paul and I split up the chapters; I wrote about half the book, and he wrote the rest. In each chapter, we decided to stick with the personal pronoun *I* because we're generally referring to our own experiences; however, the book truly benefits from our combined talents.

Dreamweaver 4 For Dummies is for anyone who wants to build sophisticated Web pages that are easy to create and maintain. Whether you're a professional or a novice, this book can get you up and running quickly with the best Web design program on the market today.

About This Book

I designed *Dreamweaver 4 For Dummies* to make your life easier as you work with this Web program. You don't have to read this book cover to cover and memorize it. Instead, each section of the book stands alone, giving you easy answers to particular questions and step-by-step instructions for specific tasks.

Want to find out how to change the background color on a page, create a nested table, build HTML frames, or get into the really cool stuff like style sheets and layers? Then jump right in and go directly to the section that most interests you. Oh, and don't worry about keeping all those new HTML tags in your head. You don't have to memorize anything. The next time you need to do one of these tasks, just go back and review that section. Feel free to dog-ear the pages, too — I promise they won't complain!

Conventions Used in This Book

Keeping things consistent makes them easier to understand. In this book, those consistent elements are *conventions*. Notice how the word *conventions* is in italics? That's a convention I use frequently. I put new terms in italics and then define them so that you know what they mean.

When I type URLs (Web addresses) or e-mail addresses within regular paragraph text, they look like this: `www.janinewarner.com`. Sometimes, however, I set URLs off on their own lines, like this:

```
www.janinewarner.com
```

That's so you can easily spot them on a page if you want to type them into your browser to visit a site. I also assume that your Web browser doesn't require the introductory `http://` for Web addresses. If you use an older browser, remember to type this before the address.

Even though Dreamweaver makes knowing HTML code virtually unnecessary, you may have to occasionally wade into HTML waters. So I set off HTML code in the same monospaced type as URLs:

```
<A HREF="http://www.janinewarner.com">Janine's Web Site</A>
```

(That's the HTML code that makes a URL a link on a Web page.)

When I introduce you to a set of features, such as options in a dialog box, I set these items apart with bullets so that you can tell that they're all related. When I want you to follow instructions, I use numbered steps to walk you through the process.

What You're Not to Read

Don't read anything in this book that doesn't interest you. Some of the material here is for people just starting out in Web design. If you've been at this for a while, this material may be too basic for you. For example, experienced designers may want to skip Chapter 4, unless you want a quick refresher course on the Hypertext Markup Language (HTML). If you've never worked with HTML before, Chapter 4 may be a good place to start because it can give you a foundation that can help you as you read other parts of the book.

If you're a graphics guru or you don't care about design issues, skip over the chapters on design and image creation. If you prefer using Photoshop to Fireworks, skip over the chapter on Fireworks.

Just pick and choose the information that you want to work with. Don't feel that you have to read everything to get the most out of it. Use this book as the reference that I intended it to be. Your time is more important than reading stuff that you don't need to know about!

Foolish Assumptions

When Macromedia developed Dreamweaver, it set out to make a professional Web development program and identified the target audience as anyone who spends more than 20 hours a week doing Web design. Fortunately for the rest of us, they also created a powerful program that's intuitive and easy to use.

Macromedia assumes that you're a *professional* developer; I don't. Even if you're new to Web design, this program can work for you, and this book can make Dreamweaver easy to use. In keeping with the philosophy behind the *For Dummies* series, this book is an easy-to-use guide designed for readers with a wide range of experience. It helps if you're interested in Web design and want to create a Web site, but that desire is all that I expect from you. In the chapters that follow, I show you all the steps you need to create Web pages, and in the glossary on the CD-ROM, I give you all the vocabulary you need to understand the process.

If you're an experienced Web designer, *Dreamweaver 4 For Dummies* is an ideal reference for you. If you're new to Web design, this book can get you up and running with this new program in a day or a weekend.

How This Book Is Organized

To ease you through the learning curve associated with any new program, I organized *Dreamweaver 4 For Dummies* to be a complete reference. You can read it cover to cover (if you want), but you may find it more helpful to jump to the section most relevant to what you want to do at that particular moment. Each chapter walks you through the features of Dreamweaver step by step, providing tips and helping you understand the vocabulary of Web design.

The following sections provide a breakdown of the parts of the book and what you'll find in each one.

Part 1: Fulfilling Your Dreams

This part introduces you to Dreamweaver and covers getting started with the basics. In Chapter 1, I give you a handy reference to toolbars and menu options, and I also describe the new features in Version 4 of Dreamweaver. And then in Chapter 2, I start you on the road to creating your first Web site, including creating new Web pages, applying basic formatting to text, and even placing images and setting links on your pages.

In Chapter 3, Paul helps you make the transition from other Web design programs to Dreamweaver. If you started your Web site with another popular HTML authoring tool, such as Microsoft FrontPage or Adobe GoLive, or if you're editing files that someone else created with another tool, this chapter provides tips and guidance for resolving common problems you may encounter when you move from other programs to Dreamweaver. You also get tips for using Dreamweaver with other Web design tools, a common challenge, especially if you're working with a team of designers.

I provide Chapter 4 as an HTML primer — whether you're new to HTML or a pro in need of a refresher course. If you prefer to work in HTML code occasionally, the Dreamweaver built-in text editor makes it a breeze while still giving you all the control you desire. This chapter also shows you how to get the most out of the Dreamweaver enhanced test editor.

Part II: Looking Like a Million (Even on a Budget)

Planning the design of your Web site is perhaps the most important part of Web site development — it can save you plenty of reorganizing time later. In Chapter 5, I start you out on the right foot with tips on Web site management, the principles of good design, and strategies that can save you countless hours. I also introduce you to the Dreamweaver enhanced site-management features, one of the most exciting advancements in Version 4. If you work with a team of designers, you'll be especially interested in the new Dreamweaver version-control features and integrated e-mail. In Chapter 6, I introduce you to some of the best and most enhanced features in Dreamweaver 4, including sophisticated template capabilities, Library items, Tracing images, the Quick Tag Editor, the Design Notes feature, and the History palette.

In Chapter 7, Paul shows you how to make the most of text formatting features in Dreamweaver. In Chapter 8, he takes you a step farther by showing you how to add graphics to your pages. He also suggests tools and strategies that can help you create the best Web graphics for your pages and includes tips on where to find free images or buy graphics that are already optimized for the Web.

Part III: Advancing Your Site

In Part III, Paul shows you how to use Dreamweaver with some of the more advanced HTML features. In Chapter 9, he covers HTML tables, which you can use to create complex page layouts that work in the most common Web browsers. A highlight of this chapter is the new Table Layout View, which makes it easier than ever to create complex Web designs. In Chapter 10, he tells you all you need to know about designing a site with HTML frames. (This chapter helps you decide when you should and shouldn't use frames and gives you plenty of step-by-step instructions for creating HTML frames in Dreamweaver.)

And in Chapter 11, Paul provides an overview of Cascading Style Sheets: how they work and how they can save you time. He describes all the style definition options available in Dreamweaver and shows you how to create and apply your first styles.

Part IV: Making It Cool

Now for the really fun stuff. In this part, you go for a walk on the wild side of HTML. In Chapter 12, Paul gets into the Dynamic HTML features, such as behaviors, timelines, and layers, which you can use to create animations and other interactive features. In Chapter 13, he leads you deeper into DHTML, enabling you to create ever more complex designs. In Chapter 14, Paul introduces you to Fireworks, the Macromedia image program for the Web, and shows you how to take advantage of the Dreamweaver integration with Fireworks to create sophisticated designs and complex images.

In Chapter 15, Paul helps you use Dreamweaver to show off your multimedia talents. He tells you how to link a variety of file types — from Shockwave to Java to RealAudio — to your Web pages. Then in Chapter 16, I address HTML forms and how you can use Dreamweaver to add interactive CGI elements, such as search engines, online discussion areas, and e-commerce systems, to your pages.

Part V: The Part of Tens

In the Part of Tens, Paul and I tell you about ten great Web sites that were created with Dreamweaver, give you ten great Web design ideas, and highlight ten tips that can save you substantial time when you're using Dreamweaver 4.

Part VI: Appendixes

Sometimes you find some of the most essential information in the appendixes — it figures that they're at the back of the book! In Appendix A, I give you a bunch of useful Web resources; in Appendix B, you find a guide to the CD-ROM and all the great software that accompanies this book. On the CD-ROM you can also find a glossary of all the terms that you need to know when you're working with Dreamweaver — and then some!

Icons Used in This Book

This icon signals technical stuff that you may find informative and interesting but isn't essential for using Dreamweaver. Feel free to skip over this stuff.

This icon indicates a tip or technique that can save you time and money —
and a headache — later.

This icon reminds you of an important concept or procedure that you'll want
to store away in your memory banks for future use.

This icon points you toward valuable resources on the World Wide Web.

Danger, Will Robinson! This icon warns you of any potential pitfalls — and
gives you the all-important information on how to avoid them.

When I want to point you toward something on the CD that accompanies this
book, I use this icon.

This icon tunes you into information in other *For Dummies* books that you
may find useful.

This icon alerts you to features of the Macromedia image editor Fireworks 4
or topics dealing with the Dreamweaver integration with Fireworks.

Where to Go from Here

Turn to Chapter 1 to dive in and get started with Dreamweaver. You find a
great overview of the program designed to get you up and running quickly, as
well as a handy reference to all the new features in Version 4. If you're already
familiar with Dreamweaver and want to learn a specific trick or technique,
jump right to the section you need; you won't miss a beat as you work to
make those impossible Web design deadlines. And most of all have fun!

Part I
Fulfilling Your Dreams

The 5th Wave   By Rich Tennant

"Sometimes I feel behind the times. I asked my 11-year-old to build a Web site for my business, and he said he would, only after he finishes the one he's building for his ant farm."

In this part . . .

Stay awake for Part I, and I'll show you that you're not dreaming as I introduce you to the wonders of this powerful Web design program. I give you a quick guide to the new features of Dreamweaver 4, and then I take you on a tour of the toolbars, menus, and panels that give Dreamweaver much of its power. In Chapter 2, you dive right into creating your first Web page. And in Chapter 3, I give you tips for adapting pages created in other Web design programs, such as Adobe GoLive and Microsoft FrontPage. Then in Chapter 4, I walk you through the basics of HTML — a great introduction for beginners and a refresher course for those already familiar with HTML.

Chapter 1

Introducing Your New Best Friend

· ·

· ·

*W*elcome to the wonderful world of Dreamweaver. If you're an experienced Web designer, you're going to love the power and sophistication of this HTML editor. If you're new to Web design, you will appreciate its simplicity and intuitive interface. Either way, this chapter starts you on your way to making the most of Dreamweaver by introducing you to the menus and panels that make this program so useful.

Dreamweaver can help you with every aspect of Web development, from designing simple pages, to fixing links, to publishing your pages on the World Wide Web. Dreamweaver can handle the simplest HTML, as well as some of the most complex and advanced features possible on the Web, such as Cascading Style Sheets and Dynamic HTML (see Chapters 11, 12, and 13 for more information on these features). It also integrates a powerful HTML text editor into its easy-to-use *What You See Is What You Get* (WYSIWYG) design environment. (Don't completely understand WYSIWYG? Then check out the glossary on the accompanying CD-ROM. You can find definitions for this term and many others.)

If you already work in another Web design program, don't worry — you can use Dreamweaver to modify existing Web pages and continue to develop your Web site without losing all the time you've already invested. (Check out Chapter 3 to find out about the best ways to work with files created in some of the other common HTML editors.) In this chapter, I introduce you to the new features in Version 4, take you on a tour of the desktop, and give you an overview of what makes Dreamweaver such a powerful Web design program.

So What's New in Dreamweaver 4?

The following list gives you a quick overview of some of the new features you'll find in Version 4:

- ✔ The Asset Panel in Dreamweaver 4 has been enhanced to provide easy access to the Dreamweaver library and templates. The Assets panel provides a central place where you keep all of the assets in your Web site, including images, colors, external URLs, scripts, and Flash and Shockwave files. You can even drag-and-drop them from the Assets Panel into your HTML document.

- ✔ The Site Window now includes icons for Design Notes so you can quickly tell if a file has a note attached to it. You can also alter the view to display design note information, such as Due Date and Status. Look for more information about using the Site Window in Chapters 5 and 6.

- ✔ The editable regions in Templates now have tabs and an outline to make it easier to see what areas of a template can be changed. I have detailed instructions on how to create and use Templates in Chapter 6.

- ✔ The new text editor now makes it possible to create JavaScript files, XML files, and any other text files in the Dreamweaver Code View, and includes live Syntax coloring. This feature is designed for Dreamweaver's most technically savvy users and is used for high-end programming.

- ✔ The Extension Manager makes it easier to add Dreamweaver extensions. See Chapter 12 for more on this feature.

- ✔ The Flash Buttons and Flash Text features are the result of improved integration with the Dreamweaver animation program, Flash. You can choose predefined Flash styles or you can add your own custom buttons or text and then easily add them to any page in your site. You find out how to use these great new features in Chapter 15.

- ✔ Thanks to Integrated Email, developers on your site can now associate their e-mail addresses with their names so that you can easily contact anyone who has checked out a file. This and other features designed to make it easier to collaborate on a Web site are covered in Chapter 6.

- ✔ The integrated HTML text editor (called the Code Inspector in Version 4) has been enhanced to enable auto-indenting, punctuation balancing, and the ability to select multiple lines and indent them all at once. Take a look at Chapter 4 for more about the text editor, as well as an introduction to HTML.

- ✔ The new Table Layout View lets you draw table cells directly on a page, drag them around, and group cells together. Layout View is accessible through the new tools at the bottom of the Objects panel.

TECHNICAL STUFF

So, what's the big deal about Dreamweaver?

Dreamweaver has gotten great reviews and attracted considerable attention because it solves common problems found in other Web programs. Many Web designers complain that WYSIWYG design tools create sloppy HTML code, alter the code in existing pages, and make manually customizing pages difficult. Most of these problems stem from the fact that people who know how to write HTML code manually are used to having total control over their HTML pages. Unfortunately, many Web design programs force you to give up that control in order to have the convenience and ease of a WYSIWYG tool.

Dreamweaver gives you both control and convenience by packaging an easy-to-use WYSIWYG tool with a powerful HTML text editor, and in Dreamweaver 4 the built-in text editor is even more powerful. Then Dreamweaver goes a step farther with a feature Macromedia calls Roundtrip HTML. With Roundtrip HTML, you can create your HTML pages in any program, open them in Dreamweaver, and not have to worry about your original HTML code being altered. (See Chapter 3 to find out more about Roundtrip HTML.)

Dreamweaver respects your HTML code. A big problem with many other WYSIWYG editors is that they can dramatically change HTML code if it doesn't conform to their rules. Unfortunately, the rules on the Web constantly change, so

many designers like to break the rules or at least add their own variations to the theme. If you create a page with custom HTML code in a text editor and then open it in a program such as Microsoft FrontPage, you run the risk that FrontPage may change your design when it tries to make your code fit the limited rules of FrontPage.

Dreamweaver promises never to alter your code, which is one of the reasons it's becoming a best friend to so many professional designers. Designers can enjoy the ease of the WYSIWYG design program and add their custom HTML touches whenever they want without having to worry about what Dreamweaver may do to their work. This decision wasn't easy for Macromedia — the company dedicated the full attention of three engineers to this problem for more than one year before it released Version 1.0.

The challenge was in figuring out how to display the HTML code created in a text editor in the WYSIWYG side of the program without ever changing the code, even if Dreamweaver has never seen your unique HTML code before. The success that Macromedia has had in solving this problem is a big part of the reason why Dreamweaver has gotten so much attention, won so many awards, and attracted the loyalty of even the most die-hard HTML coders.

✔ Because so many developers like to see the code while they work, Dreamweaver developed a Split View feature so you can simultaneously edit the HTML source on one side of your screen and the WYSIWYG on the other.

✔ Macromedia Fireworks is now more fully integrated with Dreamweaver, so images and HTML tables that were created in Fireworks and imported into Dreamweaver have their own special Property Inspector. A special interface in Fireworks even makes it possible for you to switch between

Fireworks and Dreamweaver, updating the HTML file each time you finish using Fireworks and preserving most changes you made in Dreamweaver.

✔ When you're ready to test your work, the new Dreamweaver Site Reporting feature makes it easy to look for common problems like untitled documents and missing ALT tags.

✔ If you work with a team, you need some kind of version control to ensure you don't overwrite each other's work. Dreamweaver is now set up to be easily integrated with Microsoft Visual SourceSafe and WebDAV systems.

Visualizing Your Site

Before you launch into building Web pages, take some time to plan your site and think about its structure and organization. Begin thinking about the following questions. Some of them you may not fully understand at this point and can't answer. But it's best to have answers to all these questions before you begin actually building your Web site:

✔ What do you want to accomplish with your Web site? What are your goals and objectives?

✔ Who is your target audience?

✔ Who will be working on your site? How many developers do you have to manage?

✔ How will you create or collect the text and images you'll need for your site?

✔ How will you organize the files in your site?

✔ Will you include multimedia files, such as Flash or RealAudio?

✔ Will you want interactive features, such as a feedback form or chat room?

✔ What other software will you need for specialized features (for example, Macromedia Flash for animations)?

✔ What kind of navigation system will you have for your site (that is, how can you make it easy for visitors to move from one area of your Web site to another)?

✔ How will you accommodate growth for the site?

In Chapter 2, I cover some of the site-management features of Dreamweaver before jumping into the specifics of creating your first Web pages. In Chapter 5, I provide many tips and suggestions that can help you plan your site as you answer questions like these. Taking the time to get clear on your goals and objectives can set the tone for successful Web development.

Introducing the Many Components of Dreamweaver

Dreamweaver can seem a bit overwhelming at first. It has so many features that all the panels, toolbars, and dialog boxes can be confusing when you start poking around. In the next few sections, I introduce you to the basic functions and some of the terminology of Dreamweaver. I also show you where to find various features and explain, in general terms, the function of the buttons and menu options. I cover all of these features in more detail later in the book.

The Workspace

Creating a basic Web page in Dreamweaver is remarkably easy. When you launch Dreamweaver, a blank page — called the *Workspace* — appears automatically, much like a blank document does when you open a program like Microsoft Word. You can type text directly into the Workspace and apply basic formatting, such as bold and italics, simply by selecting Text⇨Style⇨Bold or Text⇨Style⇨Italics.

You build your Web pages in the Workspace, which consists of a main window that shows the HTML page that you're working on and a number of floating panels and windows that provide tools that you can use to design and develop your pages (see Figure 1-1). The Dreamweaver Workspace consists of four basic components: the document window, floating panels, menu bar, and Status Bar.

The document window

The big, open area on the Workspace is the document window. It's essentially a blank page, but if you look at the HTML code behind it, you see that it's a simple HTML file. The document window is where you edit and design your Web page, and it is the document window that displays images, text, and other elements in much the same way that a Web browser displays them.

Pages viewed on the World Wide Web may not always look exactly the way they do in the document window in Dreamweaver because not all browsers support the same HTML features or display them equally. For best results, always test your work in a variety of Web browsers and design your pages to work best in the browsers that your audience most likely uses. Fortunately, Dreamweaver includes features that help you target your page designs to specific browsers. (For more information on browser differences, check out Chapter 13.)

Figure 1-1:
The main
Workspace
in Dream-
weaver
includes a
document
window,
menu bar,
Status Bar,
and various
floating
panels that
can be
opened and
closed
when
needed.

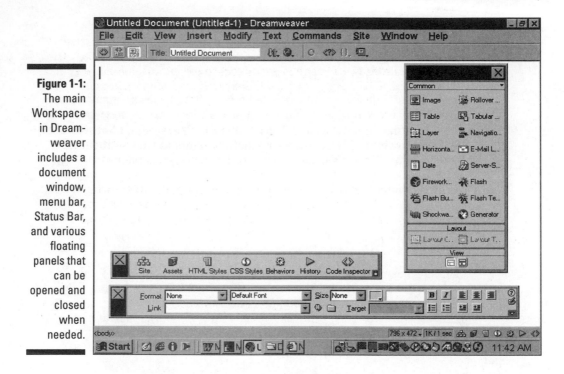

The floating panels

The floating panels in Dreamweaver provide easy access to many of the program's features. You can move the panels around the screen by selecting them and using drag-and-drop to reposition them. If you find that having all of these panels open distracts you from your ability to focus on your design, you can close any or all of them by clicking the panel's Close (X) box. You can access all the panels through the Window menu. If you want to open a panel — the Launcher bar, for example — you simply choose Window⇨ Launcher bar, and it reappears on your screen.

The panels are integral parts of this program, so I include lots more information about them throughout the book. Check out the Cheat Sheet at the front of this book for a handy reference to these panels. In Chapter 2, I cover some of the most common features, such as inserting images (the icons for the images are provided in the Common Objects panel). Chapter 2 also covers linking and the Anchor button that you find in the Invisibles panel. In Chapter 9, I explain how to use the table features available from the Insert Tables dialog box and the Tables Property Inspector. In Chapter 15, I get into using plug-in files that are also accessible from the Common Objects panel. Chapter 16 covers the HTML form options accessible in the Forms panel.

The Objects panel

The Objects floating panel contains buttons for creating HTML elements, such as tables and layers, and for inserting images, plug-in files, and other objects. Dreamweaver uses the term object to mean any element that you can put on an HTML page, from a table, to an image, to a multimedia file.

The Objects panel has the following six views or *subpanels* that offer separate sets of buttons for various functions: Common, Characters, Forms, Frames, Head, and Invisibles. Dreamweaver generally refers to these subpanels with the long name Common Objects panel or Forms Objects panel.

To switch from displaying the buttons on one subpanel to showing the buttons for one of the other subpanels, click the small arrow at the top-right corner of the panel. Figure 1-2 shows the six different panel options. You can also resize the panels and change their orientation to horizontal or vertical. And if you choose Edit⇨Preferences, you can specify whether to display only the icons in the panel or to display both the icon and its name.

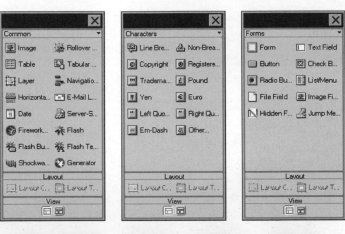

Figure 1-2: The various views (or *subpanels*) of the Objects panel provide quick access to options for frames, tables, images, and more.

The Property Inspector

Another floating panel, the Property Inspector, displays the properties of a selected element on the page. A *property* is a characteristic of HTML — such as the alignment of an image or the size of a cell in a table — that you can assign to an element on your Web page. You can keep the Property Inspector open at all times. When you select an element on a page, such as an image, the Inspector changes to display the properties for that particular element, such as the height and width, alignment, and links. You can alter those properties by changing the fields in the Property Inspector.

In Figure 1-3, the image in the upper-left corner has been selected, so the Property Inspector reveals the characteristics, or *attributes*, for that image, such as its height and width, its alignment, and the URL (*Uniform Resource Locator* or, more simply, Web address) to which it links.

At the bottom-right corner of the Property Inspector, you can see a small arrow. You can click this arrow to reveal additional attributes that let you control more advanced features.

Figure 1-4 shows the Property Inspector when a table is selected. Notice that the fields in the Inspector have changed to reflect the attributes of an HTML table, such as the number of columns and rows. (See Chapter 9 to find out more about HTML tables.)

Figure 1-3: The Property Inspector displays the attributes of a selected element, such as the image shown here.

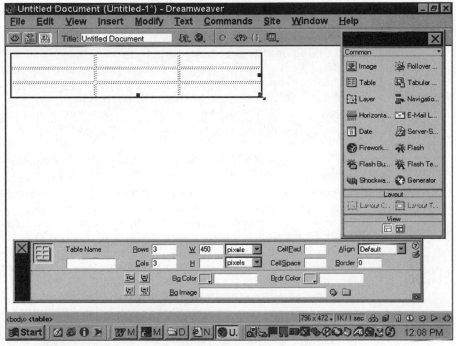

Figure 1-4:
The
Property
Inspector
displays the
attributes of
the selected
HTML table.

The Launcher bar (your way to the best goodies)

The Launcher bar, as shown in Figure 1-5, is another floating panel. The Launcher bar contains a list of shortcuts that open dialog boxes with easy access to Site features, the Library, HTML Styles, CSS *(Cascading Style Sheets)* Styles, Behaviors, History, and the HTML Code Inspector — all of which I cover in more detail later in this book. (If you're interested in DHTML features such as timelines, behaviors, and styles, be sure to read Chapters 12 and 13.)

Figure 1-5:
The
Launcher
bar provides
easy access
to various
Dream-
weaver
features.

The following list offers a description of the elements that you can access through the Launcher bar.

✔ **Site dialog box:** This box, shown in Figure 1-6, lists all the folders and files in a Web site and helps you manage the structure and organization of the site. The Site dialog box helps you organize your site and ensure that you don't break links when you publish your site online. The Site dialog box is also where you access FTP (file transfer protocol) capabilities. You can use the Connect button at the top of this dialog box to dial quickly into your server. The Get and Put buttons enable you to transfer your pages back and forth between your computer and the server. (See Chapter 2 to find out more about the Site dialog box.)

✔ **Assets panel:** The new Assets panel in Dreamweaver 4 includes the Library panel and the Reference panel. The Library panel, shown in Figure 1-7, enables you to store items in a central place so that you can easily add them to multiple pages. After an element is stored in the Library (you store an item simply by dragging the element onto the Library panel), you can then drag that element from the Library onto new pages. The Library is ideal for elements that are used throughout a Web site, as well as those that you must update frequently.

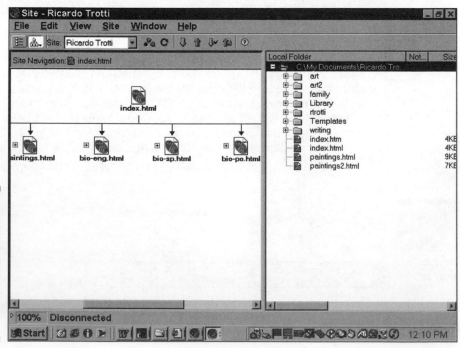

Figure 1-6:
The Site dialog box provides a view of the site structure and files in your site.

The Library feature works only if you've defined your site using the Site Definition dialog box, available by selecting Site⇨Define Sites. If you find that the Library options aren't available to you, go to Chapter 2 and follow the steps for defining a site. (For more information on the Library feature, see Chapter 6.)

The Reference panel, accessible through the tab at the top of the Library panel, provides quick access to Dreamweaver's new code reference, which defines and describes tags used in HTML, CSS, and JavaScript.

✔ **The HTML Styles panel:** Shown in Figure 1-8, the HTML Styles panel enables you to store commonly used styles for handy access. Macromedia calls these *H Styles*. Unlike CSS (Cascading Style Sheets), however, H Styles affect only one occurrence of the style: the place where you actually apply the style. If you want to be able to change a style and have it update all occurrences of that style in your document, you have to use Cascading Style Sheets. (Check out Chapter 11 for details on H Styles and CSS.) The advantage of H Styles is that they are supported by more browsers, including older versions of browsers.

Figure 1-7:
The Library panel stores items in a central place, making it easy to place the same element, such as a navigation row, on multiple pages.

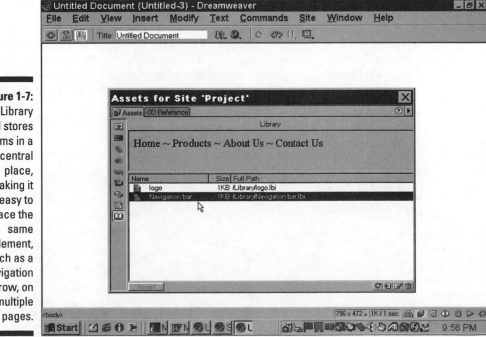

Figure 1-8:
The HTML Styles panel provides access to styles and combinations of styles to make them easy to apply to elements on your site.

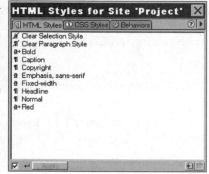

✔ **CSS Styles panel:** This box enables you to define styles by using Cascading Style Sheets (CSS). CSS styles are similar to style sheets used in desktop publishing programs such as QuarkXPress and Adobe PageMaker. You define a style and name it, and the style is then included in the CSS Styles panel, which is accessible through the tab at the top of the panel (see Figure 1-8). The CSS Styles panel provides access to the Style Definition panel, shown in Figure 1-9, where you can specify the type, size, and formatting of the style. After you define a style, you can apply it to text or other elements on a page. Style sheets are a big time-saver because they let you set several attributes simultaneously by applying a defined style. (For more information about CSS, see Chapter 11.)

Figure 1-9:
The Style Definition panel makes it easy to create new combinations of formatting features as CSS.

✔ **Behaviors panel:** In Dreamweaver, *behaviors* are scripts (usually written in JavaScript) that you can apply to objects to add interactivity to your Web page. Essentially, a behavior is made up of a specified event that, when triggered, causes an action. For example, an event may be a visitor clicking an image or section of text, and the resulting action may be that a sound file plays. Figure 1-10 shows the Behaviors dialog box with the plus sign (+) selected to reveal the drop-down list of behaviors. The left pane displays events; the right pane displays the actions triggered by those events. (Chapters 12 and 13 provide more information on creating and applying behaviors.)

✔ **History panel:** The History panel, shown in Figure 1-11, keeps track of every action you take in Dreamweaver. You can use the History panel to undo multiple steps at once, to replay steps you performed, and to automate tasks.

✔ **Code Inspector:** The Code Inspector in Dreamweaver is the best-integrated HTML text editor of any Web design program, and it's been improved for Dreamweaver 4. Notice that in Figure 1-12, the highlighted text in the WYSIWYG area is also highlighted in the HTML Code Inspector. Changes made in one immediately appear in the other. This integration makes moving back and forth between writing HTML code manually and creating it in the graphical editing environment nearly seamless.

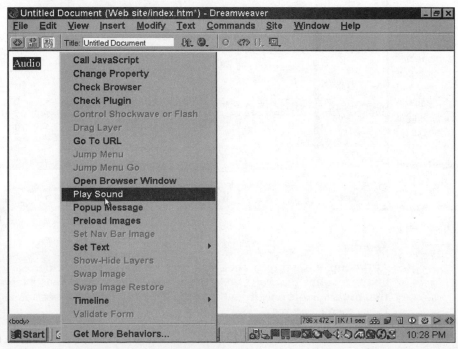

Figure 1-10:
Clicking the
+ button
opens a
drop-down
list of
behaviors.

Figure 1-11:
The History panel keeps track of all your actions in Dream-weaver, making it easy to undo or replay steps.

Figure 1-12:
The Code Inspector lets you view and edit the code behind any page you're working on in Dream-weaver.

The menu bar

At the top of the screen, the Dreamweaver menu bar provides easy access to all the features that you find in the floating panels, as well as a few others that are available only from the menu. (See the following sections for more on these menu features.)

The File menu

Under the File menu, you find many familiar options, such as New, Open, and Save. You also find a Revert option, which is similar to the Revert feature in Adobe Photoshop. This sophisticated "undo" feature enables you to return your page quickly to its last-saved version if you don't like the changes you've made. The File menu also includes access to Design Notes, a unique feature that associates private notes with HTML and other files. Take a look at Chapter 6 for more information about Design Notes and other Dreamweaver features that make collaboration easier.

Under the File menu, you can also find features that are useful for checking your work in Web browsers. Most Web design programs include some way of previewing your work in a browser. Dreamweaver takes this feature two steps farther by enabling you to check your work in a number of browsers and even test the compatibility of your pages in different versions of different browsers.

Figure 1-13 shows the Check Target Browsers dialog box, where you can specify a browser and version, such as Netscape 3.0 (still a widely used browser on the Web) or Internet Explorer 3.0. When you do a browser check, Dreamweaver generates a report listing any HTML features you have used that the chosen browser doesn't support.

Figure 1-13:
The Check
Target
Browsers
feature
produces a
list of HTML
tags on a
page that
are not
supported
by older
browsers.

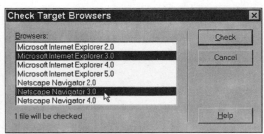

The Edit menu

The Edit menu contains many features that you may find familiar, such as Cut, Copy, and Paste. One feature that may be new to you is the second-to-last option: Launch External Editor. This feature lets you open an HTML text editor, such as BBEdit or HomeSite, that you can use in conjunction with Dreamweaver.

You also find the Preferences settings under the Edit menu. Before you start working with a new program, it's always a good idea to go through all the Preferences options to ensure that the program is set up the best way for you.

The View menu

The View menu provides access to some helpful design features, such as grids and rulers. The View menu also gives you the option of turning on or off the borders of your HTML tables, frames, and layers. This option is useful because you often want to set the border attribute of these HTML tags to zero so that they're not visible when the page displays in a browser. However, while you work on the design of your page in Dreamweaver, seeing where elements like tables and layers start and stop can be very useful. Checking the frame options in the View menu lets you see the borders in Dreamweaver even if you don't want them to be visible to your site's visitors. You can also turn the Status Bar on or off from the View menu.

The Insert menu

As shown in Figure 1-14, the Insert menu offers access to a number of features unique to Web design. From this menu, you can insert elements, such as a horizontal rule, a Java applet, a form, or a plug-in file.

Dreamweaver offers extra support for inserting Flash or Shockwave Director files, both of which are products from Macromedia. (You can find out lots more about using multimedia files, such as Shockwave and RealAudio, in Chapter 15.)

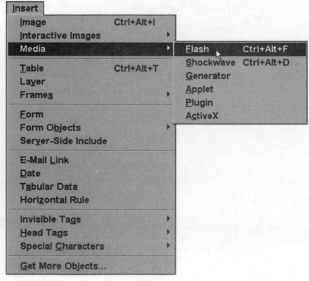

Figure 1-14:
The Insert menu makes it easy to add a variety of elements to your pages, including multimedia files.

The Modify menu

The Modify menu is another place where you can view and change object properties, such as the table attributes shown in Figure 1-15. The properties (usually called *attributes* in HTML) let you define elements on a page by setting alignment, height, width, and other specifications.

Note that you can also set nearly all these attributes using the Property Inspector. One exception to this is the Page Properties option under the Modify menu. Changing page properties (see Figure 1-16) enables you to set link and text colors for the entire page and specify the background color or image.

The Text menu

You can easily format text with the Text menu by using simple options, such as bold and italic, as well as more complex features, such as font styles and custom style sheets. Text formatting options have evolved dramatically on the Web. Just a couple of years ago, you didn't even have the option of specifying a particular font style or controlling leading and spacing. Today, although these options aren't yet universally supported, you have more control than ever over the look of your Web pages.

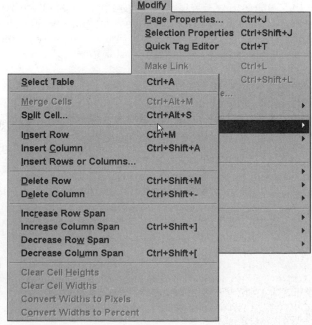

Figure 1-15: The Modify menu makes it easy to change object properties, such as the table attributes shown here.

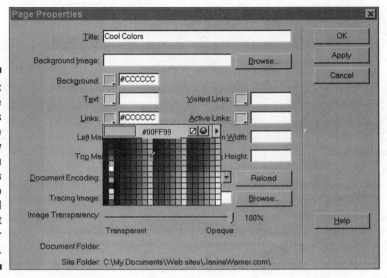

For example, if you choose a particular font for your text, that font must be available on the user's computer for the text to display properly. Because of this limitation, HTML enables you to specify several font possibilities to improve your odds that a font you want can be displayed. The browser searches the user's computer for one of these fonts in the order in which you list them. Dreamweaver recognizes the importance of specifying more than one font and the safety of using the more popular fonts.

The Commands menu

The Commands menu, shown in Figure 1-17, gives you access to a host of new options in Dreamweaver 4. These options include the Start and Play Recording features, which let you quickly save a series of steps and then repeat them. To use this feature, choose Command⇨Start Recording, perform whatever actions you want to record — for example, adding a table with three rows and two columns — and then choose Stop Recording. Then to perform that action, choose Play Recording. You can download an action by choosing Command⇨Get More Commands, a feature that automatically launches a browser and takes you to the Macromedia Web site. Once there, you can download new commands to add functionality to Dreamweaver.

The Clean Up HTML option on the Commands menu helps you correct bad HTML code, and the Clean Up Word HTML feature is designed especially to correct the common problems caused by the Save As HTML feature in Microsoft Word.

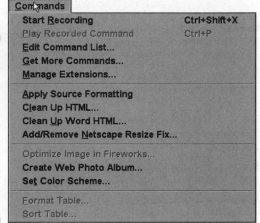

Figure 1-17:
The
Commands
menu offers
easy access
to some of
Dream-
weaver's
most
advanced
features.

The Add/Remove Netscape Resize Fix option on this menu inserts or removes a JavaScript script that is designed to help correct a Netscape bug by automatically reloading the page when users resize their browser windows.

Another great feature under the Commands Menu is the Set Color Scheme Command. This option includes a list of background and text colors that are specially designed to work well together on the Web.

The Site menu

The Site menu provides access to the options you need to set up your site, a process required before many of the other Dreamweaver features will work properly. (This process is covered in detail in Chapter 2.) The Site menu also gives you easy access to Check In and Check Out, which are options that can help you keep a team of designers from overwriting each others work. (Chapter 2 also talks about this feature.)

The Window menu

The Window menu lets you control the display of panels and dialog boxes. The window menu indicates that the three primary panels (Objects, Properties, and the Launcher bar) are visible by showing check marks next to their names. To turn these features on, click the panel name to place a check mark next to the feature you want to display; to turn the feature off, click again to remove the check mark. Other panels and dialog boxes, such as CSS Styles and HTML Code Inspector, are also listed in the Window menu for easy access.

The Help menu

The Help menu provides easy access to help options that can assist you in figuring out many features of Dreamweaver. You also find access to the Dreamweaver template and example files under Help. Templates and examples provide visual samples of common HTML designs, such as tables and frames, and provide design ideas and great shortcuts for creating complex layouts.

The Status Bar

The Status Bar appears at the very bottom of the Dreamweaver screen. On the right end of the Status Bar, you can see shortcuts to all the features available in the Launcher bar. On the left end, you find HTML codes that indicate how elements on your page are formatted. If you run your mouse pointer over text that is centered, for example, the Status Bar displays ⟨center⟩. This feature makes double-checking the kind of formatting applied to any element on your page easy. To turn the display of the Status Bar on or off, choose View⇨Status Bar.

Chapter 2

Setting Up a Web Site with Dreamweaver

In This Chapter

▶ Building a new site
▶ Making new pages
▶ Creating links
▶ Getting your Web site online

*I*f you're ready to dive in and start building your Web site, you've come to the right place. In this chapter, I show you how to create new Web pages — or an entirely new site — and how to open an existing site so that you can add to or edit your previous work.

Before you work on individual pages, you need to set up your site by using the site-management features in Dreamweaver. Whether you're creating a new site or working on an existing site, follow the steps in the next section to set Dreamweaver up to manage the site for you. The Dreamweaver site management features are great because they make it easier to keep track of the elements in your site, update your server more efficiently, and manage a site that is created by multiple developers. And with the enhancements in Version 4, all of these features are even stronger and more efficient.

You can use Dreamweaver without doing the initial site setup, but some of the features — such as the Library, which enables you to store elements for easy use throughout your site — won't work.

Creating a New Site

To set up a site in Dreamweaver, you simply create a folder on your hard drive in which you can keep your Web pages and then tell Dreamweaver where that folder is so that Dreamweaver can keep track of the structure as you create your site. You want to be sure to take this step so that you can use the Dreamweaver site-management features to their full potential.

If you're working on an existing site, you use the same steps; but instead of creating a new folder, you direct Dreamweaver to a folder that contains the existing site. (You can find out more about importing a site, as well as tips about working with sites created in other programs, in Chapter 3.)

The site setup process is important because when you finish your site and upload it to your Web server, the individual pages must remain in the same relative location to each other on the Web server as they are on your hard drive. The site-management features in Dreamweaver can help ensure that things work properly on the server by making certain that you set links and other features correctly when you create them. That way, Dreamweaver won't break links between pages when you upload your site to your Web server. The Dreamweaver site management features are also tightly integrated with its FTP capabilities so the program helps you keep track of changes and ensures that the live version of your site online reflects all the work you've done offline.

Defining a site

The following steps walk you through the process of using the Site Definition dialog box. This is where you identify your site structure so that Dreamweaver knows how to set links and can effectively handle many of the site-management features explained in later chapters.

To define a site using the Site Definition dialog box, follow these steps. (If you are opening an existing Web site, skip to Step 2. Just make sure that the entire Web site directory — a single folder containing the entire contents of your Web site — is on your hard drive.)

1. **In Windows Explorer or the Macintosh Finder, depending on the system you use, create a new folder for housing your Web site.**

   In Windows Explorer, the command is File⇨New⇨Folder.

   In the Macintosh Finder, the command is File⇨New Folder.

   You can call this folder anything you like; it's just a container that represents the server space where your Web site will reside later. All the files, subfolders, and images for your Web site should go in this folder.

2. **Choose Site⇨New Site.**

   The Site Definition dialog box appears, as shown in Figure 2-1. Make sure that the Local Info category is selected in the left side of the dialog box.

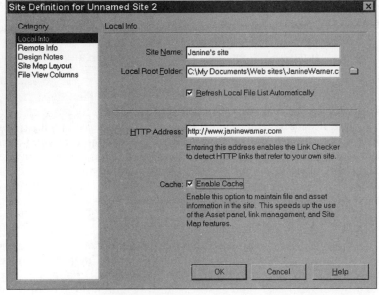

Figure 2-1:
The Site
Definition
dialog box
enables you
to set up a
new or
existing
Web site in
Dream-
weaver.

3. **In the Site Name text box, type a name for your site.**

   You can call your site whatever you like. After you name it here, the
   name appears as an option on the drop-down list in the Site dialog box.
   You use this list to select the site you want to work on when you open
   Dreamweaver, which is especially helpful if you're working on multiple
   Web sites.

4. **Use the Browse button (it resembles a file folder) next to the Local
   Root Folder text box to locate the folder on your hard drive that you
   created in Step 1 to hold your Web site.**

   If you're working on an existing site, follow the same step to locate the
   folder that holds the site you want to start working on in Dreamweaver.

5. **If Refresh Local File List Automatically isn't already selected, click to
   place a check mark in the box next to this option if you want
   Dreamweaver to automatically update the list of all the new pages you
   add to your site.**

6. **Under Link Management Options, type the URL of your Web site in the
   HTTP Address text box.**

   The HTTP Address is the URL, or Web address, that your site will have
   when it is published on a Web server. If you do not yet know the Web
   address for your site or you do not plan to publish it on a Web server,
   you can leave this box blank.

7. Check the Enable Cache option.

Dreamweaver creates a local cache of your site to be able to quickly reference the location of files in your site. The local cache speeds up many of the site management features of the program and takes only a few seconds to create.

8. Click OK to close the Site Definition dialog box.

If you haven't checked the Enable Cache option, a message box appears asking whether you want to create a cache for the site. Figure 2-1 shows what the dialog box should look like when all of the areas in the Local Info tab are filled in.

Setting up Web server access

To make your life simpler, Dreamweaver incorporates FTP capability so that you can easily upload your pages to a Web server. Integrating this feature also enables Dreamweaver to help you keep track of changes you make to files on your hard drive and ensure that they match the files on your Web server.

Note: FTP *(File Transfer Protocol)* is used for copying files to and from servers elsewhere on a network, such as the Internet. FTP is the protocol you use to send your Web site to your server when you're ready to publish it on the Web. (For a glossary of this and other terms, see the CD ROM.)

You enter information about the Web server where your site will be published on the Remote Info page of the Site Definition dialog box. You access this page by selecting Remote Info in the Category box on the left side of the Site Definition dialog box. The Remote Info page opens on the right side of the box, as shown in Figure 2-2.

If you aren't going to publish your site on a server, choose None from the Remote info drop-down list. If you're going to send your site to a server on a network, choose Local/Network from the Server Access drop-down list; then use the Browse button to specify that server's location on your network. Two new options have been added in Dreamweaver 4: Source Safe Database and WebDAV. These enable you to integrate Dreamweaver with version control systems, used to keep track of changes when a team of developers is working on a site. These options only work if you have Microsoft's Source Safe or are using WebDAV.

The most common way to publish a Web site after you develop it is to use FTP to send it to a remote server, such as those offered by commercial service provider. If that is how you're going to publish your site, the step-by-step instructions that follow walk you through the process.

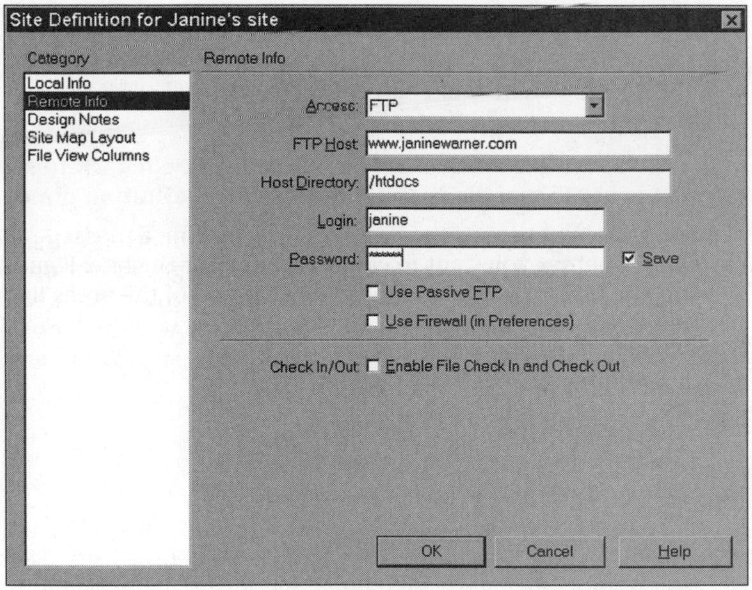

Figure 2-2:
The Site
Definition
dialog box
specifies
the access
information
for a remote
Web server.

Site Definition for Janine's site

Category
Local Info
Remote Info
Design Notes
Site Map Layout
File View Columns

Remote Info

Access: FTP

FTP Host: www.janinewarner.com

Host Directory: /htdocs

Login: janine

Password: ******   ☑ Save

☐ Use Passive FTP
☐ Use Firewall (in Preferences)

Check In/Out: ☐ Enable File Check In and Check Out

OK   Cancel   Help

If you're using a remote server, such as an Internet service provider, ask your provider for the following information:

FTP host name

Path for the host directory

FTP login

FTP password

Then choose FTP from the Server Access drop-down list in the Remote Info page of the Site Definition dialog box and follow these steps:

1. **In the FTP Host text box, type the hostname of your Web server.**

   It should look something like `ftp.host.com` or `shell.host.com` or `www.host.com`, depending on your server.

2. **In the Host Directory text box, type the directory on the remote site in which documents visible to the public are stored (also known as the *site root*).**

   It should look something like `public/html/` or `www/public/docs/`.

3. **In the text box next to Login and Password, type the login name and password required to gain access to your Web server. If you check the Save box, Dreamweaver stores the information and automatically supplies it to the server when you connect to the remote site.**

4. **Put a check mark in the Use Passive FTP or Use Firewall options only if your service provider or site administrator instructs you to do so.**

   If you aren't on a network and use a commercial service provider, you shouldn't need to check either option.

5. **If you don't want to check any other settings, click OK to save your Web Server Info settings and close the Site Definition dialog box.**

   If you want to continue reviewing the settings in other categories, choose Check In/Out, Site Map Layout, or Design Notes from the Category box on the left side of the screen (I explain each of these settings in the following sections). Then continue with the applicable instructions in one of the following three subsections. Otherwise, skip to the section "Creating New Pages."

Using Check In/Out

The Check In/Out category was designed to keep people from overwriting each other's work when more than one person is contributing to the same Web site (a valuable feature if you want to keep peace on your Web design team). When a person working on the Web site "checks out" a file, other developers working on the site are unable to make changes to that page. When you check out a file, you see a green check mark next to the filename. If someone else has checked out a file, you see a red check mark.

To use the Check In/Out feature, check the box next to Check In/Out. In Dreamweaver 3, this was a separate option in the Category box in the Site Definition dialog box. In Dreamweaver 4, this feature is available at the bottom of the Local Info box. The Check In/Out page expands when you check it and is visible in the bottom part of right side of the box, as shown in Figure 2-3.

Using this feature, you can track which files a particular person is working on. If you're the only person working on a Web site, you shouldn't need this feature, but if you want to use this tracking mechanism, check the box next to Check Out Files when Opening and then fill in the name you want associated with the files (presumably your name or nickname, if you prefer) in the Check Out Name field and then include your Email Address in that field. (The addition of the Email Address field in Dreamweaver 4 is needed for the new Dreamweaver integration with e-mail, which facilitates communication among developers on a site. You find more information about integrated e-mail in Chapter 6.)

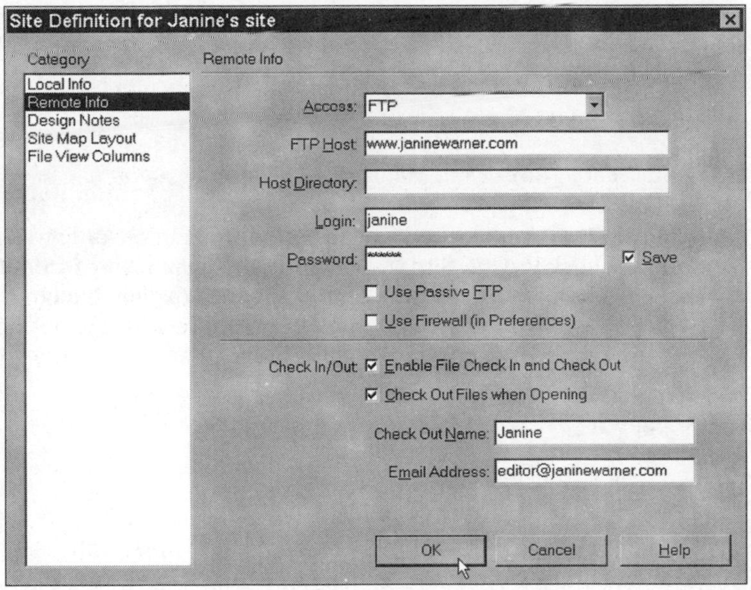

Figure 2-3:
The Check
In/Out
feature
helps you
keep track
of develop-
ment when
more than
one person
is working
on the site.

```
┌─────────────────────────────────────────────────────────────────┐
│ Site Definition for Janine's site                            [×]  │
├─────────────────────────────────────────────────────────────────┤
│ Category              Remote Info                                 │
│ Local Info                                                        │
│ Remote Info                Access: [FTP              ▼]          │
│ Design Notes                                                      │
│ Site Map Layout          FTP Host: [www.janinewarner.com    ]    │
│ File View Columns                                                 │
│                     Host Directory: [                        ]    │
│                                                                   │
│                            Login: [janine            ]           │
│                                                                   │
│                         Password: [********]       ☑ Save         │
│                                                                   │
│                          ☐ Use Passive FTP                        │
│                          ☐ Use Firewall (in Preferences)          │
│                                                                   │
│                Check In/Out: ☑ Enable File Check In and Check Out  │
│                              ☑ Check Out Files when Opening        │
│                                                                   │
│                   Check Out Name: [Janine                    ]    │
│                                                                   │
│                    Email Address: [editor@janinewarner.com   ]    │
│                                                                   │
│                    [   OK   ]    [ Cancel ]    [  Help  ]          │
└─────────────────────────────────────────────────────────────────┘
```

Using Design Notes

If you sometimes forget the details of your work or neglect to tell your colleagues important things about the Web site you're all working on, the
Dreamweaver Design Notes feature can save you some grief.

Design Notes enable you to record information and associate it with a file or
folder. Design Notes work like the comment tag, which lets you add text to a
page that won't display in a browser. But Design Notes takes this concept a
step further, enabling you to add comments to any element, including images,
multimedia files, and even folders. And unlike the comment tag, which is
embedded directly in the HTML code of a page, visitors can't see Design
Notes when they view your Web site — even if they look at the HTML source.
You can choose to upload Design Notes so that they are available to others
with access to your server, or you can prevent them from ever being loaded
to your public site.

To access the Design Notes page, choose Design Notes from the Category box
in the Site Definition dialog box (see Figure 2-4). The settings on this page let
you control how Dreamweaver uses Design Notes:

✔ **Maintain Design Notes:** Click to place a check mark in this box to ensure
  that the Design Note remains attached to the file when you upload it,
  copy it, or move it.

✔ **Upload Design Notes for Sharing:** Choose this option to include Design Notes when you send files to the server via FTP.

✔ **Clean Up:** This button enables you to delete Design Notes that are no longer associated with files or folders in your site.

When you create graphics in Macromedia Fireworks, you can save a Design Note for that file that is also available in Dreamweaver. To use this integrated feature, save the Fireworks image to your local Web site folder. When you open the file in Dreamweaver, the Design Note is displayed when you right-click on the image. This feature is a great way for graphic designers to communicate with other members of the Web design team.

Activating Site Map Layout

If you have trouble keeping track of all of your files and how they are linked in your site, you're not alone. As Web sites get larger and larger, this task becomes increasingly daunting. Dreamweaver includes a Site Map Layout feature to help you track your Web pages. This is not a Site Map like those you often see on Web sites that's visible to visitors of your site; Site Map Layout is a site management feature in Dreamweaver that you can use to visually manage the files and folders that make up your site. To access the settings for the Site Map Layout feature, choose Site Map Layout from the Category box in the Site Definition dialog box. The Site Map Layout page opens on the right side of the box, as shown in Figure 2-5.

Figure 2-4:
The Design Notes page lets you specify whether Design Notes are included when sending files to the Web server.

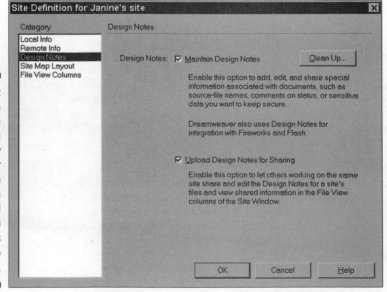

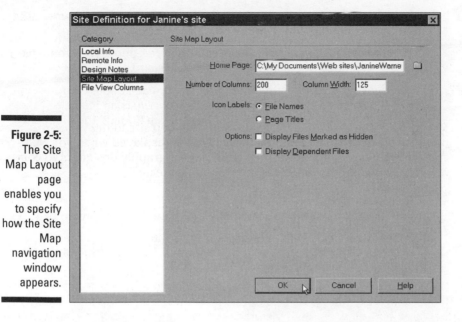

Figure 2-5:
The Site
Map Layout
page
enables you
to specify
how the Site
Map
navigation
window
appears.

You can use this feature to automatically create a site map of all the pages in your Web site. This is a useful management tool because it gives you a visual reference of the hierarchy of your Web site and all its links.

To create a site map from the Site Map Layout page of the Site Definition dialog box, follow these steps:

1. **In the Home Page text box, type the path to the main page of your site or use the Browse button (resembles a file folder) to locate it. If you have already filled out the Local Info page, this field should automatically be filled in.**

   This text box specifies the home page for the site map and provides Dreamweaver with a reference for where the Web site begins. If you don't specify a home page and Dreamweaver cannot find a file called index.html or index.htm (the most common names for a home page), Dreamweaver prompts you to select a home page when you open the site map.

2. **Set the Number of Columns field to the number of pages you want displayed per row in the site map.**

3. **Set the Column Width, in pixels, to represent how wide you want the site map.**

4. **In the Icon Labels section, click either the File Names option or the Page Titles option if you want the filename or page title of each page to be displayed in the site map.**

   You can manually edit any filename or page title after you generate the site map.

5. **In the Options section, you can choose to hide certain files, meaning that they won't be visible in the Site Map window.**

   If you select the Display Files Marked as Hidden option, files you have marked as hidden are displayed in italic in the site map.

   If you select the Display Dependent Files option, all dependent files in the site's hierarchy are displayed. A *dependent file* is an image or other non-HTML content that the browser loads when it loads the main page.

6. **When you have adjusted all the settings, click OK.**

   A message window appears asking if you want to create a cache file for the site. This helps Dreamweaver keep your links up to date and improves the performance of the Site Map.

7. **Click Create to generate a cache file and launch the site map process.**

   Dreamweaver scans all the files in your sites and launches the dialog box to display a site map like the one shown on the left side of the Site dialog box shown in Figure 2-6.

8. **Click OK to generate the site map.**

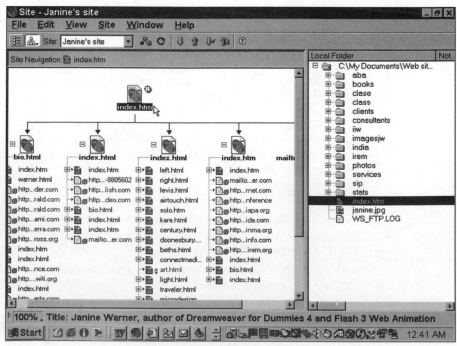

Figure 2-6: The Site Map provides a quick visual reference to the locations of pages and links in your site structure.

Creating New Pages

Every Web site begins with a single page. The front page — or *home page* — of your site is a good place to start. Dreamweaver makes it easy: When the program opens, it automatically creates a new page. To create another page, simply choose File⇨New.

Creating a new page to start a Web site may seem obvious, but consider this: You may want to create a bunch of new pages before you get too far in your development, and you may even want to start organizing the new pages in subdirectories before you have anything on them. This process enables you to organize your pages before you start setting links. After all, you can't set a link to a page that doesn't exist. So if you plan to have five links on your front page to other pages in your site, go ahead and create those other pages, even if you don't put anything on them yet.

When I first start building a Web site, I often create a bunch of pages with nothing but a simple text headline across the top of each. I make a page like this for each area of my site and often place them in subdirectories. For example, if I were creating a site for my department at a big company, I might have a page about my staff, another about what we do, and a third with information about the resources that we provide. At this initial stage, I'd create four pages — one for the front page of the site and three others for each of the subsections. With these initial pages in place, I benefit from having an early plan for organizing the site, and I can start setting links among the main pages right away. (See Chapter 5 for more tips about Web site planning and organization.)

Designing your first page

Before you get too far into design or organization, I want to give you a general idea about how to do basic tasks in Dreamweaver, such as formatting text and setting links.

If you're ready to plunge right in, click to insert your cursor at the top of the blank page and type a little text. Type anything you like; you just need something that you can format. If you have text in a word processor or another program, you can copy and paste that text from the other program into your Dreamweaver page. After you enter the text on your page, dive into the following sections, where I show you how to play around with formatting your text.

Creating a headline

Suppose that you want to center a line of headline text and apply a heading tag to make it large and bold, like the one shown in Figure 2-7. To create a headline, follow these steps:

1. **Highlight the text you want to format.**

2. **Choose Text⇨Format⇨Heading 1.**

   Heading 1 is the largest option, Heading 2 is the next largest, and your choices go all the way down to Heading 6, the smallest heading size.

3. **With the text still selected, choose Text⇨Alignment⇨Center.**

   The text automatically centers. Now you should have a headline at the top of your page that looks something like the headline shown in Figure 2-7.

   Alternatively, you can use the Property Inspector to apply the same formatting you applied using the drop-down menus from the menu bar. Choose Window Properties to open the Property Inspector. Figure 2-7 shows the Property Inspector with the Format drop-down list open.

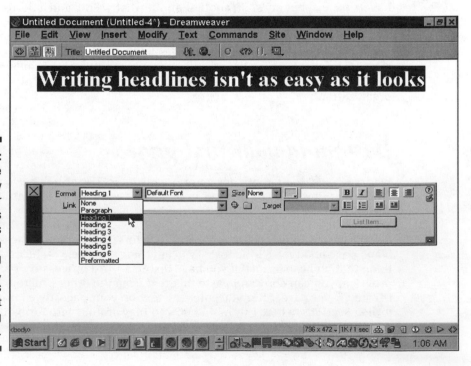

Figure 2-7: The Property Inspector provides easy access to common formatting features, such as alignment and heading sizes.

Indenting text

Type a little more text after your headline text. A single sentence is enough. To indent that text, follow these steps:

1. **Highlight the text you want to indent.**

2. **Choose Text➪Indent.**

   The text automatically indents.

If you want to continue adding text and you don't want it to be indented, choose Text➪Format➪None to transition back to plain text mode without the indent.

If you just want to indent a line or two, the Indent option in the Text menu is ideal. If, however, you want to create the effect of a narrower column of text on a page, an HTML table is a better option. You can find information about creating HTML tables in Chapter 9.

Adding images

Adding an image to your Web page is simple with Dreamweaver. The challenge is to create a good-looking image that loads quickly in your viewer's browser. For more information on finding and creating images, as well as keeping file sizes small, see Chapters 8 and 14. For now, I assume that you have a GIF or JPEG image file ready, and I walk you through the steps to link your image to your page. (Don't know what a GIF or JPEG is? Check out the glossary on the CD-ROM that accompanies this book.) If you don't have an image handy, you can find a few GIF and JPEG files on the CD-ROM included at the back of this book. You can use any image on your Web site, as long as it's in GIF or JPEG format.

You need to do two important things before inserting an image on a Web page. First, save your HTML page in your Web site's folder on your hard drive. This step is important because Dreamweaver can't properly set the path to your image until it can identify the relative locations of the HTML page and the image. Until you save the page, Dreamweaver doesn't know what folder the page will be in.

For this same reason, you need to make sure that the image file is where you want to store it on your Web site. Many designers create a folder called Images so that they can keep all their image files in one place. If you are working on a very large site, you may want an Images folder within each of the main folders of the site. An important thing to remember is that if you move the page or image to another folder after you place the image on your page, you break the link between the page and the image, and an ugly, broken GIF icon appears when your page is viewed in a browser. If for some reason you do end up breaking an image link, simply delete the broken image icon that appears in its place and insert the image again by following these steps for linking an image to your Web page:

1. **Click the Image icon in the Objects panel.**

   The Image dialog box opens. (If the Objects panel isn't visible, choose View⇨Objects to display the Objects panel in the Dreamweaver work area.)

2. **Click the Select button.**

   A dialog box opens, displaying files and folders on your hard drive.

3. **Navigate to the folder that has the image you want to insert.**

4. **Double-click to select the image you want.**

   The image automatically appears on your Web page.

   If you haven't already saved your page, a warning box appears to tell you that Dreamweaver cannot properly set the link to the image until you save the page. You see this message because Dreamweaver needs to know the location of the HTML page relative to the image to create the link. If you see this box, cancel the step, save your page by choosing File⇨Save, and then repeat the preceding steps.

5. **Click the image on your Web page to display the image options in the Property Inspector. Figure 2-8 shows an image being aligned right on the page with the Objects panel visible.**

   Use the Image Property Inspector to specify image attributes, such as alignment, horizontal and vertical spacing, and alternative text.

   The Image Property Inspector dialog box enables you to specify many attributes for images that you use in your Web site. Table 2-1 describes those attributes. If you don't see all the attributes listed in the table, click the triangle in the bottom-right corner of the Image Property Inspector.

Table 2-1		Image Attributes
Abbreviation	*Attribute*	*Function*
Image	N/A	Specifies the file size
Image Name	Name	Identifies image in scripts
Map	Map Name	Use the Map name text box to assign a name to an image map. All image maps require a name.

Abbreviation	Attribute	Function
Hotspot tools	Image map coordinates	Use the Rectangle, Oval, and Polygon icons to create image map hotspots on an image. (See Chapter 8 to find out how to create an image map.)
W	Width	Dreamweaver automatically specifies the width of the image based on the actual size of the image file.
H	Height	Dreamweaver automatically specifies the height of the image based on the actual size of the image file.
Src	Source	The *source* is the link or the filename and path to the image. Dreamweaver automatically sets this when you insert the image.
Link	Hyperlink	This field shows the address or path if the image links to another page. (For more about linking, see "Setting Links" later in the chapter.)
Align	Alignment	This option enables you to align the image. Text automatically wraps around images that are aligned to the right or left.
Alt	Alternate Text	The words you enter here are displayed if the image doesn't appear on your viewer's screen because the viewer either has images turned off or can't view images. Special browsers for the blind also use this text and convert it to speech with special programs, such as screen readers.
V Space	Vertical Space	Measured in pixels, this setting inserts blank space above and below the image.
H Space	Horizontal Space	Measured in pixels, this setting inserts blank space to the left and right of the image.
Target	Link Target	Use this option when the image appears in a page that's part of an HTML frameset. The Target specifies the frame into which the linked page should open. I cover creating frames and how to set links in frames in Chapter 10.

(continued)

Table 2-1 *(continued)*

Abbreviation	Attribute	Function
Low Src	Low Source	This option enables you to link two images to the same place on a page. The Low Source image loads first and is then replaced by the primary image. You may find this option especially useful when you have a large image size because you can set a smaller image (such as a black-and-white version) as the Low Source, which displays while the main image downloads. The combination of two images in this way can also create the illusion of a simple animation.
Border	Image Border	Measured in pixels, this attribute enables you to put a border around an image. I nearly always set the image border to 0 (zero) when linking an image to get rid of the colored border that automatically appears around a linked image.
Refresh	Refresh Image	This button resizes the image. Use this feature if your image size changes after you link it to the page and you need to reset the size so that it displays properly.
Edit	N/A	Use the Edit button to launch an image editor, such as Fireworks, to make changes to the image.

Setting Links

Dreamweaver is truly a dream when it comes to setting links. The most important thing to keep in mind is that a link is essentially an address (URL) that tells a viewer's browser what page to go to when the viewer selects the text or image with the link.

If that page is within your Web site, you want to create a *relative link* that includes the path that describes how to get from the current page to the linked page. A relative link shouldn't include the domain name of the server. Here's an example of a relative link:

```
<A HREF="staff/boss.html">The boss</A>
```

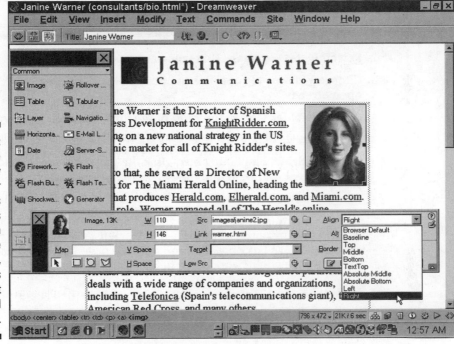

Figure 2-8:
The Image
Property
Inspector
provides
easy access
to common
image
attributes,
such as
alignment
and
spacing.

If you link to a page on a different Web site, you want to create an *absolute link*. An absolute link does include the full Internet address of the other site. Here's an example of an absolute link:

```
<A HREF="http://www.janinewarner.com/books">Janine's
        Books</A>
```

If all that HREF code stuff looks like Greek to you, don't worry. The following section shows you how Dreamweaver makes it possible for you to set links without even knowing what the code means. If you want to know more about all that "Greek stuff," Chapter 4 provides an introduction to HTML and includes a section on setting links.

Linking pages within your Web site

Linking from one page in your Web site to another — an *internal link* — is easy. The most important thing to remember is to save your pages in the folders that you want to keep them in before you start setting links. If you set a link and then move the page that you linked to a new location, you break the link.

Here's how you create an internal link:

1. **In Dreamweaver, open the page on which you want to create a link.**

2. **Select the text or image that you want to act as a link.**

3. **Choose <u>W</u>indow⇨<u>P</u>roperties to open the Property Inspector, if it's not open already.**

4. **Click the folder icon to the right of the Link text box.**

   The Select File dialog box opens, as shown in Figure 2-9.

5. **From the Select File dialog box, click the page that you want your image or text to link to and then click the Select button.**

   Alternatively, you can double-click the image or text to select it.

   The link is automatically set and the window closes. If you haven't already saved your page, a message box opens, explaining that you can create a relative link only after you save the page. You should always save the page you're working on before you insert images.

If the page is part of a frameset, use the Target field in the Property Inspector to specify which frame the linked page should open into. (You find out more about setting links in frames in Chapter 10.)

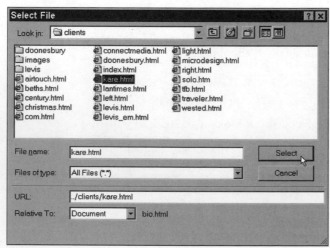

Figure 2-9:
The
Property
Inspector
includes a
link box to
easily set
links from
images or
text.

Setting links to named anchors within a page

If you like to create really long pages, using anchor links to break up naviga-tion within the page is a good idea. A *named anchor link,* often called a *jump link,* enables you to set a link to a specific part of a Web page. You can use a named anchor to link from an image or text string on one page to another place on the same page, or to link from one page to a specific part of another page. To create a named anchor link, you first insert a named anchor in the place that you want to link to. You then use that anchor to direct the browser to that specific part of the page when a viewer follows the link.

Suppose that you want to set a link from the word *Convertible* at the top of a page to a section lower on the page that starts with the headline *Convertible Sports Cars.* You first insert a named anchor at the *Convertible Sports Cars* headline. Then you link the word *Convertible* from the top of the page to that anchor.

To insert a named anchor and set a link to it, follow these steps:

1. **Open the page on which you want to insert the named anchor.**

2. **Click to place your cursor next to the word or image that you want to link to.**

   You don't need to select the word or image; you just need a reference point that is displayed when the link is selected. For this example, I would place the cursor to the left of the headline *Convertible Sports Cars.*

3. **Choose Insert⇨Named Anchor.**

   The Insert Named Anchor dialog box appears.

4. **Enter a name for the anchor.**

   You can name anchors anything you want; just make sure that you use a different name for each anchor on the same page. Then be sure that you remember what you called the anchor, because you have to type the anchor name to set the link. (Unlike other Web design programs, Dreamweaver doesn't automatically enter the anchor name.) In this example, I would choose *convertible* as the anchor name because it would be easy for me to remember.

5. **Click OK.**

   The dialog box closes, and a small anchor icon appears on the page where you inserted the anchor name. You can move an anchor name by clicking the anchor icon and dragging it to another location on the page.

If you're curious about what this named anchor looks like in HTML, here's the code that appears before the headline in my example:

```
<A NAME=convertible></A>
```

6. **To set a link to the named anchor location, click to select the text or image that you want to link from.**

   You can link to a named anchor from anywhere else on the same page or from another page. In my example, I would link from the word *Convertible* that appears at the top of the page to the anchor I made next to the headline.

7. **In the Property Inspector, type the pound sign (#) followed by the anchor name.**

   In my example, I would type **#convertible** in the Link text box. The HTML code for this line looks like this:

```
<A HREF="#convertible">Convertible</A>
```

   If you wanted to link to an anchor named *convertible* on another page with the filename coolcars.html, you would type **coolcars.html# convertible** in the Link text box.

Linking to pages outside your Web site

Linking to a page on another Web site — an *external link* — is even easier than linking to an internal link. All you need is the URL of the page to which you want to link, and you're most of the way there.

To create an external link, follow these steps:

1. **In Dreamweaver, open the page from which you want to link.**

2. **Select the text or image that you want to act as a link.**

3. **Choose Window⇨Properties to open the Property Inspector, if it's not open already.**

4. **In the Link text box, type the URL of the page you want your text or image to link to (see Figure 2-10).**

   The link is automatically set.

Figure 2-10:
To set a link
to another
Web site,
highlight the
text or
image and
type the URL
in the Link
text box in
the Property
Inspector.

Setting a link to an e-mail address

Another common link option goes to an e-mail address. E-mail links make it easy for visitors to send you messages. I always recommend that you invite visitors to contact you because they can point out mistakes in your site and give you valuable feedback about how you can further develop your site.

Setting a link to an e-mail address is almost as easy as setting a link to another Web page. Before you start, you need to know the e-mail address to which you want to link. The only other thing you need to know is that e-mail links must begin with the code *mailto:*. Here's an example of the full line of code behind an e-mail link:

```
<A HREF="mailto:editor@janinewarner.com">Send a message to
           the Janine</A>
```

To create an e-mail link in Dreamweaver, follow these steps:

1. **In Dreamweaver, open the page on which you want to create a link.**

2. **Select an image or highlight the text that you want to act as the link.**

3. **Choose <u>W</u>indow⇨<u>P</u>roperties to open the Property Inspector, if it's not already open.**

4. **In the Link text box, type** mailto: **followed by the e-mail address, as shown in Figure 2-11.**

   The link is automatically set. Even if the page is part of a frameset, you don't need to specify a target for an e-mail link. (To find out more about framesets and targets, see Chapter 10.) When a visitor clicks an e-mail link, the browser automatically opens an e-mail message window where the user can type a subject and message before sending it.

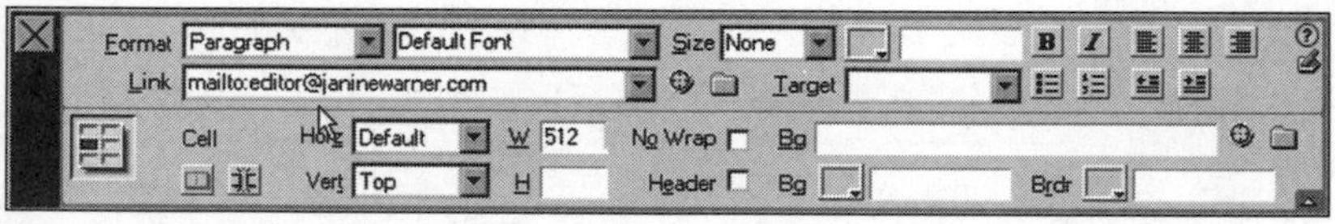

Figure 2-11:
To specify
an e-mail
link, type
mailto: and
the e-mail
address in
the Link text
box.

Putting Your Web Site Online

In the section "Creating a New Site" earlier in this chapter, I tell you how to set up a site and enter the address, login name, and password for your server. In this section, I show you how to put pages on your server and retrieve them by using the built-in FTP capabilities of Dreamweaver.

To transfer files between your hard drive and a remote server, follow these steps:

1. **Choose Site⇨Open Site and select the name of the site you want to work on from the drop-down list.**

   The Site dialog box appears, as shown in Figure 2-12.

2. **Click the Connects to Remote Host button.**

   If you're not already connected to the Internet, the Connect button should start your dial-up connection. If you have trouble connecting this way, try establishing your Internet connection as you usually do to check e-mail or surf the Web; then return to Dreamweaver and choose Connect. After you're online, Dreamweaver should have no trouble establishing an FTP connection with your host server.

   If you have trouble establishing a connection to your Web Server, refer to the section "Setting up Web server access" earlier in this chapter and make sure that the server information is set up correctly.

   After you establish the connection, the directories on your server appear in the left pane of the Site dialog box. If the files on your local hard drive don't appear in the right pane of the dialog box, use the small arrow at the bottom-left corner of the dialog box to open the right pane.

3. **To *upload* a file (that is, transfer a file from your hard drive to your Web server), drag the file or folder from the right pane (which shows the files on your hard drive) to the left pane (which shows the files and folders on the server).**

Figure 2-12:
The Site
dialog box
features a
row of
buttons
across the
top that
control FTP
functions.

4. **To *download* a file (that is, transfer a file from your Web server to your hard drive), drag files or folders from the left pane to the right pane.**

   The files are automatically copied when you transfer them. When the transfer is complete, you can open the files on your hard drive or use a Web browser to view them on the server.

If you're using the Check In/Out feature, don't just drag and drop the file. Instead, highlight the file or files you want to work on in the left pane (which shows files on the server) and choose the Check Out Files button at the top of the Site dialog box. The file automatically downloads to your hard drive and appears in the right pane. A green check mark next to the name indicates that you have checked out the file. Remember that until you check the file back in by highlighting it in the right pane and choosing the Check In button at the top of the Site Dialog box, other people working on your site aren't able to work on the file.

If you're not happy with the FTP capabilities in Dreamweaver, you may want to get a dedicated FTP program, such as Fetch for the Macintosh or WS_FTP for Windows. You can download either of these shareware programs from www.shareware.com.

Chapter 3

Working with Files Created in Other Visual Editors

*T*he Hypertext Markup Language *(HTML)* was designed as a text-based standard to ensure that information could be transferred easily between various programs, computers, and operating systems without altering the original data. In the days before visual HTML editors, this process worked well (visual HTML editors use a graphic interface to edit HTML instead of coding text by hand). Since the advent of new visual HTML editing tools, particularly ones that attempt to add lots of nifty new features, there's been a problem with adherance to the HTML standards. This may not be a problem when you work with only one HTML editor, but if you decide to try a different HTML editor at a later point, you may experience problems caused by the differences between HTML output from each program.

The main reason you run into problems when working with pre-existing sites is that some makers of visual HTML programs don't think about those folks who may want to use more than one tool for a job. Many of the early visual HTML editors such as PageMill and NetObjects Fusion suffered from this problem. While these programs made it much easier for novices to create Web sites, the ease of use came at the price of standards compliance. Dreamweaver was the first visual HTML editor to address this problem through a feature called *Roundtrip HTML*. Roundtrip HTML is designed to minimize the problem of transferring code between Dreamweaver and other HTML editors, and has several perks:

✔ Roundtrip HTML is a built-in Dreamweaver feature that is always active — you don't have to go to any extra effort to activate it.

✔ Roundtrip HTML lets you create HTML pages in any program and open them in Dreamweaver without your original HTML code being altered after it opens in Dreamweaver.

✔ With Roundtrip HTML, you can save HTML documents in Dreamweaver and reopen them in a different editor without problems. This feature is really designed to allow you to collaborate easily with other people who may be using different editing tools — the original goal of HTML.

✔ Using Roundtrip HTML, you can go back and forth between Dreamweaver and other editors countless times without having to worry about the problem of Dreamweaver changing your HTML in an undesirable way; hence the name Roundtrip HTML. (But unfortunately, you may still have to worry about some other programs changing your HTML if you do any work outside of Dreamweaver and save it before going back to Dreamweaver. I tell you more about Roundtrip HTML later in this chapter in the section "The Diverging Standard.")

TECHNICAL STUFF

Moving files from one computer platform to another

HTML files are easy to transfer from one platform to another because they are just text files. You should be able to open an HTML file created on a Macintosh computer in a text editor or Web program on a PC, and vice versa. The HTML code itself doesn't change between platforms.

However, you may have problems with links getting broken when you move an entire site to a different platform because filenames may change from lowercase to uppercase. For example, if you have a graphic in your site that's called Myimage.gif and you link to it on your page as myimage.gif, there won't be a problem if you're running it locally on a Mac or PC, or even if you upload it to a Windows NT or Windows 2000 server. But if you upload your site to your server and it's running UNIX (a lot of Web servers do), the graphic won't show up because UNIX servers make a distinction between upper- and lowercase. The server is looking for myimage.gif, whereas the image that's stored on the server is called Myimage.gif. For safety's sake, I always recommend using lowercase for all links and filenames in a Web site. If you don't, just make sure that you keep track of exactly what case your filenames are in and check that all references to them utilize the same case. Be aware that case does matter online, even if it may not on your local computer.

Another problem that arises when moving files across platforms is that line breaks may not convert properly. *Line breaks* (also called *line returns* and *line feeds*) are basically invisible return characters at the end of a sentence in HTML. The problem is that Mac OS, Windows, and UNIX all use different characters to represent a line break. This discrepancy becomes painfully evident if you open a page in Notepad or another simple text editor that only recognizes certain kinds of line breaks: All the text on your page appears as one long line that extends off the page, making it nearly impossible to read.

Fortunately, Dreamweaver enables you to specify the type of line breaks that it outputs to avoid this problem. Although you don't normally have to worry about line breaks when uploading files to a server, you can run into problems when transferring files between platforms for editing purposes. To customize your line breaks for a particular operating system, choose Edit⇨ Preferences and then choose Code Format from the Category box in the Preferences dialog box, as shown in the following figure. You can select the appropriate line break for the operating system that you or another person working with your HTML files is using. For Windows programs such as Notepad, choose the Windows option. For Mac programs such as SimpleText, choose the Mac option.

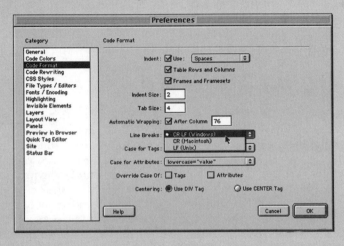

In this chapter, I show you some of the differences among Web design programs and provide tips on how best to leverage the work you've started in another HTML program when you move to Dreamweaver. If you're more concerned with creating Web sites from scratch rather than dealing with existing sites, you may want to skip ahead to Chapter 4.

Corralling Your HTML Files

Theoretically, compatibility among Web design programs should never be a problem because HTML files are, at their heart, just ASCII (or plain-text) files. You can open an HTML file in any text editor, from Macintosh SimpleText to Windows Notepad.

However, some HTML editors take a radically different approach to Web design. NetObjects Fusion, for example, creates pages in a special format and then generates HTML pages only when you publish your site. Fusion also creates very complex HTML code that can be difficult to work with in other editors. Similarly, Adobe GoLive and Microsoft FrontPage include special tags and extensions that aren't part of the HTML standard and are only used and understood by these particular programs. Programs like GoLive and FrontPage also tend to create very complex, verbose, and even redundant code, which adds to download time. Some older programs, such as Adobe PageMill, even change HTML code when it doesn't adhere to certain stringent and limited rules of syntax that only the older program utilizes. This probably all sounds confusing, but the fact of the matter is that the only people that have to worry about these problems are the ones writing the HTML! Despite all the differences in these programs, the end result as it appears in the browser to the typical Web surfer is usually the same, even though the code looks different.

The Diverging Standard

Understanding the differences between HTML programs can get complicated, but you don't have to know much HTML to appreciate the concept. The incompatibilities among Web design programs stem from the fact that HTML isn't a clear standard that's universally supported by browsers and design programs. Instead, HTML is a rapidly changing and evolving language that suffers from too many cooks taking the recipe off in their own directions. Because no clear HTML standard exists, and because many programs utilize their own proprietary HTML tags, Dreamweaver helps to solve the problem of switching back and forth between various Web design programs with its Roundtrip HTML feature. With Roundtrip HTML, any code that is not understood by Dreamweaver is left alone, rather than altered or deleted. Dreamweaver assumes that the code may be valid, even if it doesn't adhere to HTML standards, and works around it — preserving the original code. When it comes time to upload your site, and you want to get rid of all those extra proprietary tags from the other programs, Dreamweaver has a great Clean Up HTML feature to do the trick. (To find out more about cleaning up HTML, see the section later in this chapter, "Cleaning Up Your HTML.")

The Roundtrip HTML feature is important because not all Web design programs use the same rules to create HTML code. In some Web design programs, if you open a page that was created in a different program, the design of the page can be altered substantially. If the program changes even a single tag, the effect on your Web page can be dramatic. Roundtrip HTML addresses this problem and makes it easy to convert and use files from other HTML editors in Dreamweaver. Though not foolproof, the Dreamweaver Roundtrip HTML goes a long way toward solving the problem of moving HTML code back and forth between editing programs.

Importing Web Sites

The first thing you have to do when you move a Web site from another program into Dreamweaver is to import the site. You have two options for importing an already existing Web site: from your hard drive (where you store a site under development), or from the Web server where your site resides for public viewing on the Web.

Importing a site from your hard drive

To import an existing site stored on your hard drive into Dreamweaver, follow these steps:

1. **Choose Site⇨New Site.**

   The Site Definition dialog box appears, as shown in Figure 3-1.

2. **In the Site Name text box, type a name for the site that you're importing.**

   Call your site whatever you like. This name is used only in the drop-down list to identify the site. This list comes in handy when you work on multiple sites in Dreamweaver.

Figure 3-1: Use the Site Definition dialog box to create a new site or to import an existing site into Dreamweaver.

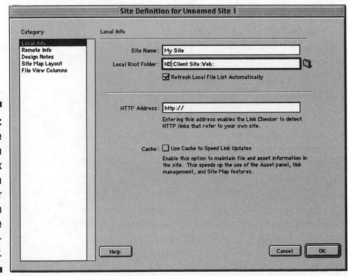

3. Click the Browse button (it resembles a file folder) to the right of the Local Root Folder text box to locate the folder on your hard drive that contains your existing Web site.

You need to locate the folder that contains the actual home or start page for your site (the home page is usually named index.htm or welcome.htm).

Next, it's time to enter the information for your remote server so that you can upload your files when they're ready. (This step actually isn't required right now because you'll be working on your site locally first, but when you want to upload your site, you'll need to fill in the info. So, I'll show you the steps, anyway.)

4. Choose Remote Info from the Category list on the left; then choose FTP *(File Transfer Protocol)* from the Server Access pop-up menu that appears at the top of the dialog box.

This opens the Remote Info page shown in Figure 3-2.

5. Type the address of your server, for example, www.mydomain.com.

Your server address, host directory, login ID, and password should have been provided to you by your *Internet Service Provider* (ISP).

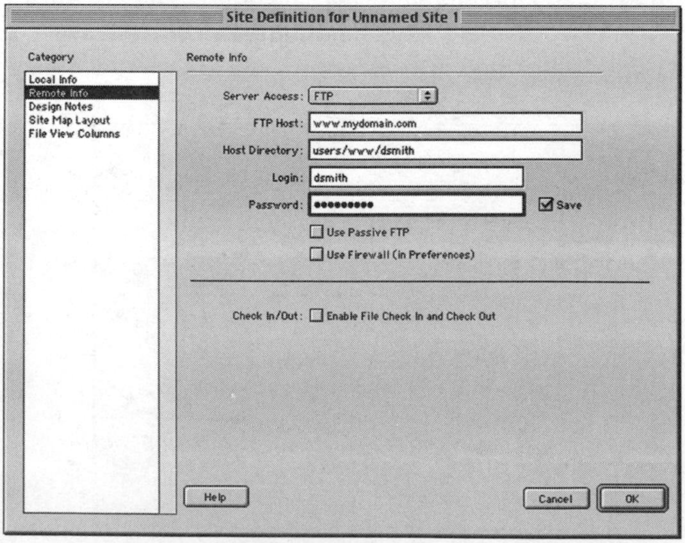

Figure 3-2:
You can enter Web server information into the Site Definition dialog box to upload your files to your Web server directly from Dream-weaver.

6. In the Host Directory text box, enter the path to your Web site.

This path represents the location of your site on the host server. Just like you have paths representing the locations of files on your hard drive, a server uses paths to represent the location of HTML files. This information is also provided by your Internet Service Provider and usually looks something like this:

```
users/www/public/yourdirectoryname
```

or

```
htdocs/yourdirectoryname
```

7. **In the Login text box, type the login name that you use to access the Web server where you store your site.**

   Again this is provided by your Internet Service Provider when you set up your account.

8. **In the Password text box, type your password.**

   Your password appears as asterisks (*) to help protect your privacy.

9. **Check the Save box if you want Dreamweaver to record your name and password so that you don't have to enter it every time you log on to your server.**

   Clicking the Save box to save your password in Dreamweaver means that anybody can open your site and upload changes to your server. Choose this option only if you're sure that no one else will be accessing your computer.

10. **Click OK to finish.**

    The Site Definition dialog box disappears and your site, with all its pages and associated graphics, appears in the Dreamweaver Site window, ready for you to work with.

When you first create a new site, Dreamweaver asks if you want to create a *cache file* for the site. The cache file helps keep your links up-to-date and improves the performance speed of the site map. Click Create when prompted by Dreamweaver to create the cache file.

Downloading a site from a Web server

If you don't already have a copy of an existing Web site on your computer's hard drive, you can use Dreamweaver to download any Web site to which you have access to on the Web (you'll need the Web server address, user ID, and password to do this).

To download a Web site, follow the same steps for importing a site provided in the preceding section, making sure that you include the relevant Remote information for your server. Then, instead of selecting an existing root folder with a local home page as in the previous section, specify an empty folder that you will then use to import the remote site into. After you finish entering the Remote Info into the Site Definition box, click OK and you're ready to download the site into the blank Site window.

1. **Click the Connect button in the Site window to log on to your remote server.**

   The computer makes a remote connection using the FTP information that you supplied (if it doesn't connect, the information you supplied is wrong). When you're connected, the remote site appears in the left panel of the Site window, as shown in Figure 3-3.

2. **The left pane of this site window represents the files on the remote server and the right pane represents the files on your local hard drive. Click in the left pane of the Site window and then select the files and folders that you want to retrieve from the server by clicking and highlighting them. You can shift-click to select multiple files.**

3. **With the files and folders that you want to retrieve selected, click the Get File(s) button to automatically copy the site from your server to your hard drive.**

   You can also manually drag and drop the folders and files from the left pane to the right pane using your mouse.

   When the files appear in the right pane after you copy them, it means that they have been successfully imported and saved locally to your hard drive. The files are saved in the folder you selected earlier in the Site Definition dialog box.

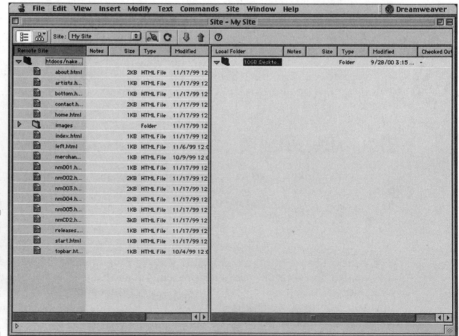

Figure 3-3: Connecting to a remote site and preparing to download files.

Working on Sites Created in Other Visual Editors

Many visual Web design programs promise to make working in HTML fast and easy. If you've fallen for that promise with other programs and then found that they weren't quite as good as you originally thought, you're not alone. Fortunately, you'll probably find that things go a bit more smoothly with Dreamweaver, which benefits from being a relative newcomer and learning from other's mistakes.

To help you out with the transition from another program, Dreamweaver makes the transition process easier with some special features. In most cases, individual pages can transfer without problems from any other program to Dreamweaver. Sometimes though, you'll find that the transition process is a bit too complicated and it's better to start from scratch. The following sections describe the most popular HTML editors and what you need to know if you're moving files from one of these programs to Dreamweaver.

Microsoft FrontPage 2000

Microsoft FrontPage 2000 (the previous version is FrontPage 98) offers some powerful features, as well as an attractive bundle of programs for Web developers. FrontPage 2000 and FrontPage 98 are Windows-only programs, but you may still be able to get your hands on a rather outdated version of FrontPage for the Macintosh called FrontPage 1.0 that Microsoft never updated.

In addition to an HTML editor, FrontPage 2000 ships with Image Composer, a graphics program designed for creating images for the Web. FrontPage also includes *Web components* — CGI *(Common Gateway Interface)* scripts that you can use to add interactive features, such as a search engine or a simple discussion area, to your Web site. Web components work only if their corresponding programs reside on the Web server that you use, but many commercial service providers now offer FrontPage Web components. Another attractive feature in FrontPage is its site-management capabilities, which simplify managing links and organizing files and folders.

FrontPage, however, does have some shortcomings, and it has frustrated many Web designers with its complexity and poor code output. Because this product has so many features, many users get lost using it. If you just want to edit a single HTML file, for example, FrontPage can be very confusing because it wants to keep everything in tidy "webs" so that it can track and manage links. Dreamweaver is proving to be much more appealing to professional Web site developers, in part because it's more flexible — whether you want to edit a single page or an entire site. FrontPage also lacks the sophistication of an integrated text editor such as HomeSite. FrontPage does include a built-in text editor, but it's a very basic one that's about as sophisticated as Windows Notepad.

If you want to move from FrontPage to Dreamweaver, make note of any FrontPage Web components that you've used, such as search engines or forms. Dreamweaver doesn't offer these built-in features, and you won't be able to continue editing them in Dreamweaver the way you did in FrontPage. Though the components should still work, thanks to the Dreamweaver Roundtrip HTML, you'll be sacrificing some of the convenience of FrontPage's built in components for Dreamweaver's more standard approach to creating code. If you've used a number of components, have gotten used to the way they work in FrontPage, and feel that you can't live without them, you might be better off sticking with FrontPage for awhile.

If you've used the Dynamic HTML features in FrontPage, you need to pay special attention to those features as you convert your site to Dreamweaver. Microsoft FrontPage isn't as good as Dreamweaver at creating DHTML features that work in both Netscape Navigator and Microsoft Internet Explorer, so you probably want to improve your DHTML code if you expect viewers to use any browser other than Internet Explorer. Because DHTML is much more complex than HTML, you probably don't want to edit this code manually — converting from other editors to Dreamweaver can get pretty tricky. You may find that the simplest solution is to delete the DHTML features that you created in FrontPage and re-create them in Dreamweaver. (For more on DHTML, check out Chapters 12 and 13.)

NetObjects Fusion

If you've been working in NetObjects Fusion, you face a more dramatic transition to Dreamweaver than you would coming from any of the other HTML editors that I discuss in this chapter. That's because Fusion takes a unique approach to Web design and HTML code output.

Using complex HTML tables and a transparent graphic to control spacing, Fusion provides down-to-the-pixel design control. This feature is enticing to many graphic designers because they can create complex layouts with much less effort in Fusion. The problem is that Fusion generates very complex code to achieve this control, and that code doesn't convert well to other editors or lend itself to easy hand editing.

Unfortunately, if you want the cleanest HTML code possible, which speeds up download time and makes editing pages easier as they change and evolve, your best bet is to dump the code that Fusion creates and re-create your designs from scratch. I'm sorry to break this to you, but if you've been using Fusion, you should probably start over with Dreamweaver; the transition process is just too daunting for most people, unless you're dealing with a really small site. Move all your images into image directories and then start over with your design work.

Adobe GoLive

Previously called GoLive CyberStudio, GoLive is now Adobe's flagship HTML editor, replacing the earlier PageMill program. GoLive offers some great features for easy page design and a lot of similarities with Dreamweaver, but also brings many of the same problems as pages created in NetObjects Fusion (see preceding section). GoLive uses a grid to provide down-to-the-pixel layout control in much the same way that Fusion does. So, like Fusion, GoLive outputs very complex code that is difficult to edit in other programs.

Because you can see the alignment grid in GoLive, you are more aware of the complex table that GoLive creates in the background. You have the option not to use the grid, however. If you avoided using it, converting your pages to Dreamweaver should be a much easier task. If you did use the grid to create your Web pages and your page designs are highly complex, you may find that re-creating your pages from scratch in Dreamweaver is your best option. The code used to create the complex HTML tables that GoLive uses in its grids is extremely difficult to edit outside of GoLive. If you're working with someone who uses GoLive, try to get them to avoid using the Layout Grid feature when designing their pages before bringing them into Dreamweaver.

If you've added any JavaScript actions to your pages in GoLive, you won't be able to edit them in Dreamweaver, although the actions will still work. Likewise, Dynamic HTML features and animations created in GoLive can't be edited in Dreamweaver without doing the coding manually. If your page contains any actions or DTHML features, you might find it easiest to re-create the page in Dreamweaver if it still needs to be edited after you import the site.

Microsoft Word

Although Microsoft Word is a word processor and is not considered an HTML editor per se, it does have rather extensive HTML output capabilities. You're likely to encounter pages that have been output from Microsoft Word at some point, due to its tremendous popularity in the marketplace. The problems you may find in HTML code generated from Word are similar to the problems generated from FrontPage: They both tend to output verbose and redundant code that deviates from HTML standards. Word should give you fewer problems than some of the other visual editors, however, and Dreamweaver does include a special command for working with Microsoft Word–generated HTML.

Other HTML editors

A few years ago there were lots of different visual HTML editors being used. Today there are only a few major ones left. The few that I discuss here seem to have captured most of the market. Still, you may find yourself inheriting sites built in older visual editors such as Adobe PageMill, Claris HomePage, or Symantec VisualPage, to name a few. Each of these should present fewer problems than either Fusion or GoLive, which tend to be the hardest to work with. In any case, as you consider how best to convert your work into Dreamweaver, look for unusual code output, non-standard rules about HTML tags and syntax, and sophisticated features — such as Dynamic HTML and CGI scripts. These are the elements of an HTML page that are most likely to cause problems when you import them into Dreamweaver.

For the most part, you can open any HTML page with Dreamweaver and continue developing it with little concern. If you run into problems, remember that you always have the option of re-creating the page from scratch in Dreamweaver — a sure way to get rid of any unwanted code. As a final option, you can continue to use both programs together, utilizing the Dreamweaver Roundtrip HTML feature to preserve the code between edits, at least until you're ready to make the complete switch to Dreamweaver.

Cleaning Up Your HTML

All visual HTML editing tools, even Dreamweaver, sacrifice ease of use for what often comes out as fat, complicated, and oftentimes redundant code. If you're an HTML pro, you may know what to look for and how to "trim the fat," so to speak. If not, don't worry. Dreamweaver includes some great features for cleaning up and trimming messy HTML code. Using the Clean Up HTML features in Dreamweaver ensure that your code is the cleanest and most efficient possible, save for hiring an expert to do it by hand.

Using the Clean Up Word HTML feature

Because Microsoft Word tends to output so much verbose and redundant code, Dreamweaver includes a special feature to help you clean up any code inherited from a Word-generated HTML document. This feature can really trim down the messy output that Word tends to generate, including unnecessary Word-specific tags, redundant `<FONT>` tags, invalidly nested tags, and so on.

To use the Clean Up Word HTML feature, follow these steps:

1. **Open the Word-generated HTML document in Dreamweaver by selecting File⇨Open.**

2. **After the page is open, choose Commands⇨Clean Up Word HTML from the menu.**

   Dreamweaver takes a while to detect the version of Word used to output the document. Then the Clean Up Word HTML dialog box appears, as shown in Figure 3-4. If Dreamweaver can't detect the version of Word automatically, you can select the correct version from the Clean Up HTML From drop-down list box near the top of the dialog box.

3. **Click to check or uncheck the boxes in the dialog box to set the preferences for how you would like Dreamweaver to clean up the code.**

   You can choose from the following listed check box options. I recommend checking all of them:

   • **Remove all Word specific markup:** Removes all Word-specific HTML. You can also select more specific options individually by using the Detailed tab.

Figure 3-4: The Clean Up Word HTML feature offers a number of options for cleaning up Microsoft Word– generated HTML files.

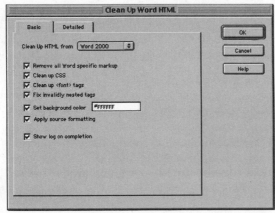

   • **Clean up CSS:** Removes all Word-specific CSS *(Cascading Style Sheets)* and cleans up any CSS code as needed. You can also select more specific options individually by using the Detailed tab.

   • **Clean up <FONT> tags:** Removes HTML tags that convert the default body text to Size 2 HTML.

   • **Fix invalidly nested tags:** Removes the font markup tags inserted by Word outside the paragraph and heading (block-level) tags.

- **Set background color:** Word sets a default background of gray for all of its pages. This option lets you enter a *hexadecimal color value* (a six-digit HTML color code) if you want to use a different background color. The default value set by Dreamweaver is white.

- **Apply source formatting:** Applies the source formatting options that you specify in Dreamweaver's HTML Format Preferences. Check this box to format your document consistently with the other HTML documents you create in Dreamweaver.

- **Show log on completion:** Displays an alert box with details about the changes made to the document as soon as the clean up is finished.

4. **When you're finished setting the options, click OK to complete the clean up.**

Always test the file by viewing it in the browser to make sure the conversion didn't delete or alter any important information and the file looks the way you want it to before you delete the original.

Using the Clean Up HTML feature

Dreamweaver also includes a generic Clean Up HTML command that can be very useful for cleaning up code generated by other programs and even by Dreamweaver itself. It's similar to the Clean Up Word HTML command except that it can be used with any other HTML editor. This feature is really handy, and I use it all the time. It's a good idea to get in the habit of using it for every file you work on — just before it's ready to publish — even if the file has never seen any editor other than Dreamweaver. The Clean Up HTML options can help you trim down your HTML code and make it as efficient as possible.

To use the Clean Up HTML feature, follow these steps:

1. **Open an existing document and choose <u>C</u>ommands⇔C<u>l</u>ean Up HTML.**

The Clean Up HTML dialog box appears, as shown in Figure 3-5.

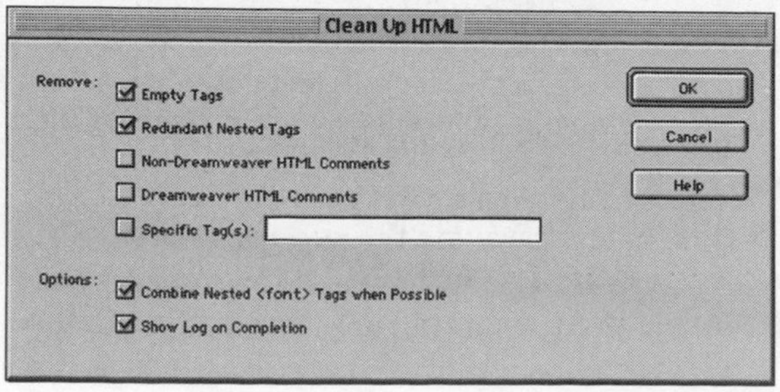

Figure 3-5:
The Clean
Up HTML
feature
offers
options for
cleaning up
HTML
output.

Clean Up HTML	
Remove:	
☑ Empty Tags	OK
☑ Redundant Nested Tags	Cancel
☐ Non-Dreamweaver HTML Comments	Help
☐ Dreamweaver HTML Comments	
☐ Specific Tag(s):	
Options:	
☑ Combine Nested <font> Tags when Possible	
☑ Show Log on Completion	

2. **Click to check or uncheck the boxes in the dialog box to set the preferences for how you would like Dreamweaver to clean up the code.**

Choose from the following Remove options:

- **Empty Tags:** Removes any tags that have no content between them, a common problem with heavily edited HTML pages. For example, `<B></B>` and `<FONT SIZE="2"></FONT>` are considered empty tags.

- **Redundant Nested Tags:** Removes all redundant instances of a tag, another common problem with pages created in visual editors.

- **Non-Dreamweaver HTML Comments:** Removes all comments that were not inserted by Dreamweaver. Make sure that you no longer need the comments before you run this option. This tool can be really useful when working with Fireworks-generated HTML, as Fireworks tends to insert a lot of unnecessary comments into the code.

- **Dreamweaver HTML Comments:** Removes all comments that were inserted by Dreamweaver. If you don't need the comments in your code, they are best removed. Be aware, however, that removing Dreamweaver comments turns template-based documents into ordinary HTML documents, and Library items into normal HTML code. That means that these documents are not automatically updated whenever the original template or Library item changes. So don't check this option if your page uses Library items or is template-based and you want to continue to have the page update automatically. (See Chapter 6 to find out more about using templates and Library items.)

- **Specific Tag(s):** Removes the tags specified in the adjacent field.

Choose from the following general options:

- **Combine Nested `<FONT>` Tags when Possible:** Consolidates two or more `<FONT>` tags when they control the same range of text. This is one of the most useful options in the Clean Up HTML command because almost all HTML editors (including Dreamweaver) create nested `<FONT>` tags that are redundant and add unnecessary code.

- **Show Log on Completion:** Displays an alert message with details about the changes made to the document as soon as the clean up is completed.

3. **When you've finished setting the options, click OK.**

The dialog box disappears; Dreamweaver performs the clean up and produces an alert message detailing the specifics of the clean up operation if you clicked the Show Log on Completion option. Preview your file again before saving it.

On rare occasions, the clean-up operation produces unpredictable results if there were errors or inconsistencies in the original code. If this is the case, close the document without saving it and reopen it to revert to the original version. You can then try selecting fewer clean-up options or just skip the clean up altogether. If the clean up doesn't produce any problems, save the file and move on to the next one.

Chapter 4

Getting into HTML

• •

• •

*W*hen you first look at the code behind a Web page, you may be overwhelmed by what you see. You may decide that learning all those hieroglyphics isn't worth it. Besides, you're learning to use Dreamweaver so you shouldn't need to edit or write HTML code. But having a basic understanding of HTML — what it looks like, where it comes from, and why it works the way it does — is helpful no matter what you do on the Web. Even if you don't want to write HTML code manually, understanding a little about how HTML works can help you appreciate what Dreamweaver has to offer. And if you really want to understand how the Web works — if you want to be able to create really sophisticated Web pages and have the most possible control over your designs — you should at least learn the basics of the Hyper Text Markup Language.

Although Dreamweaver is a great program, you'll discover that being able to manually tweak the raw HTML code every once in a while can help you overcome some of the program's limitations. Dreamweaver provides a number of options for manually manipulating the code: a built-in text editor complete with advanced HTML options, such as color coding and syntax checking, as well as tried-and-true HTML code editors HomeSite (for Windows) and BBEdit (for Macintosh) bundled with it.

In this chapter, I provide an introduction to HTML and show you the basics so you can make some sense of it even if you've never worked with HTML before. If you're an old pro, you may find this chapter is still a good refresher course.

If you really want to get into HTML, check out *HTML 4 For Dummies,* 3rd Edition, by Ed Tittel and Natanya Pitts (published by IDG Books Worldwide, Inc.).

Accessing HTML Code

You have two ways to access HTML code in Dreamweaver: the built-in Code Inspector or any text or HTML editor you associate with Dreamweaver in the Preferences⇨File Types/Editors option. The most integrated way is to use the built-in HTML Code Inspector. To get to it, use one of the following three methods:

- ✓ Choose Window⇨Code Inspector
- ✓ Click Code Inspector in the Launcher bar
- ✓ Press F10

The HTML window is a basic text editor that's fully integrated into Dreamweaver. If you type new text or apply any formatting in the WYSIWYG editor, you immediately see your changes reflected in the HTML Source window. If you select text or another element in one window, the same element appears highlighted in the other (see Figure 4-1). This feature makes it easy to find your place as you move back and forth between the two, and you can learn a lot of HTML this way.

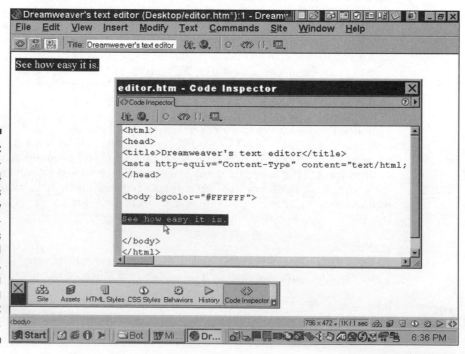

Figure 4-1: Dreamweaver 4 features many enhancements to its integrated text editor, including color coding and syntax checking.

If you add tags or text in the text editor, the WYSIWYG editor displays the results after you save the file. Try applying bold or centering some text in the WYSIWYG editor, and then notice that the `<B>` . . . `</B>` and `<CENTER>` . . . `</CENTER>` tags appear in the text editor. This impressive feature provides an interactive way to learn HTML and is a great way to keep track of what Dreamweaver is doing when you apply formatting in the WYSIWYG editing environment. With Dreamweaver 4, you can even color-code the tags in the HTML Color Preferences.

Another way to work in HTML with Dreamweaver is to use the HTML text editor that's bundled with Dreamweaver. This program — either HomeSite (for Windows) or BBEdit (for Macintosh) — is a sophisticated text editor designed for writing HTML code. If you have another preferred text editor, you can associate it with Dreamweaver (you'll find information about how to do so at the end of this chapter). You won't benefit from the integration Dreamweaver has with HomeSite and BBEdit, but you can use any program you choose to edit your pages.

Both HomeSite and BBEdit provide a list of tags that you can easily insert into your HTML file, as well as wizards and other features for creating more complex code, such as tables and frames. Keep in mind that any changes you make to your Web page in these programs don't immediately show up in the Dreamweaver window. You must save your work, leave the text editor, and then return to Dreamweaver. When you toggle back to the WYSIWYG editor in Dreamweaver, you're prompted with a dialog box stating `This file was edited outside of Dreamweaver. Do you want to reload it?` Click Yes to see your changes reflected in Dreamweaver. (With both BBEdit and HomeSite, you can keep both Dreamweaver and the text editor open at the same time and move back and forth between them.)

Understanding Basic HTML

HTML uses *tags* (set off in brackets like these: `< >`) to format words and images on a page. You insert HTML tags around words and image descriptions to specify how these elements should be displayed in a browser. For example, if you want several words to appear in bold type, simply put the tag `<B>` before the words and `</B>` after the words that you want to set in bold.

Most tags have an *open* (or *start*) *tag* followed by a similar *close* (or *end*) *tag*. The close tag is distinguished by the forward slash (/), which indicates that the formatting should stop. Together, these tags tell the browser where your formatting should begin and end.

Some HTML tags may seem strange to you at first, especially if you're used to formatting text for print. The difference stems in large part from the fact that HTML was designed to be so universally functional that nearly every computer on the planet could display pages created for the Web. But not every computer has the same size monitor or the same fonts. So you're generally limited to relative descriptions in HTML. For example, instead of making an absolute description for a font, such as "headline 24-point, bold," basic HTML uses a heading tag such as <H1>. The heading tags all show emphasis for the text that you enclose in them relative to one another. Heading 1, written <H1>, is the largest heading size, followed by <H2>, <H3>, and so on, down to <H6>, which, somewhat counter-intuitively, is the smallest heading size. The actual size of the headings varies for different types of computers and Web browsers. But relative to each other, Heading 1 clearly shows more emphasis than Heading 2, and so on, down to Heading 6.

The advantage of relative tags is that they enable viewers to decide how a Web page should display in their browsers, which takes the best advantage of their systems while still providing general guidelines about the importance of elements on a page. In Netscape Navigator, for example, the default font is Times, but viewers have the option to use any font. So, for one viewer, <H1> may be 24-point Times and bold, but for another, it may be 30-point Helvetica. However, no matter which font your viewers select, <H1> is always going to be bigger than <H2>, and so on down the line. Your job as Web designer is to organize the page so that the information and layout make sense at any setting and then try to get over your frustration at not having more control!

Creating a Simple HTML Page

HTML code is simply text typed in a document. This means that you can use any text editor or word processing program to create an HTML document: SimpleText, Notepad, Microsoft Word, Corel WordPerfect, or any one of the other 250 or so word processing programs out there. Simply type the tags that you see in the following section, and you can create a Web page. For this chapter's examples, I recommend using the HTML Source editor (called the Code Inspector) that is built into Dreamweaver because you can easily see what you create in the WYSIWYG editor of Dreamweaver.

You should also get in the habit of previewing your work in a browser. Dreamweaver does an excellent job of displaying HTML code accurately in its WYSIWYG editor; but if you view your pages in various browsers, you can begin to appreciate the differences in the way tags display. Because you can try something in HTML and then look at it right away in a browser to see the effect, figuring out HTML is relatively easy.

Viewing HTML document source code

Many people suggest that you can learn HTML by looking at the source code of Web pages. Most browsers give you the option to display the HTML code behind any Web page that you're viewing. In Netscape Navigator, choose View⇨Page Source; in Internet Explorer, choose View⇨Source (other browsers may use different command words, such as Document Source or HTML Code). Although looking at Web pages can be a great way to learn new tricks, be aware that it's also an easy way to pick up bad habits.

You'd be surprised at how many people make mistakes in their HTML code or use redundant tags. Fortunately — or unfortunately, as the case may be — many browsers forgive this and do a decent job of displaying the page, even if its creator forgot a closing tag here or left out a set of quotation marks there. The problem is that other browsers, and even other versions of the same browser, may have trouble displaying pages with these same errors. A browser may distort the intended view or even crash when confused by bad syntax. So be forewarned: Just because a page looks okay in Netscape Navigator or Internet Explorer doesn't mean that the code behind the page is without errors.

Word processing programs, such as Microsoft Word, save files in a special file format that browsers can't read. If you use a word processing program to create an HTML file, make sure that you save the file as Text Only. If you work on a Windows 3.x machine, change the .txt file extension to .htm (in Windows 95, 98, and NT, it's now okay to use .html). On a Macintosh or UNIX system, use .html. Newer versions of Microsoft Word also have a Save As HTML option that automatically converts Word files into HTML. You can use Dreamweaver to open HTML files created in Word just as you would open any other HTML files.

Table 4-1 provides some of the basic HTML codes and describes what they do.

Table 4-1		Basic HTML Codes
HTML Tag	*Close Tag*	*Function*
<HTML>	</HTML>	Identifies the page as an HTML document.
<HEAD>	</HEAD>	Defines the header area of the page and contains the <TITLE> and <META> tags.
<TITLE>	</TITLE>	Contains the page title that is displayed at the top of the browser.
<META>	No close tag	Various uses, but most commonly used for search engine information, such as keywords and descriptions.

(continued)

Table 4-1 *(continued)*

HTML Tag	Close Tag	Function
<BODY>	</BODY>	Defines the body of the page — the area that is displayed in a browser.
<P>	</P>	Optional, but recommended. Inserts a paragraph break.
 	</BR>	Optional. Inserts a line break.
<HR>	No close tag	Inserts a horizontal rule that displays as a gray line.

The simplest HTML document

All HTML documents start and end with the same basic code. At the top of the page, you should put the open HTML tag (<HTML>) to indicate to a browser that this is an HTML document. Similarly, at the very end of the page, use the close HTML tag (</HTML>). Follow the open HTML tag with the header information (the <HEAD> tag). Put the <TITLE> inside the <HEAD> tag. The <TITLE> tag often confuses people because the text within it doesn't display in the Web page itself. Instead, the contents of the <TITLE> tag appear in the browser's title bar. The <META> tag also goes inside the <HEAD> tags. The <META> tag has many uses, including embedding keywords and descriptions for search engines (see the following example). <META> tag contents do not display in a browser. After you close the header area with the </HEAD> tag, open the body text of the document with — surprise! — the <BODY> tag. All the words, images, and other HTML code that make up the document go between the <BODY> and </BODY> tags.

A very simple HTML document looks like this:

```
<HTML>
<HEAD>
<TITLE>A Simple HTML Page</TITLE>
<META DESCRIPTION="This is a simple HTML page.">
<META KEYWORDS="HTML, simple, page">
</HEAD>
<BODY>
This is a simple HTML document.
</BODY></HTML>
```

To distinguish the tags from the text, I've written all the tags in this chapter in uppercase. Even though you can write HTML in uppercase, lowercase, or even mixed case without incident, I recommend that you stick to uppercase to make your code easier to read. Dreamweaver lets you choose the case you prefer in the Preferences dialog box and then leaves the case the way you type it if you add tags manually. To change Dreamweaver's HTML preferences, choose Edit⇨Preferences and select HTML Format from the Category section.

The <P> and <BR> tags

In the preceding simple HTML example, I put each tag (or set of tags) on a separate line for clarity. Pressing Enter (or Return) after each line in my example, however, doesn't affect how the lines break when the HTML file is displayed in a browser. In your word processor, you can press Enter or Return as many times as you want in HTML code without affecting how the document appears in a browser. To create actual line breaks that *do* appear in a browser, you use the paragraph (<P>) or break (<BR>) tags. The break tag inserts a line break. The paragraph tag adds even more space by breaking the line and adding another blank line below it. In Figure 4-2, you can see how the <P> tag that I added in the following code has a different result than the <BR> tag.

```
<HTML>
<HEAD><TITLE>Paragraph and break tags</TITLE></HEAD>
<BODY>
Remember that the spaces and returns in HTML code don't
          affect the display. You have to use break and
          paragraph tags if you want the returns to show up
          in the browser. Even though I didn't put any
          returns around this break tag <BR> or this <P>
          paragraph tag in the code, the lines break when
          displayed in the browser.
Similarly, the return in this code before the beginning of
          this sentence doesn't appear in the display in the
          browser.</P>
</BODY></HTML>
```

Because you can use two different kinds of line breaks, Dreamweaver offers you two ways to use the Enter key (the Return key on a Macintosh) to insert these breaks in your pages when you are working in the WYSIWYG environment. Simply pressing the Enter key inserts a <P> tag; if you want a <BR> tag, press and hold down the Shift key while you press the Enter key. (On the Mac, press and hold down the Option key while you press the Return key.) This difference makes choosing between the two tags as you work in Dreamweaver easy. It also means that you don't need to memorize these tags or try to remember which tag is which because Dreamweaver takes care of that for you.

If you're working in the HTML Source window, in BBEdit, or in HomeSite, pressing the Enter (or Return) key inserts a line break in the text file but doesn't insert a <P> or <BR> tag. The line break separates your text, visually, when you view it in the text editor, but an actual line break is not displayed when you view the file in a browser.

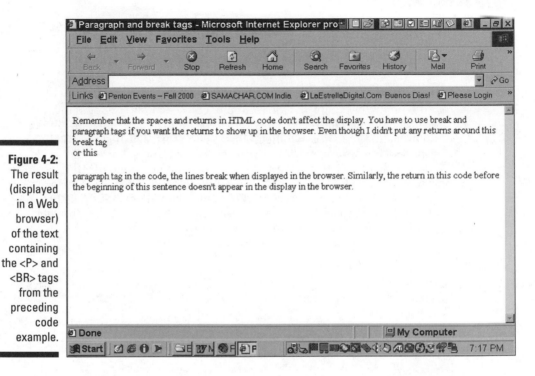

Figure 4-2:
The result
(displayed
in a Web
browser)
of the text
containing
the <P> and

 tags
from the
preceding
code
example.

The <HR> tag

Another tag that you can use to create space on a Web page is the <HR>, or
horizontal rule tag. The <HR> tag creates a gray, sometimes three-dimensional-
looking line that can act as a divider on your Web page. To insert a rule using
the WYSIWYG editor, choose Insert⇨Horizontal Rule. In a text editor, simply
type <HR> (there is no close tag). The <HR> tag attributes (available from
the Property Inspector) enable you to control the height, width, and alignment of the rule. Using these options enables you to make the line thicker
and specify how far it stretches across the page. When you fill in each of
those boxes, the editor automatically generates code that looks something
like this:

```
<HR WIDTH="50%" SIZE="4" ALIGN="CENTER">
```

The <BODY> tag

The <BODY> tag, which designates the main area of the page, includes attributes to specify background color, text color, and other features that can make
a dramatic difference in how your page looks. You can write the <BODY> tag
simply as <BODY> with no attributes, in which case the browser displays its
default colors. Dreamweaver automatically generates this simple <BODY> tag

when you create a new page. In most browsers, the default is a gray or white background, black text, and blue links that turn red after they're selected. Using attributes, you can change these colors. The following code would create a page with a white background, green text, and black links:

```
<BODY BGCOLOR="#FFFFFF" TEXT="# #3333FF" LINK="#000000">
```

BGCOLOR stands for background color, and the "#FFFFFF" is a *hexadecimal* (a number system that computers use) color code that specifies that the background should be white.

Fortunately, you don't have to worry about hexadecimal color codes because Dreamweaver calculates them for you when you choose a color from a color palette or color wheel in the WYSIWYG editor. You can set text and link colors the same way.

In the following example, all the tags introduced in this chapter so far are used on one page. Notice the colors in the <BODY> tag, the use of the horizontal rule, and the spacing created by the <P> tags. Figure 4-3 shows this code displayed in Internet Explorer.

```
<HTML>
<HEAD>
<TITLE>Attributes</TITLE>
</HEAD>
<BODY BGCOLOR="#FFFFFF" TEXT="#0E7769" LINK="#000000">
<P align=CENTER>This text should be centered because I use
          the center attribute in the paragraph tag. Because
          of the attributes used in the body tag, the
          background of this page is white and the text is
          green. (You can't tell that from the black and
          white image in Figure 4-3, but if you type this
          code into Dreamweaver and display it in a browser,
          it will be green.)
<P>This text should not be centered and should be separated
          by a return and space. Below, you can find the
          horizontal rule tag with its attributes set to
          span only half the page and to be centered.
<P>
<HR WIDTH="50%" SIZE="4" ALIGN="CENTER">
<BR>
The horizontal rule inserts a gray line. I've set this line
          to be thicker (size "4") and narrower than the
          default. It's also a little hard to see against
          the white background.
</BODY>
</HTML>
```

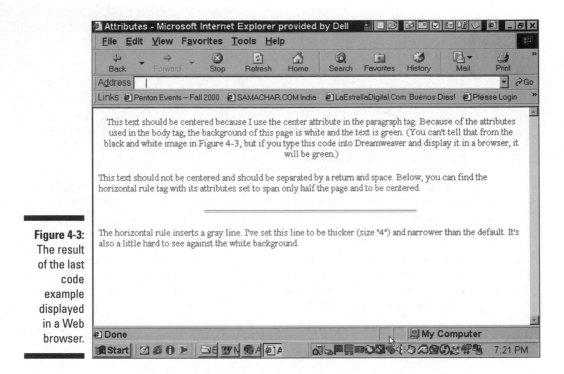

Figure 4-3:
The result
of the last
code
example
displayed
in a Web
browser.

The following text appears in the browser window shown in Figure 4-3:

This text should be centered because I use the center attribute in the paragraph tag. Because of the attributes used in the body tag, the background of this page is white and the text is green. (You can't tell that from the black and white image in Figure 4-3, but if you type this code into Dreamweaver and display it in a browser, it will be green.)

This text should not be centered and should be separated by a return and space. Below, you can find the horizontal rule tag with its attributes set to span only half the page and to be centered.

The horizontal rule inserts a gray line. I've set this line to be thicker (size "4") and narrower than the default. It's also a little hard to see against the white background.

Setting hyperlinks

Perhaps the most magical feature made possible by HTML is the capability to link to another page with hyperlinks. Many people who are new to HTML think that it must be really complicated to set hyperlinks to other pages in a Web site, and even harder to set links to another site on the Web. Fortunately, it's not that complicated, but it is a little more involved than just putting bold tags around text.

Dreamweaver automates the process of setting links to make it easier. However, understanding the basics of how links work behind the scenes helps you appreciate how links get broken and how to fix them. I start with the easy part, even though you may think it's hard at first.

You set links by using the <A HREF> tag, which I call the *link tag*. The link tag does have a close tag, but it's just </A>. The attribute for the link tag is the address of the page (or the URL) of the site you want to link to. For example, if you want to link from the word *Macromedia* on your Web page to the Macromedia Web site, the code looks like this:

```
<A HREF="http://www.macromedia.com">Macromedia</A>
```

The comment tag

A special tag that you should know about is the comment tag (<!--comment-->), which enables you to include information in your HTML document that you don't want displayed to your viewers. You can use comment tags anywhere in a document; you generally use them if you want to make notes to yourself or to someone else who may work on the file. The browser ignores all text between the <!-- and -->, so you have to make sure that all your comments appear between them. The comment tag doesn't use a closing tag because all of its contents appear between the brackets.

In the Dreamweaver WYSIWYG editor window, comment tags appear in a small yellow box with an exclamation point (you can choose not to display the comment tags in Preferences, if you prefer). To add a comment tag in the WYSIWYG editor, choose Insert⇨Comment. You can also type your comments manually in the HTML Source window, HomeSite, or BBEdit. Beware, however, that a comment tag appears on the HTML page and is visible to anyone who views your source code on the Web.

Dreamweaver's special Design Notes features is a better option if you want to put notes on your page for other designers on your team that are not visible to anyone else Design Notes enable you to attach a comment to a page, an image, a folder, or to any other element in a Web site. You can choose to upload these comments to your server so that others working on the site can also see them (as long as they have access to the server), or you can opt never to put your notes on the Web at all, ensuring they stay completely private. (For more information about Design Notes, see Chapter 6.)

Creating links from one page in your Web site to another gets a little more complicated. The tag is the same, but instead of specifying the full URL of a Web site, you indicate the filename of the page that you're linking to. For example, if you want to link from your home page to a page called help.html in the same folder, the tag looks like this:

```
<A HREF="help.html">This text links to the help page</A>
```

Setting links to pages in your own Web site may seem pretty straightforward, but it gets more complicated. The link tag in the previous example looks simple because the files are in the same folder. But you may not want to keep all the files for your Web site in one place. I recommend that you organize them in separate folders for the same reason that you probably don't like all your papers in one file folder in your file cabinet or all your files in one folder on your hard drive. However, when an HTML file isn't in the same folder as the file you want to link it to, you have to write a slightly more complicated link tag that specifies the path to the page. (Check out Chapter 5 for more on organizing your Web site's files and directories.)

To set a link to a file within another folder, you need to include the folder name and the filename in the link tag, which is called the *path*. Thus, to go from an index.html file in the Web site to tools.html in the books folder, the link looks like this:

```
<A HREF="books/tools.html">Books about HTML Tools</A>
```

This path tells your browser that the tools.html file is in the books folder on your hard drive or server. Fortunately, Dreamweaver automatically sets link paths like this one when you use the Browse feature to set links in the WYSIWYG editor. (The Browse feature is accessible by clicking the folder icon in the Property Inspector. Then you simply locate the file you want, select it, and Dreamweaver figures out the path for you.) You can find the steps you need to create all kinds of links with Dreamweaver in Chapter 2.

Naming the Main Page

Name the home page in your Web site index.htm because most servers are set up to serve the index file when somebody types just your domain name (for example, if a user types www.macromedia.com). If you don't have an index file, the browser displays a list of all the files and folders in your site instead.

The main file in your site isn't the only place that you should name a file index.htm. This technique also works for the main HTML page in other folders, especially if you want to provide a direct address to that section of the site. For example, if you want to create a special section for a product and your sales force wants to go directly to that page, you can create a folder using the product name. Then, using index.htm as the main file, all a visitor needs in order to access the page is the folder name added to the URL.

Here's what it could look like: Say your domain name is www.close.com, and you want *friends* to be an easily accessible section. If you create a folder called *friends* and make best.htm the main page, users would have to type the URL as www.close.com/friends/best.htm. If you rename best.htm to index.htm, a visitor to the site could type www.close.com/friends as the URL, and the browser would automatically load the page.

Cross-platform issues and testing

Before you send your Web site to your Web server, it's a good idea to test your links on your local hard drive. If you've set relative links, you can test your links by simply opening any linked HTML file on your computer with any browser and selecting the hyperlinks to move through the site.

Testing is almost as big a part of Web design as creating the HTML in the first place. Always thoroughly test your work before you put it online. But be aware that just because your graphics and links work on your hard drive doesn't mean that they will work on the server. Cross-platform differences become especially important in testing.

Relative versus absolute links

You should set *local links,* those that go to HTML documents or other files within your own Web site, as *relative* rather than *absolute.* An absolute link looks something like this:

```
<A HREF="http://www.your_name
.com/file_name.htm">
```

The same hyperlink set as a relative link looks like this:

```
<A HREF="file_name.htm">
```

Reserve absolute links — full URLs including the `http://` — for links to other Web sites.

I can give you two good reasons for using relative links within your Web site: First, you want to be able to test your links on your local hard drive. If you use absolute links, the files have to reside on the server in order for the links to work; otherwise, your browser will try to go to the Web address to find the specified page. Second, absolute links make the browser work harder and often take longer to load because the browser has to request the domain name each time instead of just going directly to a nearby file.

UNIX, Macintosh, and Windows computers have distinct naming requirements that can cause problems when you move a site from one computer to another. This fact surprises many new developers because HTML files are ASCII text and can be opened by any text editor on any computer system. The links, however, aren't so universal.

For example, you can call files `just about anything you want.html` on a Mac server; however, on a UNIX server, you can't have spaces or special characters in filenames, and you must make sure that the case is the same in the hyperlink as in the filename. You can also use long filenames on Windows 95, 98, and NT. But if you work in DOS or Windows 3.x, you should limit yourself to the *8.3* (say "eight-dot-three") *rule,* which requires that none of your filenames have more than eight characters and none of the extensions more than three.

The most common problems occur when you create a Web site on a Macintosh or Windows computer and then send it to a UNIX server. Because most of the servers on the Internet are UNIX machines, you need to be aware of one of the biggest differences right away: UNIX systems are case-sensitive, and Windows and Macintosh aren't. This difference means, for example, that if you create a file called index.html and refer to it in your HTML links as `INDEX.HTML`, it'll work on a Macintosh or Windows system but not on a UNIX server. Many HTML authors have tested and retested their work locally only to see all of their links fall apart when they put the site online. Using the Dreamweaver link features ensures that the case is the same in the code and the filename. But if you change the case in a filename or manually enter the name in the wrong case, you can cause broken links on a UNIX server.

Getting help with HTML Rename!

HTML Rename! is a software program designed to help you deal with filename problems. If you've already built a site and haven't been careful about the filenames, or if you're moving a site from one system to another and need to change the filenames, HTML Rename! can save you hours of time and trouble. This is also a great tool if you have developers working on different platforms — for example, if all your designers use Macs and all your programmers use Windows and UNIX.

HTML Rename! automatically converts filenames so that they conform to a specific file-naming convention. For example, if you built a site on a Macintosh or Windows machine without realizing that you couldn't use special characters or spaces when you published your site to a server, this program can go through and strip out all the special characters for you.

HTML Rename! can process an entire Web site at once, even if you have hundreds or thousands of pages. And it not only changes the filenames, it also changes their references in the HTML code so that all of your links still work. This capability to automatically find all link references is a crucial and invaluable aid because pages in a Web site can be linked from multiple locations.

HTML Rename! 2.0 works with a wizard that walks you through the process, helping you to select the folder with the Web site that you want to change and then choose the filename convention you want (such as Windows 3.x or UNIX). You have the option of letting HTML Rename! 2.0 automatically change all the filenames for you, or you can set it to alert you to filenames that are problematic and then rename them yourself. Either way, you get a chance to review all the name changes at the end of the process so you can ensure that you like them. As a bonus, the report it generates also lists any broken links or files that are not referenced anywhere in your site. The CD that comes with this book includes a trial version of HTML Rename! 2.0.

Working with HTML text editors

Dreamweaver is designed to work with other HTML editors, such as BBEdit and HomeSite. Both of these text editors are bundled with Dreamweaver 4, but you can use any text editor (including Microsoft Word, Notepad, or SimpleText). After you have associated your preferred editor in Dreamweaver, you can launch it from within Dreamweaver by selecting Edit⇨Launch External Editor or by clicking External Editor in the title bar of the HTML window. The following exercise shows you how to associate an editor. If you make changes to a page in the external editor and then switch back to Dreamweaver, you are prompted to reload the file. Your changes are immediately reflected in Dreamweaver.

To associate an external editor with Dreamweaver:

1. **Choose Edit⇨Preferences.**

   The Preferences dialog box opens.

2. **Select External Editors from the Category list on the left.**

   The External Editors panel opens in the right-hand side of the Preferences dialog box.

3. **Click the Browse button next to the HTML box and locate the text editor you want to use on your hard drive.**

   The Select External Editor dialog box opens. You can then navigate around your hard drive until you locate the editor you want to select. Double-click the name of the editor to associate it with Dreamweaver.

4. **Choose an option from the Reload Modified Files drop-down list located just below the HTML Editor text field in the Preferences dialog box.**

   Choose one of the following options:

   • **Always:** Automatically reloads a page when you switch back to Dreamweaver.

   • **Never:** Never reloads a page.

   • **Prompt:** Prompts you and gives you a choice with each transition.

5. **From the Save on Launch drop-down list, choose Always, Never, or Prompt to specify how Dreamweaver treats documents before launching the external editor.**

6. **Use the two windows at the bottom of the page to associate file extensions with external editors.**

   For example, you can associate all GIF files with Macromedia Fireworks. Then, if you have a GIF selected in a Dreamweaver page and choose Edit from the Property Inspector, Fireworks automatically starts and loads the selected image so that you can easily edit it.

7. **When you save the changes, they are reflected in Dreamweaver.**

Several file extensions, such as GIF and JPEG, are already listed in the left pane, and you can add more. In the right pane, you can add any programs that you have on your hard drive, such as Fireworks or Photoshop, and then associate them with the extensions.

To add extensions, click on the plus sign (+) on the left and type any extension. You can remove extensions and programs by selecting the element from the list and choosing the minus sign (-).

To associate an extension with a program, select the extension in the list on the left, click on the plus sign (+) above the right window, and then browse to find a program on your hard drive.

You can associate multiple programs with each extension. Click the Make Primary button to indicate the program you want to launch automatically if you choose to edit an element or file within Dreamweaver.

Appreciating Roundtrip HTML

If you like to write your own code but still want the advantage of a WYSIWYG editor once in a while, you'll appreciate what Macromedia calls *Roundtrip HTML*. Roundtrip HTML is a built-in Dreamweaver feature that is always active, and it essentially guarantees that if you open a file in Dreamweaver that you created in another program, Dreamweaver won't automatically change your code. This is not true of all HTML editors. Remember, HTML has changed a lot as it has evolved into new versions and there are many different ways to write code, especially if you create custom tags for your site. Each Web design program has its own rules about how to create HTML so if you open a page in a program such as Microsoft FrontPage and you use tags that program doesn't understand, it may automatically change your code in an effort to make your page fit the rules it thinks should be applied to HTML. This is why many savvy Web designers have avoided WYSIWYG editors.

Macromedia understood this problem and built in several features in Dreamweaver to help ensure that even custom code is maintained. When Dreamweaver comes across HTML code that it doesn't understand, it assumes that you've made a mistake. When that happens, Dreamweaver alerts you to the possible mistake by highlighting those tags in yellow in the WYSIWYG editor window as well as in the HTML Source window. Dreamweaver displays any content between the yellow highlighted tags as regular text, complete with HTML brackets, because it can't understand what you intended. If you find that you've made a mistake in your code and correct it, Dreamweaver integrates the correction and displays your formatted content properly. If you want to keep the code the way you've written it, just ignore the yellow highlighting — Dreamweaver won't change it. You can find more information about Roundtrip HTML in Chapter 3.

If you use a lot of custom code, you can specify in the Dreamweaver preferences that it *never* change the code on certain pages. This feature is crucial to sophisticated developers who sometimes create a special tag or combination of tags and don't want another program to alter their work.

The Changing Face of HTML

Now that you understand the basics of HTML code, I have to warn you that things are changing quickly. As graphic designers demand greater control, HTML is evolving. Today, the newest HTML tags let you set the exact font face, color, and size, and even create styles, much like you would in a desktop publishing program. That's a welcome and exciting part of the evolution of the language, but it's also a reason to exercise caution. Keep in mind that although HTML and the browsers we view it with have evolved, not everyone on the Web has kept up with the times. Many of your potential audience members don't have the latest browser or a fast computer and modem. If you don't create your design with these differences in mind, your pages may not appear on their computers exactly the way you intend.

Fortunately, the creators of Dreamweaver considered this problem. You can choose the level of HTML that you want to use and test your pages in Dreamweaver to identify tags and features that may not be supported in different browsers. You can use this feature by choosing File➪Check Target Browsers and then selecting the browser level that you want to verify. The current options in Dreamweaver are Netscape Navigator 2.0, 3.0, and 4.0, as well as Internet Explorer 2.0, 3.0, 4.0, and 5.0.

Writing HTML for Different Browsers

The saving grace of browser differences is that when a browser doesn't understand an HTML tag, the browser ignores the tag. So, if you're considering using a feature that adds to your design, such as font face or background colors in a table, you shouldn't hesitate just because not all browsers can view that feature. Your only real loss in most cases is that outdated browsers won't display it. Often this simply means that your users with the newest browsers enjoy the benefit of the feature and users with older browsers don't even know what they're missing.

You still need to be on the lookout, however, for inconsistent support and the problems that using the latest tags can cause. For example, if you use a black background and white text in a table, you may find that some browsers can't display the black background within a table (a relatively new HTML feature), but it can still display the white text. The text is then unreadable against the light gray or white background that the browser does display.

When you get into the more sophisticated features supported by Dreamweaver, such as DHTML and Cascading Style Sheets, browser differences can be even more serious. A powerful animation effect and sophisticated interactivity that displays well in the latest browsers may not display at all in older browsers, such as Netscape Navigator 3.0 and Internet Explorer 3.0, both of which are still common on the Web. Dreamweaver tries to help you avoid this problem by providing its File⇨Check Target Browsers feature, but you still have to change or remove these features yourself if you want your pages to work well in older browsers. Many designers today are creating two versions of pages — one that works in older browsers and another with the latest features for newer browsers. Dreamweaver 4 includes conversion features to help automate the process of creating a second version of your Web pages that works in older browsers. You can find more information about those features, as well as the Check Target Browsers feature, in Chapters 10 and 13.

Your best bet is to test your pages by previewing them in a variety of browsers. Dreamweaver gives you a list of the features that won't work, but until you see your designs in an older browser, you can't appreciate what they look like or what remains of your designs when the more advanced tags are ignored. Often, by experimenting with combinations of tags and using tags that maintain some of your design when other tags don't work, you can salvage your work and create pages that look great in the newest browsers and are still presentable in older browsers. Use the Check Target Browsers feature as a guide, but use the actual browsers to view your pages and ensure that they look okay to you.

The following two Web sites are a big help for solving this issue of how your pages look in various browsers:

  ✔ BrowserWatch (www.browserwatch.com) can help you find out about the variety and limitations of the browsers that your viewers may use.

  ✔ Shareware. com (www.shareware.com) provides access to older versions of browsers.

Web TV is the ultimate test: Although Dreamweaver is better than any other Web design program on the market when it comes to designing for multiple browsers and the diversity of the Internet, it still doesn't test for all the variables. If you want your pages to look okay to people using Web TV, for example, you need to test your pages yourself in the Web TV browser to see how they look. Fortunately, you don't need a Web TV to do so; you can download a simulator by visiting www.webtv.com and following the link to the Developer's Area.

Part II
Looking Like a Million (Even on a Budget)

The 5th Wave   By Rich Tennant

"Just how accurately should my Web site reflect my place of business?"

In this part . . .

No matter how great the content is on your Web site, the first things viewers always notice are the design and the images. This part helps you get organized and introduces you to the design rules of the Information Superhighway so that you can make your pages look great, even if you're new to the Web.

Chapter 5

Designing a Well-Planned Site

· ·

In This Chapter

▶ Defining Web site goals and objectives

▶ Building a new site

▶ Changing and fixing links

▶ Synchronizing your site

▶ Setting the tone for your site

▶ Testing your site with the new Dreamweaver 4 Site Report feature

· ·

*O*ne of the most common mistakes new Web designers make is plunging into developing a site without thinking through all of their goals, priorities, budget, and design options. The instinct is to simply start creating pages, throw them all into one big directory, and then string stuff together with links. Then, when they finally test it out on their audience, they're often surprised when users say the site is hard to navigate and users can't find the pages they want to use.

Do yourself a favor and save yourself some grief by planning ahead. By having a plan, you also stand a much better chance of creating an attractive Web site that's easy to maintain and update. In this chapter, I cover many of the common planning issues of Web design and help you begin developing your site before you even start using Dreamweaver. Then I show you how enhancements to Dreamweaver 4 make it even easier to manage a team of developers and how to get the most out of the Dreamweaver site management features, such as site synchronization and integrated e-mail. If you do find yourself in the unfortunate predicament of trying to fix broken links, I show you how Dreamweaver makes that task easier now. And finally, I give you some pointers on what constitutes good design. If you build your site based on these principles, you can help ensure that your site is one that viewers keep coming back to because they know they will find what they're looking for when they get there.

Preparing for Development

One of the first things I recommend is that you hold a brainstorming session with a few people who understand the goals you have for your Web site. The purpose of this session is to come up with possible features and elements for your Web site. A good brainstorming session is a nonjudgmental free-for-all — a chance for all involved to make any suggestions that they can think of, whether realistic or not.

Not discrediting ideas at the brainstorming stage is important. Often an unrealistic idea can lead to a great idea that no one may have thought of otherwise. And if you stifle one person's creative ideas too quickly, that person may feel less inclined to voice other ideas in the future.

After the brainstorming session, you should have a long list of possible features to develop into your site. Now the challenge is to edit that list down to the best and most realistic ideas and then plan your course of development to ensure they all work well together when you're done. Read the "Web site planning questionnaire" sidebar for help in defining the objectives for your Web site.

Developing a New Site

In a nutshell, building a Web site involves creating individual pages and linking them to other pages. You need to have a home page (often called the *front page*) that links to pages representing different sections of the site. Those pages, in turn, can link to subsections that can then lead to additional subsections. A big part of Web site planning is determining how to divide your site into sections and deciding how pages link to one another. Dreamweaver makes it easy to create pages and set links, but how you organize those pages is up to you.

If you're new to this, you may think you don't need to worry much about expandability in your Web site. Think again. All good Web sites grow, and the bigger they get, the harder they are to manage. Planning the path of growth for your Web site when you get started makes a tremendous difference later. Neglecting to think about growth is probably one of the most common mistakes among new designers. They jump right into the home page, add a few pages, and then add a few more, throwing them all into one directory. Before they know it, they're working in chaos.

Web site planning questionnaire

The following questions can help you assess the goals for your Web site. Your answers to these questions should shape your planning process and become an important reference whenever you're faced with a decision about your Web site.

1. Who is your target audience?

Base all of your design and navigation decisions on this answer. If you're creating a game site for schoolchildren, you need to make very different decisions than if you're creating a site for a bunch of busy CEOs. Keep your audience in mind and make sure that they can find what they want quickly. Whenever possible, gather together a group of people from your target audience to test your work as you develop your site.

2. Why do you want a Web site?

Before you even run Dreamweaver, spend some serious time thinking through the answer to this question. Then you probably need to mentally prepare yourself for the fact that your answer may change and evolve over time. The important thing is to realize that the answer to this question should also drive the decisions you make about your site.

If you want a Web site because you think it may be fun, keep that as your goal and don't get too serious about it. If you want your site to generate money, base your decisions on financial issues and spend time projecting costs and revenues. As you answer this question, consider what you can realistically expect to gain from your Web site. Will your Web site become a vehicle for attracting new customers, better serving existing ones, or both?

3. What are your three main objectives?

Do yourself a favor and define your three main objectives by writing them down on a piece of paper. Then put the list some place where you're forced to look at it on a regular basis (tape it to the refrigerator or pin it up on the bulletin board next to your desk). Then, every time you're faced with a decision about your Web site, refer to this list and make sure that your choice fulfills your objectives.

4. What do you want people to do when they visit your site?

Build your site with clear goals in mind for your users. Do you want them to learn more about your product? Do you want them to have fun? Do you want them to purchase your product online? Keep your desired result in mind as you start on the early planning.

5. How much do you want to spend?

Web sites can become a black hole for money and time, so setting a budget is an important part of the planning process. Nobody wants to waste money developing a Web site. But sometimes if you don't spend the money required to create something valuable, you're just wasting the tight budget you *were* willing to invest. Make sure that you give your Web project the resources it deserves and then stick to your plans and budget. Remember, you can always start small and add more later if further site development proves cost-effective.

Managing your site's structure

Managing the structure of a Web site has two sides: the side that users see, which depends on how you set up links, and the behind-the-scenes side that depends on how you organize files and folders.

What the user sees

The side that the user sees is all about navigation. When users arrive at your home page, where do you direct them from there? How do they move around your site? A good Web site is designed so that users can navigate easily and intuitively and create their own path to the information most relevant to them. As you plan, make sure that users can access key information easily from more than one place in the site. Make sure that they can move back and forth between pages and sections and return to main pages and indexes in one step. Setting links is easy in Dreamweaver; the challenge is to make sure that they're easy for visitors to follow.

What you see

The second side to managing your Web site structure happens behind the scenes (where your users can't see the information, but you want some kind of organizational system to remember what's what). Before you get too far into building your site with Dreamweaver, spend some time thinking about the management issues involved in keeping track of all the files you create for your site. By *files*, I mean all the images, HTML pages, animations, sound files, and anything else you put in your Web site. As you create pages for your Web site, it's best to organize them in separate folders or directories.

I've seen many Web developers get 20 or 30 pages into a growing Web site and then realize that having all of their files in one folder was a mistake. In fact, it's more than a mistake; it's a mess. And to make matters worse, if you start moving things into new folders after the site grows, you have to change all the links. Not realizing this, some people start moving files around and then find that they have broken links and don't remember where things are supposed to go. Fortunately, Dreamweaver 4 includes site management tools that let you move pages around without breaking links; but starting out with a good plan is still better than having to clean up the structure later.

Before you build those first few pages, think about where you're likely to add content in the future. After you've put together a list of the key elements you want in your site, you're ready to create a storyboard or outline. Use the list and outline to create logical sections of a site that anticipate growth. For example, you may start with one page that lists all your staff; however, after they see how cool it is, staff members may want to develop their own pages. If you're providing information for your sales team, you may find that you want a separate section for each product. As you add new sections, such as the ones I mention here, create new subdirectories to store their respective files. Creating subdirectories also makes it easier to manage a site that's built by multiple people. If each subsection has a separate folder, then each developer can better manage his or her own files.

Naming your site

Dreamweaver lets you call your files any name that works on your operating system, even something like `don't forget this is the photo the boss likes`, but be aware that your Web server may use a different operating system that's more restrictive. Many of the servers on the Web are run on UNIX machines, which are not only case-sensitive, but they also don't allow spaces or special characters, except for the underscore (_). So coming up with names that work and that you — and everyone else on your site development team — can remember can be difficult.

Keeping track of the information on the pages in your Web site is much easier if you develop a naming structure that makes sense to everyone working on the project. For example, say your Web site is a newsletter that includes articles about the happenings in your town. Simple names like fire.html and truck.html may make sense to you this week because you're familiar with the top stories. But six months from now, if you're looking for that article on the big car accident, you may not remember that you called it truck.html. Adding dates to the end of filenames can help you identify the files that you may need months — or even years — down the road. Remember that you can't use spaces, but you can use the underscore. So a good filename may be, fire8_12_2001.html or truck8_19_2001.html to help you remember that these articles were added in August of 2001.

Under construction? No hard hats here!

All good Web sites are under construction — always. It's the nature of the Web. But build your site in such a way that you can add pages when they're ready instead of putting up placeholders. Don't greet your viewers with a guy in a yellow hat who seems to say, "You clicked this link for no good reason. Come back another day, and maybe we'll have something for you to see." Instead of creating "Under Construction" placeholders, create directory structures that make adding new pages later easy. You can let readers know that new things are coming by putting notices on pages that already have content — a message like "Come here next Thursday for a link to something even cooler" is a great idea. But never make users click on a link and wait for a page to load, only to find that nothing but a guy with a hard hat is waiting for them.

Another option is to create a folder for each new update and name it with a date. For example, a folder named stories8_2001 could contain all the stories from the August, 2001 issue. Then you can put truck.html and any other stories from that issue in the stories8_2001 folder, and you can find them by date as well as by filename. Talk to other people who may work on the site and make sure that you create a system that makes sense to everyone and is easy to explain if a new person joins the team. Whatever you do, don't name files randomly and throw them all in one directory. You should also consider documenting your naming system. Printing out a list of all the filenames in your site can provide a handy reference if you're looking for a particular file.

Organizing images and handling links

Before I go on, I want to make a few points about organizing images in a Web site. I've heard many HTML teachers and consultants suggest that you place all of your images in a single folder at the top level of the directory structure and call it Images or Graphics. You may also find that some other HTML authoring tools require you to keep all of your images in one folder.

The advantage of keeping all images in one folder is that the path to all of your images can be the same, so you have to go to only one place to look for them. However, the problem with using just one folder is that if all of your images are in one place, you're likely to end up with a long list of image files, and you're likely to lose track of which image is which.

A good alternative is to store your images in multiple *image* folders within the subfolders that hold the HTML files where those images appear. For example, keep all of your staff photos for your staff pages in an *images* folder within a subfolder called *staff*. If you have images that link throughout the site — a menu bar, for example — you may want to create an images folder at the top level of your directory structure for those.

Dreamweaver makes no distinction between a folder called *images* and a folder by any other name, so you can call these folders whatever you like, including my personal favorite: *Goofy_pictures*.

Managing links

From the Site dialog box in Dreamweaver, you can move or rename local files, and Dreamweaver automatically adjusts all related links. This feature can save you tons of time, especially if you're trying to organize a large, haphazard site.

One thing to note, however, is that this feature works only on local files. In order to rearrange files and automatically correct corresponding links, you need to have your entire site, or a self-contained section of it, stored on your local hard drive. You can use the FTP features in Dreamweaver to download a site before you work on it. Before this feature will work, you have to turn on the link-management options in Dreamweaver.

To turn on the Dreamweaver link-management options in Preferences, follow these steps:

1. **From the Dreamweaver menu bar, choose Edit⇨Preferences.**

    The Preferences dialog box opens.

2. **Select General from the left side of the Preferences dialog box.**

3. **Choose Always or Prompt from the Update Links When Moving Files pop-up menu.**

    Choose Always to automatically update all links to and from a selected document whenever you move or rename it. Choose Prompt to first view a dialog box that lists all the files affected by the change.

    If you choose Prompt, you are given the following two options whenever you move or rename a file: Update, to update the links in the file(s), or Don't Update, to leave the file(s) unchanged.

4. **Click OK to save your changes and exit the Preferences dialog box.**

If Check In/Out is enabled, Dreamweaver automatically attempts to check out the file before making any changes.

Changing and moving links

After you enable link-management options in the Preferences dialog box, you can use the Site Window to rename or rearrange files and folders with drag-and-drop ease.

To rename or rearrange files, follow these steps:

1. **Choose Site⇨Open Site and select the name of the site that you want to work on.**

    The Site dialog box opens.

2. **Use the plus (+) and minus (–) signs to open and close folders in the Local Folder pane on the right of the Site Window.**

3. **Click to select a file or folder you want to change.**

4. **Drag that file or folder anywhere in the window to move it.**

    This window works just like the Explorer window on a PC or the Finder on a Mac. For example, in Figure 5-1, I simply dragged the bio.html file onto the main folder icon to move it to the top level of the site. The Update Files dialog box appears as shown because I chose Prompt in the Preferences dialog box.

5. **To rename a file in the Site dialog box, select the file, right-click (Windows) or Ctrl+click (Mac), and type the new name.**

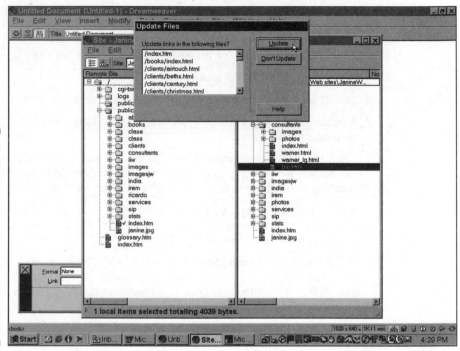

Figure 5-1:
The Update
Files dialog
box shows
you which
links will be
changed
when you
move or
rename a
file in the
Site
Window.

Making global changes to links

If you want to globally change a link to point at a new URL or to some other
page on your site, you can use the Change Link Sitewide option to enter the
new URL and change every reference automatically. You can use this option
to change any kind of link, including mailto, ftp, and script links. For example,
if the e-mail address that you list at the bottom of every page on your site
changes, you can use this feature to fix it automatically — a real time-saver.
You can also use this feature when you want a string of text to link to a different file than it currently does. For example, you could change every instance
of the words *Enter this month's contest* to link to `/contest/january.htm`
instead of `/contest/december.htm` throughout your Web site.

To change all links from one page on your site to another using the Change
Link Sitewide feature, follow these steps:

1. **Select a file in the local pane of the Site dialog box.**

   If the Site dialog box isn't already open, choose Site⇨Open Site and
   select the name of the site you want to work on.

2. **From the menu at the top of the Site dialog box, choose** **S**ite⇨**Change Link Site**w**ide.**

   In the Change Link Sitewide dialog box that appears, use the Browse button to locate another file or type a filename and relative path into the Into Links To box.

3. **Click OK.**

   Dreamweaver updates any documents that link to the selected file.

Remember that these changes occur only on the local site until you change them on the remote server. To automatically reconcile these changes, use the Dreamweaver Synchronize Files option that I describe in the "Synchronizing Local and Remote Sites" section later in this chapter.

To change an e-mail link or a link to a remote URL, follow these steps:

1. **From the menu at the top of the Site dialog box, choose Site⇨Change Link Sitewide.**

   If the Site dialog box isn't already open, choose Site⇨Open Site and select the name of the site you want to work on.

2. **In the Change Link Sitewide dialog box that appears, type the URL or e-mail link that you want to change in the top text box, labeled Change All Links To (see Figure 5-2).**

3. **In the second text box labeled Into Links To, type the new URL or e-mail address that you want to use.**

4. **Click OK.**

   If you selected Prompt in Link Update Preferences (described at the beginning of this section), Dreamweaver displays the Update Files dialog box listing all of the places where the change will be made. Choose Update to make the change to all of the files listed; choose Don't Update to cancel. If you chose Always in the Link Update Preferences, Dreamweaver automatically executes the changes, updating all documents that contain the specified URL or e-mail address when you choose OK. (Figure 5-2 shows the process with the Prompt dialog box.)

Again, remember that these changes will not be reflected on the live site until you FTP the changes to your server. The best way to do this is to use the Dreamweaver Synchronize Files option that I describe later in this chapter.

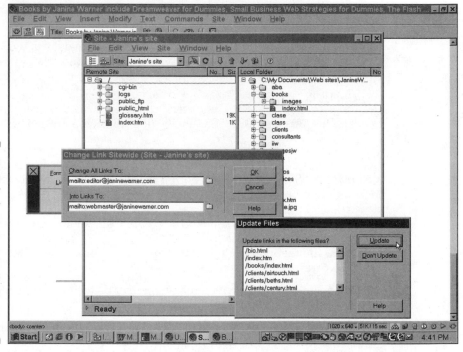

Finding and Fixing Broken Links

If you're trying to rein in a chaotic Web site, or if you just want to check a site because you fear that a few broken links may exist, you'll be pleased to discover the Check Links feature. You can use Check Links to verify the links in a single file or an entire Web site, and you can use it to automatically fix all the referring links at once.

Here's an example of what Check Links can do. Assume that someone on your team (because you would never do such a thing yourself) has changed the name of a file from new.htm to old.htm without using the Dreamweaver automatic link update process to fix the corresponding links. Maybe this person changed the name using another program or simply changed the name in the Finder on the Mac or in the Explorer in Windows. Changing the filename was easy, but what this person may not have realized is that if he or she didn't change the links to the file when the file was renamed, the links are now broken.

If only one page links to the file your dumb teammate changed, fixing it isn't such a big deal. As long as you remember what file the page links from, you can simply open that page and use the Property Inspector to reset the link the same way you would create a link in the first place. (You can find out all the basics of link creation in Chapter 2.)

But many times, a single page in a Web site is referred to by links on many other pages. When that's the case, fixing all the link references can be time-consuming, and it's all too easy to forget some of them. That's why Check Links is so helpful. First, it serves as a diagnostic tool that identifies broken links throughout the site (so you don't have to second-guess where someone may have changed a filename or moved a file). Then it serves as a global fix-it tool. You can use the Check Links dialog box to identify the page a broken link should go to, and then you can have Dreamweaver automatically fix all links referring to that page. The following section walks you through the process.

Checking for broken links

To check a site for broken links, follow these steps:

1. **Choose Site⇨Open Site and select the name of the site you want to work on.**

   Link checking works only for sites listed in the Dreamweaver Site dialog box. For more information about the Site dialog box and how to set up a new site or import an existing one, see Chapter 3.

2. **Choose Site⇨Check Links Sitewide.**

   The Check Links Sitewide dialog box opens, as shown in Figure 5-3, and displays a list of filenames with broken links. This process is quick; even on a site with hundreds of pages, Dreamweaver usually takes less than one minute to check all the links.

Figure 5-3:
The Link Checker dialog box displays a list of broken links and "orphans."

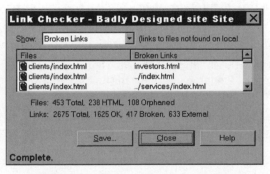

If you find broken links, the next section, "Fixing broken links," shows you how Dreamweaver automatically updates multiple link references.

Fixing broken links

Broken links are one of the most embarrassing problems in Web design. After you identify a broken link in your site, you should feel compelled to fix it immediately. Nothing can turn your users off faster than clicking on a link and getting a "File Not Found" page. Fortunately, Dreamweaver makes fixing broken links simple by providing quick access to files with broken links and automating the process of fixing multiple links to the same file.

If you want to test your site for broken links, read the preceding section, "Checking for broken links," and then use the following steps to fix any broken links you find. If you discover a single broken link on your own, you can always open the page and reset the link to fix it the same way you created it. (You can find out how to create links in Chapter 2.)

After using the Link Checker to identify broken links, follow these steps to use the Link Checker dialog box to fix them:

1. **With the Link Checker dialog box open, double-click a filename that Dreamweaver has identified as a broken link.**

   The page and its corresponding Property Inspector open. The Link Checker dialog box should remain open and visible.

2. **Select the broken link or image on the open page.**

   In the example in Figure 5-4, I've selected a broken image, and I'm fixing the link to the refering GIF.

3. **In the Property Inspector, click the folder icon to the right of the Link text box to fix a link to another page, or click the folder icon next to the Src text box to fix a link to an image.**

   The Select HTML File or Select Image Source dialog box appears.

   If you already know the location of the file that you want to link to, you can type the correct filename and path in the Link text box to fix a link to a page, or in the Src text box to replace a missing image.

4. **Browse to identify the file that you want to link to.**

5. **Click the filename and choose the Select button; then click OK.**

   The link automatically changes to reflect the new filename and location. If you're replacing an image, the image file reappears on the page.

If the link that you correct appears in multiple pages, Dreamweaver prompts you with a dialog box asking if you want to fix the remaining broken link references to the file. Click Yes to automatically correct all other references. Click No to leave other files unchanged.

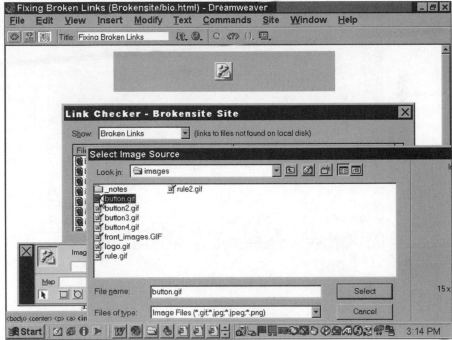

Figure 5-4:
Use the
Select
Image
Source
dialog to fix
broken links.

Using the New Dreamweaver Site Reporting Feature to Test Your Work

Before you put your site online for all the world to see, run a report using the new Dreamweaver 4 Site Reporting feature. You can create a variety of reports, and even customize them, to identify problems with external links, redundant and empty tags, untitled documents and missing Alt text. These are all easy things to miss — especially when you're working on a tight deadline — and they can cause real problems for your viewers if you leave them unfixed. Before Dreamweaver added this great new feature, finding these kinds of mistakes was a tedious and time-consuming task. Now you can run a report that identifies these errors for you and use Dreamweaver's new tools to fix mistakes across your entire site with the push of a button. The following steps walk you through the process.

Follow these steps to produce a Site Report of your entire Web site:

1. **Define the site you want to test and then select it using Site➪Open Site.**

   See Chapter 2 for step-by-step instructions if you need them.

2. **Choose Site➪Reports.**

   The Reports dialog box appears (see Figure 5-5).

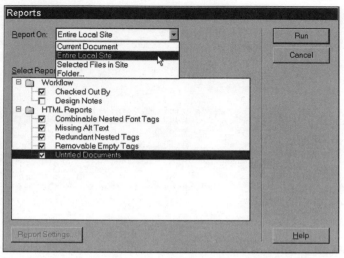

Figure 5-5:
You can
select any
or all of the
options in
the Reports
dialog box
to run simul-
taneously.

3. **From the Report On pull-down menu, choose Entire Local Site (see Figure 5-5).**

   You can also choose to check only a single page by opening the page in Dreamweaver and then choosing Current Document from the Report On pull-down menu. You can also run a report on Selected Files or on a particular Folder. If you choose Selected Files, you must have already selected the pages you want to check in the Site window.

4. **Select the type of report you want by putting check marks next to the report names in the Select Reports section of the Reports dialog box.**

   Table 5-1 describes the kind of report you get with each option. You can select as many reports as you want.

   Note: The Report Settings button is active only if you select Checked Out By or Design Notes, under Workflow. The Report Settings feature lets you specify your name for checking out files and make alterations to the Design Notes option.

Table 5-1	Site Report Options
Report Name	*Results*
Checked Out By	Produces a list of files that are checked out of the site and identifies the name of the person who has checked it out.
Design Notes	Produces a list of Design Notes (see Chapter 6 for more on how to use Design Notes).

Report Name	Results
Combinable Nested Font Tags	Produces a list of all instances where nested tags could be combined. For example, `<font color="#00000"><font size="2">Great Web Sites You Should Visit</font></font>` would be identified because you can simplify the code by combining the two font tags into: `<font color="#00000" size="2">Great Web Sites You Should Visit</font>`.
Missing Alt Text	Produces a list of all the Image tags that do not include Alt text. *Alt text* is used to add alternative text to an image tag. If the image isn't displayed for some reason (many people choose to surf with images turned off), the Alt text appears in place of the image. Alt text is also important to the blind because special browsers that "read" pages to site visitors can't interpret text that is part of an image, but can "read" the Alternative text included in the image tag.
Redundant Nested Tags	Produces a list of all places where there are redundant nested tags. For example, `<center>Good headlines <center>are harder to write</center> than you might think</center>` would be identified because you could simplify the code by removing the second center tag to make the code look like this: `<center>Good headlines are harder to write than you might think</center>`
Removable Empty Tags	Produces a list of all of the empty tags on your site. These often occur if you delete an image or text section without deleting all the tags associated with it.
Untitled Documents	Produces a list of filenames that don't have a title or have duplicate titles. The title tag is easy to forget because it does not display in the body of the page. The title tag contains the text that appears at the very top of the browser window and is also the text that appears in the favorites list when someone saves your page in their browser. And if that's not enough, a good title tag is key to getting good placement in many search engines, as well.

5. **Click Run to create the report(s).**

   If you haven't already done so, you may be prompted to save your file, define your site, or select a folder (see Chapter 2 for more information on defining a site in Dreamweaver.)

   The Results dialog box opens (see Figure 5-6 displaying a list of problems found on your site). You can sort the list by different categories by clicking the column heading. You can also sort by filename, line number, and description. If you run several reports at the same time, you can keep the all the results windows open at the same time.

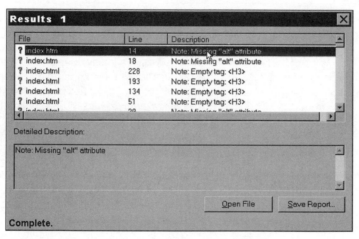

Figure 5-6:
The Results dialog box displays a list of problems found on your site.

6. **Select any item in the Results dialog to see a detailed description of the problem, as shown in Figure 5-6.**

7. **Double-click on any item to open the corresponding file in the Document window.**

8. **Use the Property Inspector or other Dreamweaver feature to fix the identified problem and then save the file.**

   Remember that your changes aren't applied to your live site until you update your server. Use the Synchronize feature, described in the next section of this chapter, to update all of your changes at once.

Synchronizing Local and Remote Sites

After you've done all of this cleanup and organization on the local copy of your Web site, you want to make sure that those changes are reflected on the live site on your Web server. Fortunately, Dreamweaver makes that easy, too, by including a feature that automatically synchronizes the files in both places. Before you synchronize your sites, you can use the Site FTP dialog box to verify which files you want to put on or get from your remote server. Dreamweaver also confirms which files are updated after you've completed the synchronization.

Follow these steps to synchronize your Web site:

1. **Choose Site⇨Open Site.**

   The Site dialog box opens.

2. **Select the Connect button to log on to your remote site.**

   Chapter 2 shows you how to set up this feature for your site.

3. **Choose Site⇨Synchronize.**

   A pop-up menu appears.

4. **From the pop-up menu, choose to make your local site the master.**

   You also have the option to make the remote site the master. This choice may be useful if multiple people are working on the same site from remote locations.

5. **Choose which option you want to use to copy the files:**

   • **Put Newer Files to Remote:** This option copies the most recently modified files from your local site to the remote site.

   • **Get Newer Files from Remote:** This option copies the most recently modified files from your remote site to the local site.

   • **Get and Put Newer Files:** This option updates both the local and remote sites with the most recent versions of all the files.

6. **Select whether or not you want to delete the files on your local or remote site.**

   Be aware that if you don't specify here that Dreamweaver should *not* delete files, files are automatically deleted if they are not on the site you designated as master. That means that if you choose the local site as the master, Dreamweaver deletes any files in your remote site that do not exist in the local copy. If you choose the remote site as the master, Dreamweaver deletes any files in your local site that do not exist on the remote site.

7. **Click OK.**

   The Site FTP dialog box displays the files that are about to be changed.

   This is your last chance before files are deleted! In the Site FTP dialog box, you have the option to verify the files you want to delete, put, and get. If you don't want Dreamweaver to alter a file, deselect it now or forever live with the consequences.

8. **Click OK.**

   All approved changes are automatically made, and Dreamweaver updates the Site FTP dialog box with the status.

9. **A dialog box appears, and you can choose to save the verification information to a local file.**

   Choose to save or not save the verification information. Having the option to save this information can be handy later if you want to review your changes.

Applying the Rules of Web Design

Before you start designing your Web site, examine some of the basic rules of good Web design. I don't mean that you should never try your own thing, break out of the mold, or make your mark. But most artists agree that before you try breaking the rules, you need a solid understanding of what the rules are and why they work.

Create a consistent design theme

Most of the best sites on the Web maintain a consistent design theme throughout the site by using the same fonts and sets of colors on every page. If you visit a well-designed site, such as `www.fortmason.org`, which was also designed in Dreamweaver, you can see how the design theme from the front page carries over to the subsequent pages. The same image that represents the Ballet section on the front page is incorporated into the design on the front of the subsection, making it easy to follow your steps as you move through the Web site The one critique I'd make of this site is that they require AOL users to have Version 4 of the AOL software, which isn't a reasonable requirement if you really want to make your site accessible to everyone on the Web. The latest Nielsen ratings for the Web rank AOL as the top attraction on the Net.

Develop an intuitive navigation system

An intuitive navigation system is one that's easy to use and follow. The Washington Post site (`www.washingtonpost.com`) succeeds in making a wide range of information accessible by placing a row of navigation buttons across the top of each page, as well as the left and right columns. This technique enables them to categorize groups of links, making it easy for viewers to find their way to any of the site's main sections and subsections. Effectively organizing all the information at The Washington Post site is a highly complex task, and their success has won them many awards in the newspaper industry. If you visit the site, you'll see that the row of navigation buttons across the top changes to indicate the page you're viewing. This valuable technique helps viewers see where they are and quickly decide if they want to visit another section of the site.

Make sure that your site loads quickly

No matter how fabulous your design, if it takes too long to download, no one will wait around to see it. The creators of the Fish Farmhouse site at `http://www.phish.com/farmhouse`, winners of the 2000 Flash Film Festival, overcame this problem by using Macromedia Flash technology. Flash enables you to create vector-based animations that load much faster than bitmapped images, such as GIFs and JPEGs. (You can find more information about Flash and other animation programs in Chapter 15.) You can find other great uses for Flash in Macromedia's Flash gallery at `www.macromedia.com`.

If you use GIF or JPEG images, reduce file sizes as much as possible. Programs such as Macromedia Fireworks and Equilibrium Debabelizer are designed to help reduce file sizes as you convert images for the Web. You can find an evaluation version of Fireworks on the CD-ROM that accompanies this book, and you can check out Chapter 14 for descriptions of the programs mentioned here and other graphics programs that you may find helpful in building your Web site.

Keep your site simple and easy to read

If you want to see your tax dollars at work, visit the White House site at `www.whitehouse.gov` (make sure you don't go to `www.whitehouse.com` by mistake — I'm not even sure that site should be legal). I can't say that I'm overly impressed with the design at the White House, but it's a clear and easy-to-read site that keeps it simple — a rule too many Web designers (and most people in government) are prone to forgetting.

Strive for original designs

Above all else, I've always admired originality. Organic Online at `www.organic.com` has won many awards for its innovative designs and powerful compositions. This is one of the few Web design companies that consistently pushes the limit of what's possible on the Web and produces effective results. Examples of award-winning work by Organic include BMW Brazil (`www.bmw.com.br`), where Macromedia Flash technology brings the site to life and lets viewers experience the inside and outside of a BMW — right down to the sound of the engine. Another great Organic site is CDNOW (`www.cdnow.com`), where interactive marketing ideas contribute to one of the most successful e-commerce sites on the Web.

Test, test, and test again

Probably the most important rule of Web design is to test, test, test. When you test your designs, you're not just making sure that you don't have broken links or missing images; you need to make sure that viewers understand your message and can easily find their way around your navigation system. The best way to ensure that you've achieved these goals is to invite people from your target audience to visit your Web site. Try to get a good cross section of potential viewers and then watch them as they move around your site. Be careful not to provide any guidance or suggestions; your goal is to see where they go on their own to make sure that they can find what they're looking for. This powerful exercise can be instrumental in helping you develop a clear and intuitive design and navigation system for your Web site. The section earlier in this chapter on checking and fixing broken links is an important guide to making sure your site works properly. You'll also benefit from following the earlier instructions on how to use the new Dreamweaver Site Reporting feature, a quick and easy way to get a report on many of the other common errors on a site and then fix them with some great time-saving tools.

Chapter 6

Coordinating Your Design Work

● ●

● ●

Strive for consistency in all your designs — except when you're trying to be unpredictable. A little surprise here and there can keep your Web site alive. But generally, most Web sites work best, and are easiest to navigate, when they follow a consistent design theme. Dreamweaver offers several features to help you develop and maintain a consistent look and feel across your site, whether you're working on a Web site by yourself or you're coordinating a team of developers.

In this chapter, I cover three of my favorite Dreamweaver features — templates, Library items, and the Tracing image — and show you how they combine to make your work faster and easier to manage. I also introduce you to Design Notes, the History panel, and the Quick Tag Editor.

Templating Your Type

Many Web design programs boast about their HTML templates. But what they really mean is that they include some ready-made page designs with the program. Dreamweaver takes this concept a few leaps farther by providing template design features that enable you to create the basic design of a page and then control which sections can and can't be altered. This is a valuable feature if you are working with a team of developers of varying skill levels. For example, if you're building a site for a real estate company and you want to let the employees update the sales listings without being able to mess up the page design, a template can be the perfect solution.

When you create a template, you create an outline of what a page should look like. Usually a template represents a design with placeholders but no actual content. You can use templates to create documents for your site that have a common structure and appearance. And here's a great bonus: When you're ready to redesign your site, simply go back and edit the template itself, and then you can automatically apply the changes to every page on the site that uses that template (for example, if you change the logo for your company or add a new navigation element that you want to appear on every page in a section). Templates are best used when you are creating a number of pages that share certain characteristics, such as background color or navigation elements. Rather than setting the correct properties for every new page or making the same changes on page after page, you can use a template to make changes to several pages at once.

Typing your template

One of the greatest advantages in using the Dreamweaver template feature is that you can specify which areas of the template can be changed. This is especially useful if you're working with people who have various skill levels in HTML, and you want a more advanced designer to create a page that a less experienced person can't mess up later. With that goal in mind, a template has editable regions and locked (noneditable) regions. Use editable regions for content that changes, such as a product description. Use locked regions for static, unchanging content, such as a logo or site navigation elements.

For example, if you're publishing an online magazine, the navigation options may not change from page to page, but the titles and stories do. To indicate the style and location of an article or headline, you can define *placeholder text* (an editable region, with all of the size and font attributes already specified). When you're ready to add a new feature, you simply select the placeholder text and either paste in a story or type over the selected area. You do the same thing to create a placeholder for an image. By default, templates are locked. You can add content to the template, but when you save the template, all content is marked noneditable automatically. If you create a document from such a template, Dreamweaver warns you that the document will not contain any editable regions. To make a template useful, you must create editable regions or mark existing content areas as editable. (The step-by-step instructions in the following section, "Creating Templates," walk you through the process.)

You can modify a template even after you've used it to create documents. Then when you update documents that use the template, the noneditable sections of those documents are updated to match the changes you made in the template.

While you're editing the template itself, you can make changes to any part of the file, be it the editable or locked regions. While editing a document made from a template, however, you can make changes only to the editable regions of the document. If you go back and change a template after it is created, Dreamweaver gives you the option of having those changes reflected in all the pages you've created with that template or only the page you are currently editing.

Creating templates

Creating a template is as easy as creating any other file in Dreamweaver, as you can see in the following steps. You can start with an existing HTML document and modify it to suit your needs, or you can create a completely new document. When you save a file as a template, the file is stored automatically in the Templates folder of the main folder for the Web site. Templates must be saved in this common folder for the automated features in Dreamweaver to work properly. If you don't already have a Templates folder in your Web site, Dreamweaver automatically creates one when you store your first template.

The Template features work only if you have defined your Web site in Dreamweaver. If you aren't sure how to do this, refer to Chapter 2, where I explain how to define a new site or import an existing one.

All elements in a template are locked by default, except the document title section, which is indicated by the <TITLE></TITLE> tags. (The document title section not being locked is an improvement in Dreamweaver 4 — in Dreamweaver 3 you couldn't make the title area editable.) For the template to be of any use for building new pages, you must make other areas of the page editable, as well. Remember that you can always return to the template and make more areas editable or remove the capability to edit certain areas later. To create a template with editable regions, follow these steps:

1. **Choose Window⇨Templates.**

2. **In the Templates panel, click the arrow in the top-right corner and choose New Template from the drop-down menu that opens.**

   A new, untitled template is added to the list of templates in the panel.

3. **With the template still selected, type a name for the template just as you would name any file in the Finder on a Mac or the Explorer on a PC.**

   The new template is added to the Templates for Site list, as shown in Figure 6-1.

Figure 6-1:
The
Templates
panel makes
it easy to
access and
organize
your
templates.

4. **After you name the new template, double-click the name to open it.**

   The template page opens in Dreamweaver as any other HTML page would, except that the filename ends with the extension .dwt.

   You can now edit this page as you would any other HTML page, inserting images, text, tables, and so on.

5. **Choose Modify⇨Page Properties to specify background, text, and link colors.**

   Next you place some text or images on the page as placeholders for information that you may want to change in the future.

6. **To make an image or text area editable, select the image or text and choose Modify⇨Templates⇨New Editable Region. (The image or text that you select as editable becomes an area that can be changed in any page created with the template. Areas that you don't mark as editable will become fixed and can be changed only if you modify the template itself.)**

   The New Editable Region dialog box opens.

7. **In the Name text box, type a name for the editable region.**

   The text or image is highlighted in the template, indicating that it is editable. You can name the region anything you want, but choosing something that corresponds to the type of information you're going to put in the area makes it easier for you to remember.

8. **To make other images or text areas editable, repeat Steps 6 and 7.**

9. **Save your template and close the file when you're finished.**

You can make an entire table or an individual table cell editable, but you can't make multiple cells editable all at once, unless you have merged them first. You have to select each cell one at a time if you want to make some of the cells in a table editable, but not others. (For more about creating HTML tables, see Chapter 9.) Layers and layer content are also treated as separate elements, but either can be marked as editable. Making a layer editable enables you to change the position of that layer. Making layer content editable means that you can change the content of the layer, such as the text or image in the layer. (For more information about layers, see Chapter 11.)

Saving any page as a template

Sometimes you get partway through creating a page before it occurs to you that it would be better to make the page a template. Other times, you may have a page that someone else created, and you decide that you want to make it into a template. Either way, it's as easy to create a template from an existing page as it is to create a new one.

To save a page as a template, follow these steps:

1. **Open the page that you want to turn into a template the same way that you open any other file in Dreamweaver.**

2. **Choose File⇨Save as Template.**

   The Save As Template dialog box appears.

3. **Use the drop-down menu next to the Site text box to select a site.**

   The menu should list all the sites that you've defined in Dreamweaver. If you're working on a new site or haven't yet defined your site, Chapter 2 shows you how to define your site.

4. **In the Save As text box, type a name for the template.**

5. **Click the Save button in the top-right corner of the dialog box to save the file as a template.**

6. **Make any changes that you want and choose File⇨Save to save the page. Follow the steps in the earlier section, "Creating Templates," to make areas editable.**

   Notice that the file now has the .dwt extension, indicating that it's a template.

7. **Choose File⇨Close to close the file.**

Using Templates

After you create all these great templates, you'll want to put them to use. You can use templates to create or modify all the pages in your Web site or just use them for specific areas or sections. Using a template to create a new page is similar to creating any other HTML page.

To use a template to create a page, follow these steps:

1. **Choose <u>F</u>ile⇨Ne<u>w</u> From Template.**

   The Template dialog box opens.

2. **Open any template by double-clicking its name.**

   You can also create a new document and then apply a template to it by dragging the template from the Templates panel onto the new file.

3. **Choose <u>F</u>ile⇨<u>S</u>ave and name the new file as you would any other HTML page.**

4. **You can now edit the page, using most of the Dreamweaver editing features.**

   Some features, such as converting layers to tables, are not available on pages created with templates.

Remember that only the editable regions of the template can be altered when you use a template to create a page. If you want to change a locked region of the page, you have to either remove the template association from the file or open the template and change that area of the file to make it editable by revising the template itself.

You can remove the template association from a file by selecting Modify⇨ Templates⇨Detach From *templatename*.dwt. This action makes the file fully editable again, but changes you make to the template are not be reflected on a detached page. To edit the template itself, choose Modify⇨Templates⇨ Open *templatename*.dwt.

You can also apply a template to an existing page. When you apply a template to an existing document, the content in the template is added to the content already in the document. If a template is already applied to the page, Dreamweaver attempts to match editable areas that have the same name in both templates and to insert the contents from the editable regions of the page into the editable regions in the new template.

You can apply a template to an existing page by using any one of the following techniques:

✔ Choose Modify⇨Templates⇨Apply Template to Page and then double-click the name of a template to apply it to the page.

✔ Drag the template from the Template panel to the Document window.

✔ Select the template in the Template panel and choose Apply from the pull-down list available through the arrow at the top right corner of the Template panel.

Making Global Changes with Templates

The greatest advantage of using templates is that you can apply changes to all the pages that use a template all at once. Suppose that you redesign your logo or want to change the positioning of key elements in a section of your site. If you've built those elements into a template, you can make the change and update all the places they are used on the site automatically — a real time saver. You can use the template update commands to update a single page or to update all the places that template has been used in the entire site.

To change a template and update the current page, follow these steps:

1. **Open a document that uses the template that you want to change.**

2. **Choose Modify⇨Templates⇨Open Attached Template.**

    The template opens.

3. **Modify the template as you would edit a new template.**

    For example, to modify the template's page properties, choose Modify⇨Page Properties.

4. **When you're finished making changes to the template, choose Modify⇨Templates⇨Update Current Page.**

    The page you have open changes to reflect the changes you've made to the template.

If you save a template after making changes, the Update Pages dialog opens automatically, prompting you to choose the page or pages you want to update. Choose All to update all pages at once, or select one or more pages to update them individually. You can also choose Don't Update if you aren't ready to apply the changes.

To change a template and update all the files in your site that use that template at once, follow these steps:

1. **Open an existing template and make the changes that you want to apply.**

2. **Choose Modify⇨Templates⇨Update Pages.**

    The Update Pages dialog box appears.

3. **From the Look In drop-down list, choose one of the following options:**

   • **Entire Site:** Select the site name to update all pages in the selected site to all of the corresponding templates.

   • **Files That Use:** Select the template name to update all pages in the current site that use that template.

   Make sure that Templates is selected in the Update option.

4. **Click Start to run the update process.**

   When the update process is completed, the Update Pages dialog opens with a report on which pages were altered. (See Figure 6-2.)

Reusing Elements with the Library Feature

The Library feature is not a common feature in other Web design programs, so the concept may be new to you even if you've been developing Web sites for a while. The more experienced you are, however, the more likely you are to appreciate the value of this feature and the time it can save you.

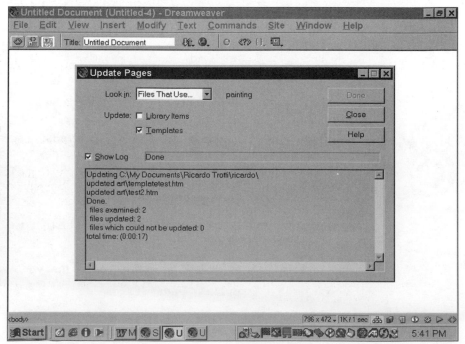

Figure 6-2: The Update Pages dialog provides a report on all pages altered when you apply changes made to a template.

The Dreamweaver Library feature was designed to automate the process of inserting and changing elements that appear on multiple pages in a Web site. You can save any element as a Library item — for example, a logo or a navigation row of images and links. You can then insert that element (or collection of elements) on any page by simply dragging it from the Library to the new page. Even better, if you ever need to change the Library element (by adding a link or image, for example), you can change the element in the Library and let Dreamweaver automatically update the change throughout the site. Libraries are not shared among sites, so each site you define must have its own Library.

A *Library item* is a snippet of code (which can contain image references and links). Like templates, Library items are a great way to share the work of your best designers with less experienced ones. For example, one designer could create a logo and another the navigation elements, and then these could be placed in the Library and made available to the rest of the team. However, you have more flexibility with Library items, because they are elements that can be placed anywhere on any page, even multiple times.

Library items can be any element from the body of a document, such as text, tables, forms, images, Java applets, and plug-in files. Library elements are efficient because Dreamweaver stores the snippet of code like a document in the Library folder and then updates the links to it from wherever the Library element is applied, which makes it easy to store one image in one place and use it all over your site. Library items can also contain behaviors, but there are special requirements for editing the behaviors in Library items.

Library items cannot contain timelines or style sheets because the code for these elements is part of the Head area of an HTML file. (For more information on behaviors and timelines, see Chapter 12; for more on style sheets, see Chapter 11.)

Creating and using Library items

The following sections lead you through the steps for creating a Library item, adding one to a page, and editing a Library item when an element changes. For these steps to work appropriately, you must do them carefully, in sequential order. Before creating or using Library items, you must first define a site or open an existing site. If you're not sure how to do this, see Chapter 2.

Creating a Library item

To create a Library item that you can use on multiple pages on your site, follow these steps:

1. **Open any existing file that has images, text, or other elements on the page.**

   A navigational row with images and links that are used throughout your Web site is an ideal use of the Library feature.

2. **From this page, select an element that you want to use as a Library item.**

3. **Choose <u>W</u>indow⇨<u>L</u>ibrary to open the Library panel; then drag the selected navigational row (or other element) into the Library panel.**

   You can also click the New Library Item button on the Library panel to add a selected item to the Library.

4. **Name the element as you name any file in the Finder on a Mac or in Explorer on a PC.**

   When you name a Library item, you automatically save it to the Library, so you can then easily apply it to any new or existing page in your site. All Library items are listed in the Library for Site dialog box shown in Figure 6-3.

Adding a Library item to a page

You can take elements out of the Library as easily as you put them in. When you add a Library item to a page, the content (or a link to it) is inserted in the document.

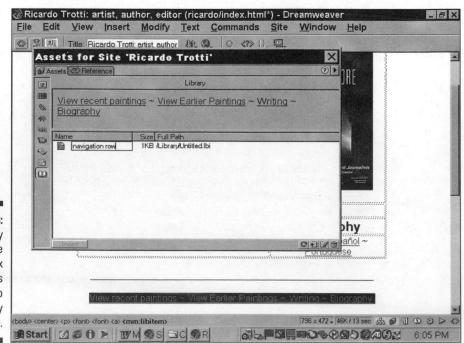

Figure 6-3:
The Library for Site dialog box provides access to Library items.

To add a Library item to a page, follow these steps:

1. **Create a new document in Dreamweaver or open any existing file.**

2. **Click in the Document window and choose Window⇨Library.**

   The Library panel opens. You can also access the Library by choosing the Assets button on the Launcher bar and then selecting Library.

3. **Drag an item from the Library panel to the Document window.**

   Alternatively, you can select an item in the Library panel and click the Insert button.

   The item automatically appears on the page. After you've inserted a Library item on a page, you can use any of Dreamweaver's formatting features to position it on the page.

Highlighting Library items

Library items are highlighted to distinguish them from other elements on a page. You can customize the highlight color for Library items and show or hide the highlight color in Highlighting preferences.

To change or hide Library highlighting, follow these steps:

1. **Choose Edit⇨Preferences and then select Highlighting from the Category section on the left.**

2. **Click the color box to select a color for Library items. Check the box next to Show to display of the Library highlight color on your pages. Leave the box blank if you don't want to display the highlight color.**

   For the Library highlight color to be visible in the Document window, you must also be sure that the Show Library Items box is checked in the Highlighting section of the Preferences dialog.

3. **Click OK to close the Preferences dialog box.**

Changing a Library item

One of the biggest timesaving advantages of the Dreamweaver Library feature is that you can make changes to items and automatically apply those changes to multiple pages. First, you edit the original Library item file; then you can choose to update the edited item in any one or all of the documents in the current site.

To edit a Library item and then update one or all of the pages on which you use that item, follow these steps:

1. **Choose Window⇨Library or click Assets on the Launcher bar and select Library.**

   The Library panel opens.

2. **Select any item listed in the Library for Site panel and double-click to open the item.**

   Dreamweaver opens a new window for editing the Library item.

   Notice that the background of the Library item is gray. Because the Library item is just a snippet of code, there is no <BODY> tag in which to specify a background color. Don't worry over this — the Library item will have the same background color or image as the page where you use the Library item.

3. **Using the editing functions, make any changes you want to the Library item.**

   For example, you can redirect the link of text items or images, edit the wording or font, or add images or text.

4. **Choose File⇨Save to save changes to the original item or choose File⇨Save As and give it a new name to create a new Library item.**

   The Update Library Items dialog opens, displaying a list of all pages where the Library item appears.

5. **Select the page or pages you want to update and choose Update. To cancel without making changes, choose Don't Update.**

   Because Library items can contain only Body elements, the Style panel and the Timeline Inspector are unavailable when you are editing a Library item. Timeline and style sheet code are parts of the Head area of a Web page. The Behavior Inspector is also unavailable because it inserts code into the Head as well as the Body.

Making Library items editable

As I say at the beginning of this chapter, you should strive for design consistency in *almost* all things. If you find that you want to alter a Library item in just one place, however, or make just a couple of exceptions, you can override the Library feature by breaking the link between the Library and the item in the document. Remember, however, that after you've broken that connection, you cannot update the Library item automatically.

To make a Library item editable, follow these steps:

1. **Open any file that contains a Library item and double-click the Library item.**

   The Property Inspector opens.

2. **Choose the Detach from Original button.**

   A warning message appears, letting you know that if you proceed with detaching the Library item from the original, it will no longer be possible to update this occurrence of it when the original is edited.

3. **Click OK to detach the Library item.**

Using a Tracing Image to Guide Your Layout

Macromedia's Tracing Image feature is unique in the world of Web design tools, although the concept dates back to the earliest days of design. The Tracing Image feature enables you to use a graphic as a guide to your page design, much like you would put thin paper over an existing image to re-create it by tracing over it.

The Tracing Image is ideal for people who like to first create a design in a program such as Photoshop or Fireworks and then model their Web page after it. By using the Tracing Image feature, you can insert an image into the background of your page for the purpose of "tracing" over it. Then you can position layers or create table cells on top of the Tracing image, making it easier to exactly re-create your design in HTML. You can use JPG, GIF, or PNG format images as Tracing images, and you can create them in any graphics application that supports these formats.

Although the Tracing image appears in the background of a page, it doesn't take the place of a background image and is never displayed in a browser.

To add a Tracing image to your page, follow these steps:

1. **Create a new page or open any existing page in Dreamweaver.**

2. **Choose View⇨Tracing Image⇨Load.**

   The Select Image Source dialog opens.

3. **Double-click the filename or highlight the image that you want to use as a Tracing image; then choose Select.**

   The Page Properties dialog box opens and the image name and its path are displayed in the Tracing Image text area.

   Alternatively, you can choose Modify⇨Page Properties and use the Browse button next to the Tracing Image text area to select a Tracing image.

4. **Use the Transparency slider to set the opacity for the Tracing image to 50%, as shown in Figure 6-4.**

   Lowering the transparency level causes the Tracing image to appear faded, making it easier to distinguish between the Tracing image and editable elements on the page. You can set the transparency level to suit your preferences, but 50% seems to work well with most images.

5. **Click OK.**

   A Tracing image appears in the document window.

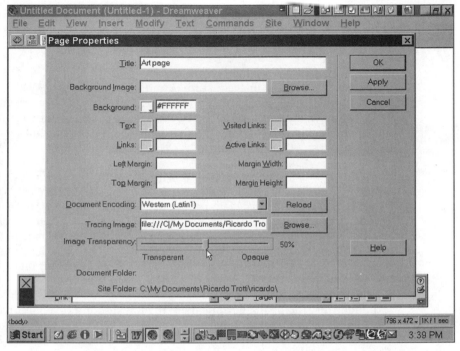

Figure 6-4:
The Tracing
Image
feature lets
you place
an image
behind your
pages that
you can use
to "trace"
your design
in HTML.

If a Tracing image doesn't appear, make sure that you have a check next to Show when you choose View➪Tracing Image➪Show.

A Tracing image doesn't replace a background image, but when you load a Tracing image, your background image or color is no longer visible in the document window. However, it still appears when you view the page in a browser. The Tracing image itself is visible only when you're editing the page in the document window; it never appears when the page is loaded into a browser.

You have even greater control over Tracing Images in Dreamweaver 4. Select View➪Tracing Image to reveal four new options:

- **Show:** Hides the Tracing Image if you want to check your work without it being visible, but don't want to remove it.
- **Align with Selection:** Enables you to automatically line up the tracing image with a selected element on a page.
- **Adjust Position:** Enables you to use the arrow keys or enter X, Y coordinates to control the position of the Tracing Image behind the page.
- **Reset Position:** Resets the Tracing Image to 0, 0 on the X, Y coordinates.

Keeping in Touch with Design Notes

Design Notes are ideal for communicating with other developers who are working on your site. This Dreamweaver feature works like the comment tag, but with a lot more privacy. Many developers use *comment tags* — HTML code that enables you to embed text in a page that won't display in a browser — to share information with each other. But anyone who views the source of your documents can see a comment tag, so it's not a very secure way to share information.

If you want to hide sensitive information, such as pricing structures or creative strategies, yet still be able to share it with other members of your development team, use Design Notes. Information saved as a Design Note in Dreamweaver can travel with any HTML file or image, even if the file is transferred from one Web site to another or from Fireworks to Dreamweaver.

To create and use Design Notes, follow these steps:

1. **Choose Site⇨Define Sites.**

   The Define Sites dialog box opens.

2. **Click to select the site you want to work on and then click Edit.**

   The Site Definition dialog box opens.

3. **In the Category list at the left, choose Design Notes.**

   The Design Notes page appears.

4. **If it's not already selected, click to select the Maintain Design Notes option.**

   With this option selected, whenever a file is copied, moved, renamed, or deleted, the associated Design Notes file is also copied, moved, renamed, or deleted with it.

5. **If you want your Design Notes to be sent with your files when they are uploaded to your server, click to select the Upload Design Notes for Sharing option.**

   If you're making notes only to yourself and don't want them to be associated with the page when you upload them to the server, deselect this option and Design Notes will be maintained locally but not uploaded with your files.

6. **Click OK in the Site Definition dialog box; then click Done in the Define Sites dialog box.**

   The Site dialog box opens.

7. **You can now add Design Notes to your files by choosing File⇨Design Notes to open the Design Notes dialog box.**

To add Design Notes to a document, follow these steps:

1. **With the file open that you want to add Design Notes to, choose File⇨Design Notes.**

   The Design Notes dialog box opens (see Figure 6-5).

2. **Choose the status of the document from the Status drop-down list box.**

   Your options are Draft, Revision 1, Revision 2, Revision 3, Alpha, Beta, Final, and Needs Attention. You can choose any status, and you should set a policy with your design team about what each status means and how you will use these options to manage your development.

3. **Type your comments in the Notes text box.**

4. **Click the date icon (just above the Notes text box) if you want to insert the current local date.**

   The current date is inserted automatically.

5. **In the All Info tab, you can add other information that may be useful to developers of your site. For example, you can name a key designer (in the Name field) and define the value as the name of that person or the priority of the project (in the Value field). You also may define a field for a client or type of file that you commonly use.**

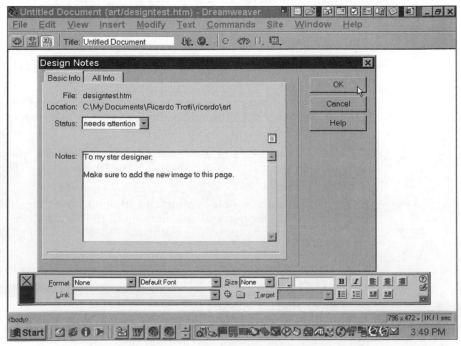

Figure 6-5:
Design Notes make it easy to associate messages with HTML or image files for other members of your development team.

Click the plus (+) button to add a new key; click the minus (–) button to remove a key.

6. **Click OK to save the notes.**

The notes you entered are saved to a subfolder named _notes in the same location as the current file. The filename is the document's filename, plus the extension .mno. For example, if the filename is art.htm, the associated Design Notes file is named art.htm.mno. Design Notes are indicated in the Site View by a small yellow icon that looks like a cartoon bubble. They are also visible in the directory that you can see on your hard drive.

Staying in Touch with Integrated E-Mail

The new Dreamweaver 4 integrated e-mail feature is another handy tool for collaborative Web design. This is not a new application in Dreamweaver, but a feature that enables you to use Dreamweaver in conjunction with any e-mail program you already use and to have easy access to the e-mail address of other members of your team when you need it.

When you're working on a site with a team of people, it's not uncommon that the page you want to work on has already been checked out by someone else, making it impossible for you to do the work you need to do on it. In Dreamweaver 4, you can now associate an e-mail address with each developer's name in the Check In/Check Out feature. Then when you find that someone else has the page you need, you can easily fire off an e-mail telling that person to check it back in so you can work on it.

Developers on your team can use the following steps to associate their e-mail address with their version of Dreamweaver as part of the Check In/Check Out set up:

1. **Choose Site⇨Define Sites.**

The Define Sites dialog box opens.

2. **Click to select the site you want to work on and then click Edit.**

The Site Definition dialog box opens.

3. **In the Category list at the left, choose Remote Info.**

The Remote Info page appears.

4. **If it's not already selected, click to select the Enable File Check In/Check Out (see Figure 6-6).**

5. **Click to select Check Out Files When Opening.**

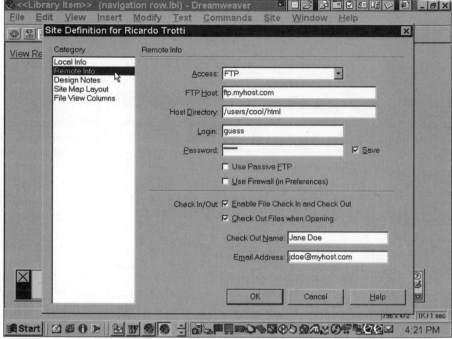

Figure 6-6:
With
Dream-
weaver 4,
you can
associate
your e-mail
address
with the
Check
In/Check
Out feature.

6. **Enter your name in the Check Out Name text box. (Nicknames are okay as long as everyone on the team knows your silly name.)**

7. **Enter your e-mail address in the Email Address text box.**

8. **Click OK to save your changes.**

Keeping the peace with version control

Version control systems enable you to better manage changes made by different team members and prevent them from overwriting each other's work. If you already use these programs, you'll be glad to know that you can now integrate both Visual Source Safe and systems that use the Web DAV protocol with Dreamweaver, which makes it possible to take advantage of the Dreamweaver site management features and still protect your code development process. If you don't know about these programs, visit the Microsoft site (www.microsoft.com) to learn more about Visual SourceSafe, or visit www.ics.uci.edu/pub/ietf/webdav/ to learn more about WebDAV protocols.

Remembering Your History

You can keep track of what you've been doing and even replay your steps with the History panel. The History panel also lets you undo one or more steps and create commands to automate repetitive tasks.

To open the History panel, shown in Figure 6-7, choose Window⇨History. As soon as you open the History panel, it starts automatically recording your actions as you do work in Dreamweaver. You can't rearrange the order of steps in the History panel, but you can replay them and undo them. Don't think of the History panel as an arbitrary collection of commands; think of it as a way to view the steps you've performed, in the order in which you performed them. This is a great way to let Dreamweaver do your work for you if you have to repeat the same steps over and over again. It's also a lifesaver if you make a major mistake and want to go back one or more steps in your development.

Here's a rundown of how you can put the History panel to use:

✔ **To copy steps you've already executed:** Use the Copy Steps option as a quick way to automate steps you want to repeat. You can even select steps individually, in case you want to replay some, but not all, of your actions exactly as you did them.

Figure 6-7:
The History panel keeps track of what you've done, making it easy to undo any move and repeat any or all of your steps.

✔ **To replay any or all of the steps displayed in the History panel:** Highlight the steps you want replayed and click the Replay button in the bottom of the History panel.

✔ **To undo the results of the replayed steps:** Choose Edit⇨Undo.

✔ **To apply steps to a specific element on a page:** Highlight that element in the document window before selecting and replaying the steps. For example, if you're applying bold and italic formatting to just a few words on a page, you can replay the apply bold and italics steps to selected text.

You can also set the number of steps that are displayed in the History panel by choosing Edit⇨Preferences and selecting General from the Category list on the left. The default is 50, more than enough for most users. The higher the number, the more memory the History panel requires to function properly.

Using the Quick Tag Editor

If you're one of those developers who likes to work in the Dreamweaver WYSIWYG editing environment but still wants to look at the HTML tags once in a while, you'll love the new Quick Tag Editor.

The Quick Tag Editor, as the name implies, lets you modify, add, or remove an HTML tag without opening the HTML Source Window. That means that while you're in the middle of working on a page, you can quickly bring up the tag you are working on without leaving the document window. You can use the Quick Tag Editor to insert HTML, edit an existing tag, or wrap new tags around a selected text block or element.

The Quick Tag Editor opens in one of three modes — Edit, Insert, or Wrap — depending on what you have selected on a page. Use the keyboard shortcut Ctrl+T (Windows) or ⌘+T (Macintosh) to change modes while the Quick Tag Editor is open.

You can enter or edit tags in the Quick Tag Editor, just as you would in the Document Source Window, without having to switch back and forth between the text editor and WYSIWYG environment.

To enter or edit tags in the Quick Tag Editor, follow these steps:

1. **With the document you want to edit open, select an element or text block.**

   If you want to add new code, simply click anywhere in the file without selecting text or an element.

2. **Choose Modify⇨Quick Tag Editor.**

   You can also press Ctrl+T (Windows) or ⌘+T (Macintosh).

The Quick Tag Editor opens in the mode that is most appropriate for your selection. For example, if you click on an image or formatted text, it opens to display the code so that you can edit it. If you don't select anything, or if you select unformatted text, the Quick Tag Editor opens with nothing in it, and you can enter the code you want to add.

If you want to edit an existing tag, go to Step 3. If you want to add a new tag, skip to Step 4.

3. **If you selected an element that is formatted with multiple HTML tags or a tag with multiple attributes, press Tab to move from one tag, attribute name, or attribute value to the next. Press Shift+Tab to move back to the previous one.**

If you aren't sure about a tag or attribute, pause for a couple of seconds and a drop-down list appears automatically, offering you a list of all the tags or attributes that are available for the element you are editing. If this "hints" list doesn't appear, choose Edit⇨Preferences, choose Quick Tag Editor Preferences, and make sure that the Enable Tag Hints option is selected.

4. **To add a new tag or attribute, simply type the code into the Quick Tag Editor.**

You can use the Tab and arrow keys to move the cursor to the place you want to add code. You can keep the Quick Tag Editor open and continue to edit and add attribute names and values as long as you like.

5. **To close the Quick Tag Editor and apply all your changes, press Enter (Windows) or Return (Mac).**

Chapter 7

Working with Text

*N*ow that you're ready to start working on your Web page, the most basic element you need to learn about is text. The very first Web pages back in the early days of the Web used to be text only, and back then text came in one color, black on a gray background. In fact, HTML was originally developed as a way to exchange text-only files between scientists and researchers, not to design pretty pages. Graphics didn't come along until later. Before Dreamweaver, though, even formatting text for things like bold and italic required a pretty thorough knowledge of HTML tags, and there were lots of tags to memorize. With Dreamweaver, formatting and working with text is much easier, and you can accomplish a lot more than you could a few years ago, even if you were an HTML expert.

After you figure out how to work with text in Dreamweaver, you'll probably come to the conclusion that HTML doesn't give you a whole lot of typographic control over your page designs. Welcome to the world of HTML design. Fortunately, things in the HTML world have progressed a lot since the early days of Web design, and thanks to some new technologies, today's Web designers have a lot more control over type than they did even a few years ago. *Cascading Style Sheets* (CSS), for example, is a kind of extended HTML that provides a way to gain greater control over the look of the type in your Web page. CSS goes a long way in giving you real typographic control and a consistent look and feel throughout a Web site, as well as saving time in designing your Web page. I tell you all about CSS in Chapter 11. But before that, you need to find out how to do the basic formatting.

In this chapter, I also discuss HTML styles, which are a unique and very convenient feature built into Dreamweaver. HTML styles make it easy for you to save and apply repetitive text attributes to documents — things like type size, color, bold, italic, and so on.

Formatting Text in Dreamweaver

In this and the following sections, I show you how to control the look of your text, including choosing formatting through the Property Inspector and using HTML styles. In Chapter 2, I touch on the basics of entering and formatting text by using Dreamweaver. In this chapter though, I go over working with text in a lot more detail.

For starters, text is entered into your document simply by typing on the keyboard while in an open document. Anytime you want to make a change to text on your page, you simply need to highlight it by clicking and dragging the mouse over an area of text (see Figure 7-1).

Understanding the <FONT> tag

HTML is really all about tags (see Chapter 4 for more information). Whenever you make changes to a type selection in Dreamweaver, you alter the contents of the HTML <FONT> tag or add additional tags that control things like bold and italic. Changing the contents of the <FONT> tag allows you to specify size, font face, color, and tells the browser how to display the type. All of these options are attributes of the <FONT> tag, so you specify them in the Property Inspector in Dreamweaver. But before you start applying these options, you need to understand a little about how they work.

Regarding font sizes, HTML uses sizes which range from 1 to 7, with 7 being the largest. HTML can also specify font sizes relative to a given browser's default font size. The actual size of the default font varies from browser to browser and from platform to platform. In most browsers, the standard default size is HTML Font Size 3, but users can change the default to any font and size in the browser's preferences. If you're used to regular font sizes, 3 sounds like it's a really tiny font size. But, actually, it's about the same size as Times 12 point on the Mac and Times 14 point on the PC. That's why the default size option in the Property Inspector in Dreamweaver is the equivalent of Font Size 3.

In addition to setting absolute font sizes, you can also set relative font sizes. HTML gives you the option of setting the font size using +1 through +7 or –1 through –7. Using these options enables you to specify a font size relative to the default of the browser, even if it's something other than font size 3. For example, if you set the font size to +2, it is displayed at +2 larger than whatever the default font size is, even if the viewer made the default size in her browser the equivalent of Times 24 point.

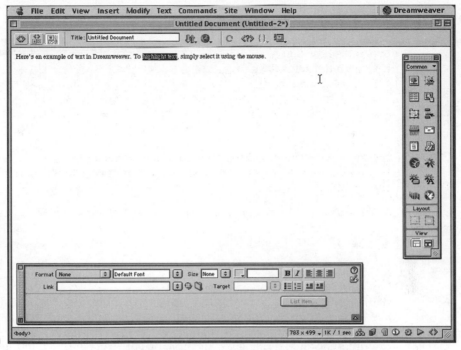

Figure 7-1:
Highlight an
area of text
on a page
by dragging
the cursor
over it.

When you specify a font face in Dreamweaver, you override the default font of the browser (the default font and size can be changed in the browser's preferences). But for the font to be displayed, it must be available on the viewer's computer. If you specify that you want to use Helvetica but your viewer's computer doesn't have Helvetica, the browser reverts to the browser's default font.

To help get around the problem of specifying specific fonts, HTML lets you specify multiple font faces and then prioritize their use. For example, if you specify Helvetica, you may also specify a similar font, such as Arial, as your second choice. Then, if Helvetica isn't available, the browser looks for Arial. If Arial is on the viewer's hard drive, the browser uses it to display the text instead. You can even take this a step further and choose a family of fonts, such as serif or sans serif, as one of your options. Then the browser at least tries to use a font in the same family if none of the fonts you've chosen is available.

To help you specify multiple font choices, Dreamweaver provides a list of common fonts and families in the font drop-down list in the Property Inspector. These are organized into groups of three or four fonts that you can apply to text, and they include some of the most popular and useful combinations of font choices. You can also edit this list to add fonts and combinations of fonts of your own choosing. Figure 7-2 shows the drop-down list for font choices in the Property Inspector. In this example, I've chosen the Verdana, Arial, Helvetica, Sans-Serif option. The browser that displays this text will try to display it first in Verdana. If Verdana isn't available on the computer, the text is displayed in Arial, Helvetica, or any sans-serif font — whichever one the computer finds first.

Figure 7-2:
Click the
arrow in the
font drop-
down list
box to
choose a
font or font
family.

HTML font sizes can be misleading when viewed between Macintosh and PC computer platforms. A given font size viewed on the Mac usually appears about two point sizes smaller than the same font size viewed on a PC because of a difference in the display standards. Be sure to take this difference into consideration, especially if you're designing a site on a Mac. Ideally, you should view the results on both platforms during development of your site in order to find a size that works best, knowing that the size you choose may look too small on a Mac or too big on a PC.

Applying font attributes

With Dreamweaver, applying a font or combination of fonts and setting font sizes and colors is easy.

To apply font attributes to text, follow these steps:

1. **Highlight the text that you want to change.**

2. **Open the Property Inspector if it isn't visible by choosing Window⇨ Properties. In the Property Inspector, choose a set of fonts from the font drop-down list (click the button to the right of where it says Default Font).**

   The font is automatically applied to the text. If you don't see the fonts you want to apply, you can create your own set by choosing Edit Font List from this drop-down list

3. **With the text still highlighted, choose the size you want from the Size drop-down list in the Property Inspector (button to the right of the Size field in the Property Inspector).**

   You can choose a size from 1 to 7 or specify sizes relative to the default font size by choosing + or − 1 through 7.

4. **With the text still highlighted, click the color square in the middle of the Property Inspector, just to the right of the Size text box.**

   When you click the color square, a pop-up color palette appears so that you can select a font color.

5. **Choose any color from the color palette (see Figure 7-3) by clicking the eyedropper over the appropriate color.**

6. **You can also click Bold (B) or Italic (I) in the Property Inspector to change the font style accordingly.**

Figure 7-3:
Click the color square in the Property Inspector to open up the color palette.

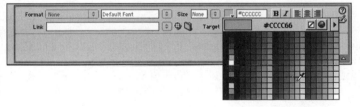

This color palette is limited to Web-safe colors (those that best display on both the Macintosh and Windows operating systems). If you want to create a custom color, click the icon that looks like a rainbow-colored globe in the top-right corner of the color palette. If you click the first icon, the square with a diagonal red line, the color reverts to the default text color for the page (the color specified as text color in Page Properties). You can also pick up a color from anywhere on the screen simply by dragging the eyedropper icon over any part of the screen and clicking over a desired color.

Generally, using Web-safe colors for text is a good idea, but you can use any color you like. Select other color palettes besides the Web-safe colors by clicking the small arrow at the top right of the color palette, and then selecting the colors from the list.

Creating Your Own HTML Styles

Now that you know how to control font attributes, you'll probably find that making font changes throughout a site can become rather boring and repetitive, especially if you need to make the same changes over and over. If you want to save some time, you can easily save commonly-used attributes as particular styles and then use them over and over again. This is what HTML styles are about. Don't confuse HTML styles with Cascading Style Sheets (discussed in Chapter 11) however. HTML styles are simply a collection of <FONT> tag and other style attributes that you can save in Dreamweaver and then easily reuse. HTML styles are really convenient but they are much more limited than Cascading Style Sheets. First of all, they only let you apply font attributes that are available as part of regular HTML. This means that you can't specify font sizes based on pixels, picas, or any other measurement other than the normal, very limited, HTML sizes. HTML styles also can't be shared among sites unless the other sites are also being edited in Dreamweaver. No other HTML program can use or modify Dreamweaver HTML styles.

Perhaps the greatest limitation of HTML styles compared with Cascading Style Sheets, however, is that if you format text to a certain style and later change the style definition, the text you formatted earlier doesn't update automatically to reflect the changes to the style. Still, in many cases, HTML styles can save time and increase productivity if your needs aren't that demanding and automatic updating isn't critical to your needs.

To create a new HTML style, follow these steps:

1. **Choose Text⇨HTML Styles.**

   A submenu appears offering you a list of predefined styles, along with the New Style option.

2. **Choose New Style.**

   The Define HTML Style dialog box opens, as shown in Figure 7-4.

3. **Select all formatting attributes, including font, size, color, style, and alignment, that you want to include in this style.**

4. **In the Name text box, type a name for your style; then click OK.**

   Your new style now appears in the submenu when you choose Text⇨HTML Styles. Any time you want to apply this style to a selected area of text, you can simply choose the style from the submenu and your text changes to reflect that style. When you quit Dreamweaver and start it up again, or even restart your computer, the HTML Style you created still remains as an option in the HTML Syles menu until you remove it.

```
┌───────────────────────────────────────┐
│          Define HTML Style              │
│                                         │
│      Name:  My Style                    │
│                                         │
│   Apply To:  ○ Selection (a)            │
│              ● Paragraph (¶)            │
│                                         │
│ When Applying: ○ Add to Existing Style (+)│
│                ● Clear Existing Style   │
│                                         │
│   Font Attributes:                      │
│                                         │
│      Font:  Verdana, Arial, Helve ↕     │
│      Size:  3                      ↕     │
│     Color:  ■  #3333FF                  │
│     Style:  B  I  Other...              │
│                                         │
│   Paragraph Attributes:                 │
│                                         │
│    Format:  Paragraph          ↕        │
│   Alignment: ▤ ▤ ▤                      │
│                                         │
│                                         │
│  Help    Clear    Cancel     OK         │
└───────────────────────────────────────┘
```

Figure 7-4:
Dream-
weaver lets
you define
and name
custom
HTML styles
to use
throughout
your page or
Web site.

To apply an existing HTML style, follow these steps:

1. **Highlight the text you want to modify and choose** T̲ext⇨HTML St̲yles.

   A submenu appears offering you a list of predefined styles that ship with Dreamweaver or any custom styles that you have created.

2. **Click to select one of the styles from this list, and the style is applied to your selected text.**

HTML styles are stored on your hard drive in a file called styles.xml. This folder is located either in the site folder (in the Library subfolder) or in the Dreamweaver configuration folder if the site root folder has not been defined.

Chapter 8

Adding Graphics

● ●

In This Chapter

▶ Creating images

▶ Using clip art

▶ Choosing a graphics program

▶ Keeping file sizes small

▶ Inserting images

▶ Using image maps

● ●

*N*o matter how great the writing may be on your Web site, the graphics always get people's attention. And the key to making a good first impression is to use images that look good, download quickly, and are appropriate to your Web site.

If you're familiar with using a graphics editing program to create graphics, you're a step ahead. If not, I'll give you some pointers and show you how to use pre-existing graphics on your Web site. In this chapter, you can find out how to bring graphics into Dreamweaver and work with some of the more popular image editing programs. I also include information about choosing other image editing programs, working with clip art, keeping image file sizes small, and working with graphics for the Web. Lastly, you can discover how to place and align images on your pages, create image maps, and set a background image using Dreamweaver.

Getting Great Graphics

You want your Web graphics to look good, but where do you get them? If you have any design talent at all, you can create your own images with Fireworks or any of the other image programs that I describe in "Creating your own images" later in this chapter. If you're not an artist, you may be better off gathering images from clip art collections (libraries of ready-to-use image files) and Web sites, as I describe in this section. If you have a scanner, you can also scan in existing photographs or logos to use.

Unfortunately, Dreamweaver doesn't have any image creation or editing capabilities of its own, so you have to use a different program if you want to create or edit images. If you bought the Dreamweaver 4/Fireworks 4 Studio, however, you're in luck; you have everything you need to create and edit images for your Web site. Otherwise, the most that you can expect from Dreamweaver in this area is that it integrates well with almost any other image editing program, though you still need to buy a separate program to create or edit your image files.

Buying clip art

If you don't want to hassle with creating your own images (or, like me, you lack the artistic talent), you may be happy to find many sources of clip art available. Clip art images, often called royalty-free images, are generally sold for a one-time fee that grants you all or most of the rights to use the image. (Read the agreement that comes with any art you purchase to make sure that you don't miss any exclusions or exceptions.) You can find a wide range of CD-ROMs and Web sites full of clip art, and even animations, that you can use on your Web site. Many professional designers buy clip art images and then alter them in an image program, such as Fireworks or Adobe Photoshop, to tailor them for a specific project or to make an image more distinct.

Here are some clip art suppliers:

- **Artville** (www.artville.com): Artville (see Figure 8-1) is an excellent source of quality illustrations and a great place to find collections of artistic drawings and computer-generated images that can provide a theme for your entire Web site.

- **Eyewire** (www.imageclub.com and www.eyewire.com): One of the world's largest sources of clip art, Eyewire includes illustrations as well as photographs.

- **PhotoDisc, Inc.** (www.photodisc.com): PhotoDisc, shown in Figure 8-2, is one of the leading suppliers of royalty-free digital imagery, specializing in photographs of a wide variety of subjects.

- **Stockbyte** (www.stockbyte.com): Stockbyte is a great source for international royalty-free photos.

- **Web Promotion** (www.webpromotion.com): A great source for animated GIFs and other Web graphics. Artwork on this site is free provided you create a link back to Web Promotion on your Web site or you can buy the artwork for a small fee.

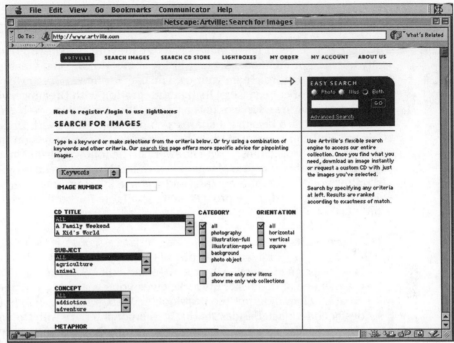

Figure 8-1:
The Artville
Web site.

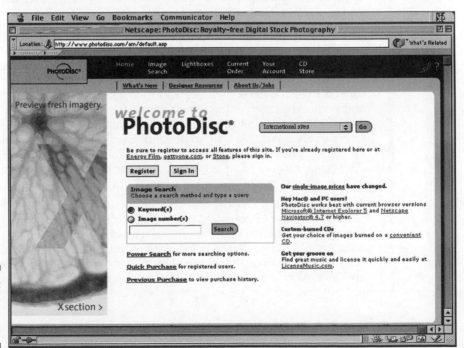

Figure 8-2:
The
PhotoDisc
Web site.

Creating your own images

The best way to get original images is to create your own. If you're not graphically talented or inclined, consider hiring someone who can create images for you. If you want to create your own images for use in Dreamweaver, I recommend Fireworks because of its tight integration with Dreamweaver and overall great features. Fireworks is a perfect tool for making Web graphics and is easy to learn because it shares a common interface with Dreamweaver. However, you can use any of the other image editing programs on the market either separately or in unison with Fireworks. The following list of image-editing programs shows you a little of what's out there. Most of these programs also allow you to scan photographs and logos using a scanner. Unless otherwise indicated, all of these programs are available for both Mac and Windows:

- **Macromedia Fireworks 4** (`www.macromedia.com/software/fireworks/`): Fireworks was one of the very first image-editing programs designed specifically to create and edit Web graphics. This program is one of the best. Fireworks gives you everything you need to create, edit and output the best-looking Web graphics, all in one well-designed product. Besides sharing a common interface with Dreamweaver, Fireworks also integrates extremely well with Dreamweaver to speed up and simplify the process of building a Web site. In Chapter 14, I cover some of the special features of Fireworks and Dreamweaver that help you to work together with these two programs.

- **Adobe Photoshop 6.0** (`www.adobe.com/products/photoshop/`): Adobe calls Photoshop the "camera of the mind." This is unquestionably the most popular image-editing program on the market and a widely used standard among graphics professionals. With Photoshop, you can create original artwork, correct color in photographs, retouch photographs and scanned images, and do much more. Photoshop has a wealth of powerful painting and selection tools in addition to special effects and filters to create images that go beyond what you can capture on film or create with classic illustration programs. The latest versions of Photoshop also add a wealth of features for creating and editing Web graphics, putting it on par with Fireworks in this department.

- **Adobe Photoshop LE** (`www.adobe.com/products/photoshop/`): The Limited Edition of Photoshop is a heavily scaled-down version of Photoshop that often comes bundled with scanners and other programming bundles. The Limited Edition offers most of the basic functions of Photoshop, but doesn't include features for compressing and optimizing graphics. Although you can still accomplish a lot with Photoshop LE, it's not the best tool for preparing images to use on the Web.

- **Adobe Illustrator 9.0** (www.adobe.com/products/illustrator/): Illustrator is one of the industry standards for creating illustrations. You can drag and drop illustrations that you create in Illustrator right into other Adobe programs, such as Photoshop or PageMaker. Illustrator also comes with an export feature that enables you to export your illustrations in GIF or JPEG format with a browser-friendly palette of colors so that your illustrations look great on the Web.

- **Adobe PhotoDeluxe 4.0 Home Edition** (Windows), Adobe PhotoDeluxe 2.0 (Mac) (www.adobe.com/products/photodeluxe/): Though not nearly as powerful as Photoshop, PhotoDeluxe makes many tasks easier by automating common features and concentrating on features for creating Web graphics. The program is designed to retouch photos (removing red-eye and improving color balance and contrast) and has the ability to crop and resize. You also find a collection of clip art included, as well as templates and wizards to help you create greeting cards, calendars, and more. PhotoDeluxe a great choice if you don't want to spend the extra money for Photoshop or don't need all the bells and whistles that Photoshop offers. This program is also geared for Web graphics output and is very easy to use and learn.

- **Equilibrium DeBabelizer** (www.equilibrium.com/debab/): DeBabelizer, by Equilibrium Technologies, is a graphics-processing program capable of handling almost every image format ever used on a computer. This one probably isn't the best program to use for creating images from scratch, but it does excel at some of the highly specialized tasks of preparing and optimizing images for the Web. One of the best features of DeBabelizer is its capability to convert images from just about any format to just about any other. If you have a bunch of images to convert, you can use DeBabelizer's batch convert feature, which enables you to automatically convert hundreds of photographs into JPEGs or convert many graphics into GIFs all at once without having to open each file separately. Be aware, though, that DeBabelizer has a pretty steep learning curve and isn't recommended for someone just starting out in creating Web graphics.

- **Jasc Paint Shop Pro 7** (www.jasc.com): Paint Shop Pro, by Jasc Software, is a fully featured painting and image-manipulation program available only for Windows. Paint Shop Pro is very similar to Photoshop, but on a more limited scale because it doesn't offer the same range of effects, tools, and filters. However, it costs less than Photoshop and may be a good starter program for novice image-makers. You can also download an evaluation version for free from the Jasc Web site.

- **Macromedia Freehand 9.0** (www.macromedia.com/software/freehand): Macromedia Freehand is an illustration program used widely both on the Web and in print. Freehand has many excellent Web features, including support for Web file formats such as GIF89a, PNG, and JPEG, as well as vector formats such as Flash (.SWF) and Shockwave FreeHand (.FHC). Thirty-day trial versions are available for free on the Macromedia Web site.

- **MicroFrontier Color It!** (www.microfrontier.com): This low-cost, easy-to-use graphics program is available only for the Macintosh and is a great tool for beginners, as well as those on a tight budget. Although it's much more limited than many of the other programs in this list, it provides enough features to create basic banners and buttons for a small business Web site. A demo version is available for free from the Microfrontier Web site.

- **Microsoft Image Composer** (www.microsoft.com/frontpage/imagecomposer/imagecomposer1.htm) and **PhotoDraw 2000** (www.microsoft.com/office/photodraw/): Image Composer was designed for creating Web graphics, so it's a good tool for the novice Web designer. Unfortunately, it's available only for Windows and only as part of the Microsoft FrontPage 2000 Web design software. Likewise, PhotoDraw 2000 is Windows-only and comes bundled with Office 2000 to offer photo-editing and drawing tools for easily making Web graphics. Either of these two tools is an adequate starting point for creating and editing images for use on the Web.

The last few years have seen a tremendous advancement in the features and capabilities of specialized Web graphics programs as well as increased competition between application vendors, especially the heavyweights like Adobe and Macromedia. Consequently, the current "best of the crop" graphics program is a toss-up between Macromedia's Fireworks and Adobe's Photoshop. One of these two programs will come out on top of almost any comparison of features and ability to produce the smallest Web graphics. If you're serious about Web graphics, I highly recommend getting one of these two programs — they're the cream of the crop and can easily pay for themselves by giving you the most professional and efficient results on your Web projects.

However, if you don't have the budget or the time to learn more complex programs, you may be better off with a more limited photo-editing program such as Adobe PhotoDeluxe, which is a capable yet far less expensive option, costing only around $49. For creating buttons, banners, and other Web graphics on a budget, consider Jasc Paint Shop Pro, MicroFrontier Color It!, or Microsoft Image Composer.

Understanding the Basics of Web Graphics

Because having a basic understanding of graphics formats and how they work on the Web is so important, I include the following sections to give you an overview of what you need to know about graphics as you create them or place them on your pages.

The most important thing to keep in mind when placing images on a Web page is that you want to keep your file sizes as small as possible. You may ask, "How small is small?" In fact, this is one of the most common questions people ask about Web graphics. The answer is largely subjective — remember that the larger your graphics files are, the longer people have to wait for them to download before they can see them. You can have the most beautiful picture of Mount Fuji on the front page of your Web site, but if it takes forever to download, most people aren't going to be patient enough to wait to see it. Also remember that when you build pages with multiple graphics, you have to consider the cumulative download time of all the graphics on the page. So smaller is definitely better. Most Web pros consider anything from about 40K to 60K a good maximum cumulative size for all the graphics on a given page. Anything over 100K is definitely a no-no if you expect people with dial-up modems to stick around long enough to view your pages. To make it easy to determine the total file size of the images on your page, Dreamweaver includes this information in the status bar of the current document window, as shown in Figure 8-3. This number indicates the total file size of all the images and HTML on your page as well as the expected download time at a given connection speed (you can set your own connection speed by choosing Edit⇨Preferences⇨Status Bar⇨Connection Speed).

Figure 8-3: The Dreamweaver Status Bar indicates the total download size of the page, including graphics and HTML, as well as the estimated download time.

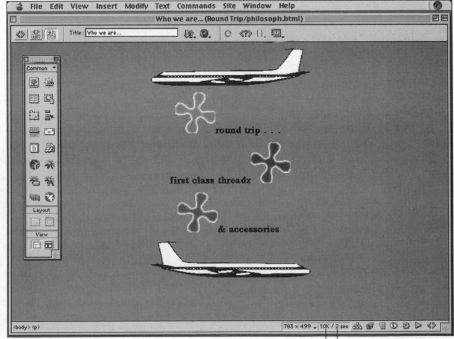

Estimated download time

Total file size for all images and HTML on the page

Achieving small file sizes requires using compression techniques and color reduction, tasks that can be achieved using any of the graphics programs I mention in the preceding section. Whatever program you use, you should understand that image sizes can be reduced to varying degrees and that the challenge is to find the best balance between small file size and good image quality. If you really want to find out the best ways to create graphics for the Web, read *Web Graphics For Dummies* by Linda Richards (published by IDG Books Worldwide, Inc.).

One of the most common questions about images for the Web is when you use GIF and when you use JPEG. The simple answer:

Use	For
GIF	Line art (such as one- or two-color logos), simple drawings, and so on
JPEG	Colorful, complex images (such as photographs)

How an image appears on a Web page

The HTML tag that you use to place images on a Web page is similar to the link tag that you use to create hyperlinks between pages. Both tags instruct the browser where to find something. In the case of the link tag, the path to the linked page instructs the browser where to find another URL. In the case of an image tag, the path in the tag instructs the browser to find a GIF or JPEG image file. The path describes the location of the image in relation to the page on which it appears. For example, /images/baby.gif is a path that would instruct a browser to look for an image file called baby.gif in the /images directory. This path also implies that the /images directory is in the same directory as the HTML file containing the link. Whenever you see a forward slash in HTML it signifies a directory (or folder) that contains other files or folders.

Trying to determine the path can get a little complicated. Fortunately, Dreamweaver sets the path for you, but you need to take care of two important steps before Dreamweaver can do this properly:

1. Save your page.

   When you save a page, Dreamweaver automatically remembers the exact location of the page in relation to the image. Saving the file is essential because the path always indicates the location of an image relative to the page containing the link (this is called a *relative link*). If you forget to save your file beforehand, Dreamweaver always prompts you to save the file before completing the link. If you don't save the file, Dreamweaver inserts an absolute link that references the image's location on your hard disk, but this link isn't valid on any other machine or when you upload your Web site. An *absolute link* to your hard drive works on your machine, but not on your Web server, or any other machine for that matter.

2. Make sure that your images and pages stay in the same relative locations when you're ready to go public with your site and move them all to a server.

That said, sometimes the best thing to do is just experiment with both formats and see which yields the best results. In time, you'll get a knack for which is the best format to use depending on the type of image you're working with.

Inserting Images on Your Pages

Dreamweaver makes placing images on your Web pages easy. All you have to do is click the appropriate icon on the Common Objects panel.

Before inserting any images into your page, it's important to save your page because Dreamweaver must know the directory location of the page so that it can properly create the image links.

To place an image in a new file, follow these steps:

1. **Choose File⇨New to start a new page.**

2. **Choose File⇨Save to Name and save the new HTML file in the folder of your choice.**

3. **If the Objects panel and Property Inspector aren't already visible, choose Window⇨Objects and Window⇨Properties to open them.**

4. **Click the Insert Image icon in the Common Objects panel (the first icon in the upper-left corner).**

   The Select Image Source dialog box appears, as shown in Figure 8-4.

Figure 8-4:
Clicking the
Insert Image
icon opens
up a dialog
box in which
you can
locate and
preview the
image you
want to
place.

5. **In the Select Image Source dialog box, browse your local drive in order to locate the image you want to place.**

    Alternatively, you can insert images simply by dragging and dropping image files from any open directory right into your Dreamweaver document, provided that they are in a valid Web graphics file format such as GIF or JPEG.

    Remember that when you work with images in Dreamweaver, as with any Web authoring tool, it's best to maintain the same directory structure on your local hard drive as you intend to use on your server when you upload your files. Starting out with all of your images and HTML files in one common folder on your computer makes them easier to track. Within this common folder, you can subdivide your images and HTML folders however you like. Mirroring the structure of your server on your local machine vastly simplifies uploading, tracking, and maintaining your site structure throughout the development cycle as well as later on when you want to update your site.

6. **Highlight the image to insert and double-click it or click once and then click the Select (or Open) button.**

    The image automatically appears on your page.

Aligning Images on a Page

After you place an image on your Web page, you may want to center or align it so that text can wrap around it. In the following two sections — "Centering an image" and "Aligning an image with text wrapping" — I show you the steps to accomplish both of these goals.

Centering an image

To center an image on a page, follow these steps:

1. **Click to select the image that you want to center.**

    The Property Inspector changes to display the image properties.

2. **From the icons for alignment options in the Property Inspector, shown in Figure 8-5, click the Center Alignment icon.**

    The image automatically moves to the center of the page.

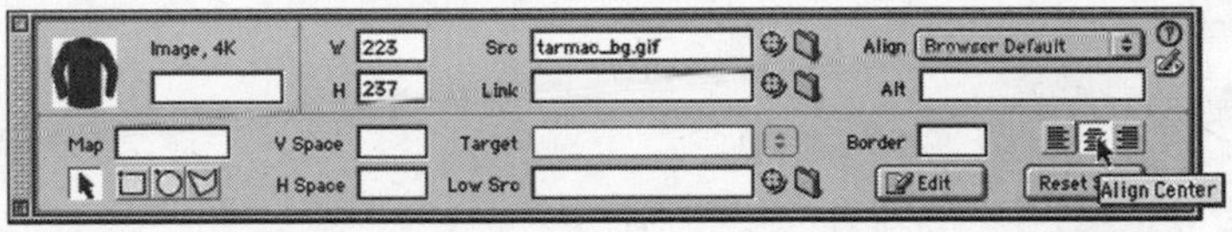

Figure 8-5:
Use the
alignment
icons in the
Property
Inspector to
center an
image.

Aligning an image to one side with text wrapping around it on the opposite side

To align an image to the right of a page and wrap text around it on the left, follow these steps:

1. **Insert the image immediately to the left of the first line of the text (see Figure 8-6).**

   The easiest way to do this is to place the cursor before the first letter of text; then select Insert⇨Image.

   Don't put spaces or line breaks between the image and the text.

2. **Select the image.**

   The Property Inspector changes to display the image attribute options.

3. **In the Property Inspector, choose Right from the Align drop-down list, as shown in Figure 8-7.**

   The image aligns to the right and the text automatically wraps around it.

To align the image to the left of the page with text wrapping around on the right, follow Steps 1 and 2 above, and then in Step 3, choose Left from the Align drop-down list instead of Right.

Creating complex designs with images

The alignment options available in HTML enable you to align your images vertically or horizontally, but you can't do both at once. Also, the alignment options don't really enable you to position images in relation to one another or in relation to text with much precision. The way to get around this limitation is to create HTML tables and use the cells in the table to control positioning, as shown in Figure 8-8.

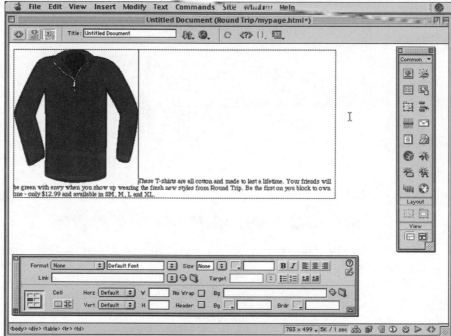

Figure 8-6:
To wrap text around an image, first place the image immediately to the left of the text with no spaces between the text and image.

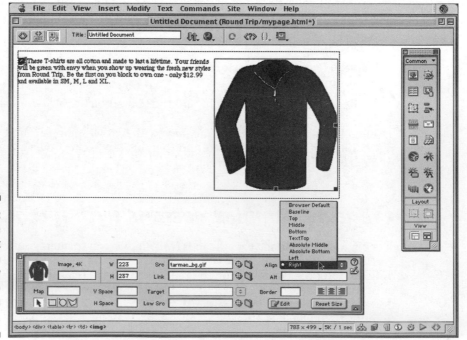

Figure 8-7:
Use the alignment options in the Property Inspector to align an image.

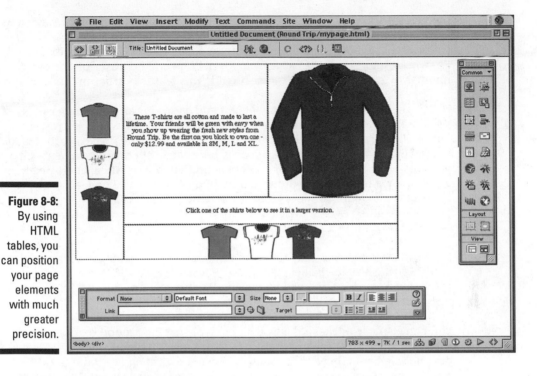

Figure 8-8:
By using HTML tables, you can position your page elements with much greater precision.

This sounds complex at first, but with a little experimentation, you can create almost any page layout using tables. Chapter 9 shows how to use tables to create more complex Web page designs.

Using the transparent GIF trick

You may find it strange that I would suggest you place an invisible image on a Web page, but that's exactly what I show you how to do in this section. A small, transparent GIF is a powerful element in Web page design because you can use it to control the exact position of other elements on a page. You'll notice that some other programs, such as Fireworks, also utilize transparent GIFs to "force" other page elements into compliance. These GIFs are automatically generated, and you can often recognize them because they use names such as shim.gif, dot clear.gif, or clear.gif. Regardless of the name, they all perform the same function.

If you're not sure how to make a clear GIF, don't worry — I include one on the CD-ROM that accompanies this book. You can do whatever you like with it. I always name this image clear.gif, and I use one on nearly every Web site I work on. See Appendix B for more information about what's on the CD.

If you want to make your own, just create a small, solid-color image, save it as a GIF, and designate the color you used as transparent. You can make a color transparent in most good graphics programs, including Adobe Photoshop, Fireworks, and Microsoft Image Composer. You can find descriptions of a number of graphics programs that provide this feature earlier in this chapter.

HTML enables you to specify any height and width for an image, regardless of its actual size. Thus, you can use a small transparent GIF with a corresponding small file size (for quick download) and then alter the image attributes for height and width to create exact spaces between other visible elements on your page. Many Web designers recommend that you create a single-pixel graphic for this purpose, but I've found that a 10 x 10 pixel image works best because some older browsers have trouble displaying a GIF that's only one pixel. Remember, even if the clear GIF is 10 x 10 pixels, you can still set the height and width to a smaller size.

Dreamweaver makes it easy to use the transparent GIF trick because it provides easy access to the height and width attributes in the Property Inspector. You may also need to specify the alignment of the image to achieve the desired effect.

You can also use a transparent GIF to control spacing around text. This method is handy when you want more than just a break between lines of text or other elements, but not as much as you get with the paragraph tag. This is also an ideal way to create larger spaces between elements with down-to-the-pixel design control.

To insert and size a transparent GIF between images, text, or other elements on a page, follow these steps:

1. **Copy the file for the transparent GIF (clear.gif) from the CD-ROM that accompanies this book to the folder on your hard drive where you're storing the images for your Web site.**

2. **With your page open in Dreamweaver, click to insert your cursor on the page where you want to insert an image or add text.**

   Don't worry if you can't put the cursor exactly where you want it; just get as close as you can. You can always reposition it later — that's what the transparent GIF trick is all about.

3. **Choose Insert⇨Image or click the Insert Image icon in the Common Objects panel to insert the image.**

   The Select Image Source dialog box appears.

4. **Browse to the file for the image that you want to place on your page, and then double-click it or click once and select Choose (or Open).**

   The image appears in your workspace.

   In these steps, I insert two image files in addition to the transparent GIF, which I use to control the spacing between them, but you can add text in this step instead of an image and still use the following steps to control the spacing between elements on your page.

5. **Choose Insert⇨Image or click the Insert Image icon in the Common Objects panel again to insert the second image.**

   The Select Image Source dialog box appears, enabling you to browse your drive for the desired image.

6. **Browse to find the clear.gif file that you copied to your hard drive in Step 1 and then double-click it.**

7. **Click OK.**

   The transparent GIF is inserted on your page and automatically selected.

8. **With the clear.gif image still selected, type** 20 **in the text box next to the W in the Property Inspector and** 20 **in the text box next to the H in the Property Inspector.**

   This sets the height and width of the image to 20 pixels each.

   I use a value of 20 pixels just for demonstration — you can set the height and width to any values you want.

   If you click clear.gif, you can see the outline of the image while it's selected. Notice that as soon as you deselect the image, it becomes invisible in Dreamweaver. You can always reselect it by clicking in the area until the cursor highlights it. If you're working with a very small GIF, say one that's only 1 pixel high by 1 pixel wide, you may have difficulty selecting it by clicking after it's been deselected. For this reason, I recommend resizing the GIF as soon as it's been placed on the page and still highlighted.

9. **Now place the third image to the right of the transparent GIF.**

   Just repeat Steps 3 through 5 to insert the image.

   After you insert your third image, you have two visible images with the space between them held by the transparent GIF, as shown in Figure 8-9. To change the space, simply increase or decrease the width of the transparent GIF.

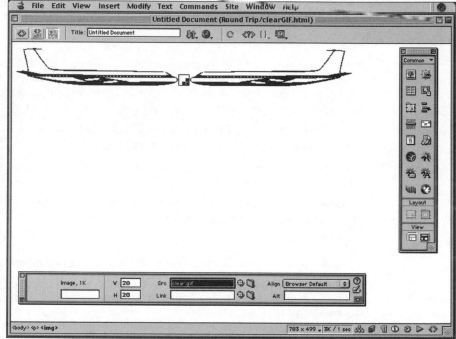

Figure 8-9:
The clear
GIF
highlighted
between
the two
airplanes
controls the
spacing
between
these two
images.

Creating a Background

Background images can bring life to a Web page, adding color and fullness. Used cleverly, a background image can help create the illusion that the entire page is one large image while still downloading quickly and efficiently. The trick is to use a small background image that creates a dramatic effect when it tiles (repeats) across and down the page

Beware, though, that certain backgrounds can make it hard to read text that's placed on top of them, so choose your background images carefully.

When you set an image as the background for your Web page, the browser repeats it across and down the page. This is why background images are often called *tiles,* because they repeat like tiles across a kitchen floor. However, if you use a long, narrow image as a background or a large image that's small in file size, you can create many effects beyond a repeating tile.

Kare Anderson's Say It Better Web site (www.sayitbetter.com), shown in Figure 8-10, uses a background image that fills the entire page. The background image creates a stripe of pink down the left-hand side of the page and fills the rest of the page with a peach color. The effect is a rich, colorful page.

In this case, the background image wasn't a small image designed to tile horizontally as well as vertically, but a narrow strip (shown in Figure 8-11) that's too wide to repeat horizontally.

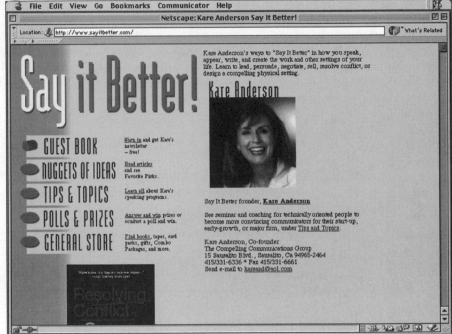

Figure 8-10:
Kare Anderson's Say it Better Web site has a fuller, richer design because a background image fills the entire page.

Figure 8-11:
The background image used in Figure 8-10, as it looks in Adobe Photoshop.

In the event that you don't want a background image to tile, your only option is to use an image that is larger than the maximum size of the largest monitor you expect people to view your site with. That way, they'll never see the next tile because it will always be out of view. Sometimes I create a background image that is something like 1200 x 1600 pixels in size. The key here is that you must be careful to keep your image file size very small. Background images of these dimensions work well only if you are using GIFs with very limited numbers of colors in them, never with JPEG images. Because GIFs can use only a couple of colors, their files sizes stay small even though their physical dimensions are huge. A GIF that size with no more than eight solid colors takes up only a few kilobytes of space. Use fewer colors, and it takes up even less space.

To set a background on a Web page, follow these steps:

1. **Choose Modify⇨Page Properties.**

   The Page Properties dialog box appears, as shown in Figure 8-12.

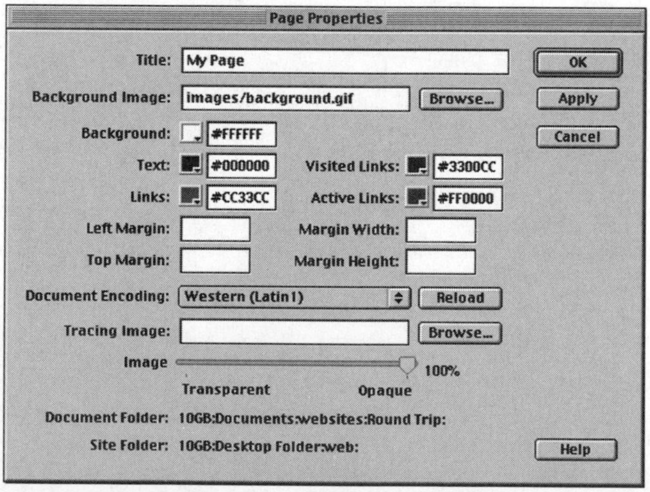

Figure 8-12:
The Page
Properties
dialog box
enables you
to set a
background
image, as
well as a
background
color, text,
and link
colors.

2. **Click the Browse button to the right of the text box next to Background Image.**

   The Select Image Source dialog box opens.

3. **Browse to find the image that you want to use as your background image.**

   When you insert an image in your Web site, you want to make sure that the image is in the same relative location on your hard drive as it is on your server. If you plan to use your background tile throughout your site, you may want to store it in a common images folder where it is easy to link to from any page in your site.

4. **Click the filename of your background image to select it.**

   The Select Image Source dialog box disappears.

5. **Click OK in the Page Properties dialog box to finish.**

   Note that if you click the Apply button, you see the effect of the background tile being applied to the page before you click OK to close the dialog box.

Creating Image Maps

Image maps are popular on the Web because they enable you to create hot spots in an image and link them to different URLs. A common use of an image map is to make a geographic map, such as a map of the United States, link to different locations depending on the section of the map selected. For example, if you have a national bank and want to make it easy for customers to find a local branch or ATM machine, you can create hot spots on an image map of the United States and then link each hot spot to a page listing banks in that geographic location. Dreamweaver makes creating image maps easy by providing a set of simple drawing tools that enable you to create hot spots and set their corresponding links.

To create an image map, follow these steps:

1. **Click to insert your cursor in the place on your Web page where you would like to place an image that contains the image map.**

2. **Choose Insert⇨Image.**

   The Select Image Source dialog box appears.

3. **Browse to find the image that you want to insert.**

4. **Double-click the filename of the image or click once and then click OK.**

   The image appears on the page.

5. **Select Window⇨Properties to open the Property Inspector if it's not already open; then highlight the image.**

   With the Property Inspector visible, just click the image so that the image properties display in the Inspector window.

6. **To draw your hot spot, choose a shape tool from the Image Map tools in the lower left of the Property Inspector (see Figure 8-13).**

   The shape tools include a rectangle, an oval, and an irregular polygon, and they allow you to draw regions on your images, called *hot spots,* each with a specific link.

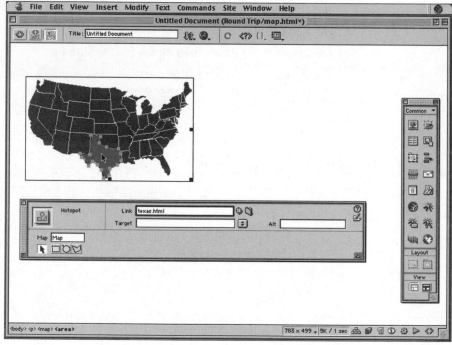

Figure 8-13:
Click and
highlight
any image
to display
the image
map tools in
the Property
Inspector.

7. **With the rectangle shape tool selected, click and drag over an area of the image that you want to make *hot* (link to another page).**

   As you click and drag, a light blue highlight appears around the region that you're making hot; this highlighted area indicates the active region. Position this region so that it covers the area that you want. If you need to reposition the hot area, select the arrow tool from the lower-left corner of the Property Inspector and then select and move the region to the location you want. You can also resize it by clicking and dragging any of the corners.

   If you want to make a shape other than a rectangle, you can use either the oval or polygon hot spot tools. The polygon tool functions a little bit differently; to make a polygon selection (such as one of the state of Texas in a U.S. map), you click the tool once for each point of the polygon shape you want to draw. Then, to close the shape, click again on the first point you drew after you finish drawing all the other points.

8. **To link a selected hot area, click the Folder icon next to the Link text box (at the top of the Property Inspector).**

   The Select HTML File dialog box opens.

9. **Browse to find the HTML file that you want to link to the hot spot on your image.**

10. Double-click the file to which you want to link.

The hot spot links to the selected page and the Select HTML File dialog box automatically closes. You can also type the path directly into the link field if you know it, saving you from having to find it on your hard drive.

11. To add more hot spots, choose a shape tool and repeat Steps 7 through 10.

12. To give your map a name, type a name in the text field next to Map, just above the shape tools.

Giving your map a name helps to distinguish it in the event that you have multiple image maps on the same page. You can call the map anything you want.

When you are finished, you see all your image map hot spots indicated by a light blue highlight.

You can go back at any point and re-edit the image map by clicking and highlighting the blue region on your image and dragging the edges to resize the image or by entering a new URL to change the link.

Part III
Advancing Your Site

The 5th Wave   By Rich Tennant

"I have to say I'm really impressed with
the interactivity on this car-wash Web site."

In this part . . .

*I*f you want to create compelling designs within the confines of the rules of HTML, you need to use HTML tables, frames, and Cascading Style Sheets (CSS). This part walks you through the maze of nested tables and merged cells, split pages framed with links, and the power and design control that you can achieve only with CSS.

Chapter 9

Coming to the HTML Table

In This Chapter
- ▶ Introducing HTML tables
- ▶ Going beyond spreadsheets
- ▶ Customizing table structure
- ▶ Creating complex designs

*W*hen most people think of tables, they think of spreadsheets and financial data. But you don't have to be a number cruncher to appreciate HTML tables. On the Web, tables are for much more than numbers; they can actually help you to create complex designs. For example, you can use a table to align elements side by side on a page and create columns of text. Whereas HTML page layout options are limited, tables provide a way to achieve much more precise alignment of page elements.

If you've ever used a desktop publishing program such as QuarkXPress or Adobe PageMaker, you've probably used text and image boxes to lay out pages. Tables work much the same way. You use the table cells (the "boxes" created at the intersection of each row and column in a table) to control the placement of text and images. Because you can make the borders of the table invisible, your viewers don't see the underlying structure of your table when they look at your Web page in a browser. You still won't get the design control you're used to in a desktop publishing program, but you can come much closer to that control by using tables.

In this chapter, I explore a wide range of uses for HTML tables and show you step-by-step how to create a variety of designs for your Web pages.

Creating Simple Tables in Layout View

Tables are made up of three basic elements: rows, columns, and cells. If you've ever worked with a spreadsheet program, you're probably familiar with what tables are all about. Tables in HTML differ from spreadsheet tables mainly in that they are much more involved to create and edit. Back in the days when you had to design Web pages in raw HTML code by hand, even simple tables were difficult to create. The code behind an HTML table is a mess of <TR> and <TD> tags that indicate table rows and table data cells. Figuring out how to type in those tags so that they create a series of little boxes on a Web page was never an intuitive process. If you wanted a complex design using tables with uneven numbers of rows or columns, you really faced a challenge.

Thank the cybergods that WYSIWYG editors such as Dreamweaver have made this process so much easier. If you've ever written HTML code manually, you can appreciate how much simpler Dreamweaver makes it to quickly create tables, merge or split cells, change a background color, or specify the width of a border. Using the Dreamweaver Layout View mode, the easiest way to work with tables in Dreamweaver, you can quickly and easily create the most complex tables simply by clicking and dragging tables cells around on the screen. When your basic table structure is complete, you can then use the Property Inspector to specify a wide range of table attributes, such as border size, alignment, colors, and so on. With Layout View, Dreamweaver also allows you to easily move table cells around your page after the table has been laid out, avoiding one of the great pitfalls of table design: changing your mind about the table structure after you've built it.

In this section, I walk you through creating a simple table. For the purposes of these steps, I create a table with two columns and two rows, but you can specify any number of rows and columns that you want.

The easiest way to work with tables in Dreamweaver is to switch to Layout View and use the special Layout Cell and Layout Table tools (see the following steps on how to do this). With these tools, which are available only in Layout View, Dreamweaver offers an enormous amount of convenience and special features that make working with tables a breeze. The ability to work in two different document viewing modes is a new feature in Dreamweaver 4. Switching between the two modes (Standard View and Layout View) can greatly simplify the process of creating and editing tables. You're already used to working in Standard View in Dreamweaver because that's the default view for working on documents. Layout View provides a special view mode that is designed to assist in the constructing and editing of tables by providing an easy to use and understand grid-like canvas, which makes table editing a snap (see Figures 9-1 and 9-2).

To create a simple table in Layout View, follow these steps:

1. **Switch to Layout View by clicking the Layout View button in the Common Objects panel or by selecting <u>V</u>iew⇨<u>T</u>able View⇨<u>L</u>ayout View.**

   You may see a message briefly describing how to use the Layout Table and Layout Cell buttons. Click `Don't show me this message again` to avoid seeing it next time.

2. **Click the Draw Layout Cell button.**

   The cursor changes to a crosshair when you move the mouse over the document area, indicating you're ready to draw a table cell.

3. **Click the mouse on the document and drag to draw a rectangular shape for your first table cell.**

   The cell is drawn and its surrounding table structure is automatically generated. A grid representing the table structure appears with the current cell shown in white.

4. **In the grid space just to the right of the cell you just drew, draw another cell of equal size using the same Draw Layout Cell button. Make sure the second cell is exactly adjacent to the first cell.**

   As you draw, notice that the cell "snaps" into place along the guidelines in the table grid. Use the grid as a guide in lining up your cells.

Draw Layout Table button

Draw Layout Cell button

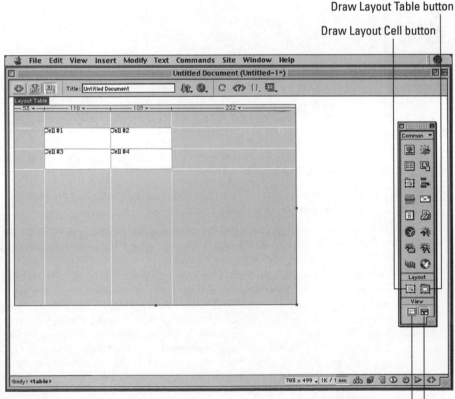

Figure 9-1:
The unique Dreamweaver Layout View allows you to easily create and edit tables on a grid system.

Standard View button

Layout View button (selected)

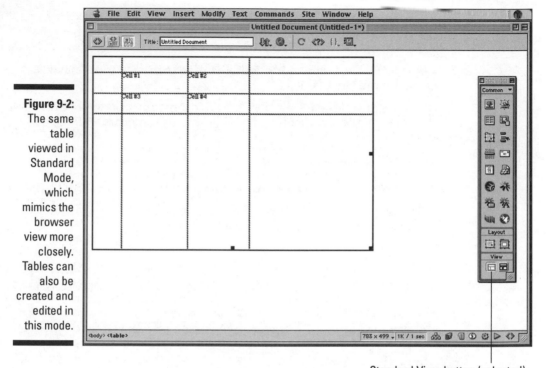

Figure 9-2:
The same table viewed in Standard Mode, which mimics the browser view more closely. Tables can also be created and edited in this mode.

Standard View button (selected)

5. **Now draw two cells just below the two you created, making a two by two cell table.**

6. **Click your mouse in the first cell you drew and type some text; then repeat that for the other three cells.**

7. **Switch to Standard View by clicking the Standard View or selecting View⇨Table View⇨Standard View to see how your table looks.**

Depending on where you started drawing your table cells, Dreamweaver may create table cells around the cells you just created to maintain their position on the page. Normally a table defaults to the top left corner of a page, so the first cells in the table are close to the top left margin. However, using Layout View, you can draw cells wherever you want them on a page, and Dreamweaver automatically generates the other cells that are needed to keep the positioning you created in Layout View. Remember, HTML won't allow you to place things anywhere on a page unless you use table cells to control their placement. Empty cells that Dreamweaver creates to fill space in a table merely act as *spacer cells* and don't show up in the browser, giving the illusion that various page elements are positioned independently on any part of the page.

Editing Tables in Layout View

One of the really wonderful things about working with tables in Layout View is that you can use the layout grid to edit, move, and resize any of the rows, columns, and cells in the table, which allows you to really use the grid as a design guide for creating any kind of layout you want. Normally, the only way to create complicated layouts in HTML is by meticulously building complex tables. But in Layout View, you can move table cells around on the grid using drag-and-drop to precisely position text or images without having to manually create spacer cells to do the job. You also have the flexibility to create *nested* tables (tables drawn within tables) for even more control over your layout. To create a nested table, simply click the Draw Layout Table button and begin drawing a table inside of another existing table the same way you did in the previous section with the Layout Cell button. For more information on nested tables see the section titled "Using nested tables: Tables within tables" later in this chapter.

Understanding Table Options

Layout View works best for creating and editing the overall *structure* of your table. When you're ready to start editing the *contents* of the table and its individual cells, it's best to work in Standard View. In Standard View, you can change HTML table attributes, such as height, width, border size, and spacing, using the Property Inspector. You can also insert things like text and images into the cells. Click the border of any table to select it, and the Property Inspector displays the table options shown in Figure 9-3. To view all the options, click the expander arrow in the lower-right corner of the Property Inspector.

Figure 9-3:
The Property Inspector provides access to attributes for a selected table or cell.

Sometimes selecting a table with the mouse can be a bit tricky. Use the HTML tag selector in the document's Status Bar at the lower-left edge of the document to select an entire table easily. You can click your mouse anywhere in your table to display the HTML tags in the status bar, then click the <TABLE> tag in the tag selector to select the entire table.

The Property Inspector gives you access to the following table options for customizing the appearance of your table:

- ✔ **Rows:** Displays the number of rows in the table. You can alter the size of the table by changing the number. Be careful, though: If you enter a smaller number, Dreamweaver deletes the bottom rows — contents and all.

- ✔ **Columns:** Displays the number of columns in the table. You can alter the size of the table by changing the number. Be careful, though: If you enter a smaller number, Dreamweaver deletes the columns on the right side of the table — contents and all.

- ✔ **W (Width):** Displays the width of the table. You can alter the width by changing the number. The width can be specified as a percentage or a value in pixels. Values expressed as a percentage increase or decrease the table's size relative to the size of the user's browser window.

- ✔ **H (Height):** Displays the height of the table. You can alter the height by changing the number. The height can be specified as a percentage or a value in pixels. Values expressed as a percentage increase or decrease the table's size relative to the size of the user's browser window. This table attribute is only recognized by version 4.0 browsers and above.

- ✔ **CellPad:** Specifies the space between the contents of a cell and its border.

- ✔ **CellSpace:** Specifies the space between table cells.

- ✔ **Align:** Controls the alignment of the table. Options are left, right, and center.

- ✔ **Border:** Controls the size of the border around the table. The larger the number, the thicker the border. If you want the border to be invisible, set the border to 0.

- ✔ **Bg Color:** Controls the background color. Click the color square next to this label and select a color from the box that appears. When you click the color square, the cursor changes to an eyedropper, enabling you to pick up a color from anywhere on the page by clicking the color. You can apply this option to a single cell or to the entire table.

- ✔ **Bg Image:** Enables you to select a background image. Specify the filename or click the folder icon to locate it. You can apply this option to a single cell or to the entire table.

✔ **Brdr Color:** Controls the border color. Click the color square next to this label and select a color from the box that appears. When you click the color square, the cursor changes to an eyedropper, enabling you to pick up a color from anywhere on the page by clicking the color. You can apply this option to a single cell or to the entire table.

The following icons appear in the bottom-left corner of the Property Inspector, from left to right and top to bottom:

✔ **Clear Row Heights:** Globally deletes all the height values for the rows in the table. When no heights are specified, the rows shrink to whatever size is needed to accommodate their contents.

✔ **Clear Column Widths:** Globally deletes all the width values for the columns in the table. When no widths are specified, the columns shrink to whatever size is needed to accommodate their contents.

✔ **Convert Table Widths to Pixels:** Converts the width of the table from a percentage to pixels.

✔ **Convert Table Widths to Percent:** Converts the width of the table pixels to a percentage of the page.

Table dimensions expressed as a percentage enable you to create a table that changes in size as the browser window is resized. If you want a table to always take up 75 percent of the browser window, for instance, percentages are a good way to specify table size. No matter what size the user resizes the browser window to, the table will always structure itself to occupy 75 percent of the window. On the other hand, if you want a table to always take up a specific number of pixels — that is, to remain the same size regardless of the browser window size — choose pixels instead of percentages for your table dimensions.

Controlling Cell Options

In Standard View, in addition to controlling the table options in the Property Inspector you can control options for the contents of individual cells within the table. Whenever you select an individual cell by clicking the cursor inside of the cell, the Property Inspector changes to display the individual properties for that cell (see Figure 9-4), allowing you to change those properties. You can also change multiple cells at the same time. Say you want to have some, but not all, of the cells in your table take on a certain color background and style of text. You can apply the same properties to multiple cells at the same time by holding down the Shift key while clicking on adjacent cells to select them. If you want to select multiple cells that are not adjacent, hold down the Ctrl key (Command key on the Mac) instead and click each cell that you want to select. Any properties you select in the Property Inspector afterwards are applied to all the selected cells.

When one or more cells are selected, the top half of the Property Inspector controls the formatting of text and URLs within table cells. The bottom half of the Property Inspector provides the following options:

- **Horz:** Controls the horizontal alignment of the cell contents.
- **Vert:** Controls the vertical alignment of the cell contents.
- **W:** Controls the width of the cell.
- **H:** Controls the height of the cell.
- **No Wrap:** Select No Wrap to prevent word wrapping within the cell. The cell will widen to accommodate all text as you type or paste it into a cell. (Normally the text would just move down to the next line and increase the height of the cell.)
- **Header:** Use to format a cell's contents using a header style of bold and centered.
- **Bg (Image):** Allows you to specify a background image for the cell.
- **Bg (Color):** Allows you to specify a background color for the cell.
- **Brdr (Color):** Allows you to change the border color of the cell.

Using the Format Table Feature

One of the best reasons for using tables is to present lots of data in a clear and structured way. Tables accomplish this because the use of rows and columns allows the reader to follow along easily when there is a lot of data to represent. One of the ways to make your data even more presentable and attractive is to colorize the rows and columns in the table. In the previous section, I show you how to change the attributes of individual cells. In this section, I show you a really great Dreamweaver feature that allows you to select predefined table formats with great color schemes to enhance your presentation. Figure 9-5 shows a sample of the Format Table feature that lets you to do this.

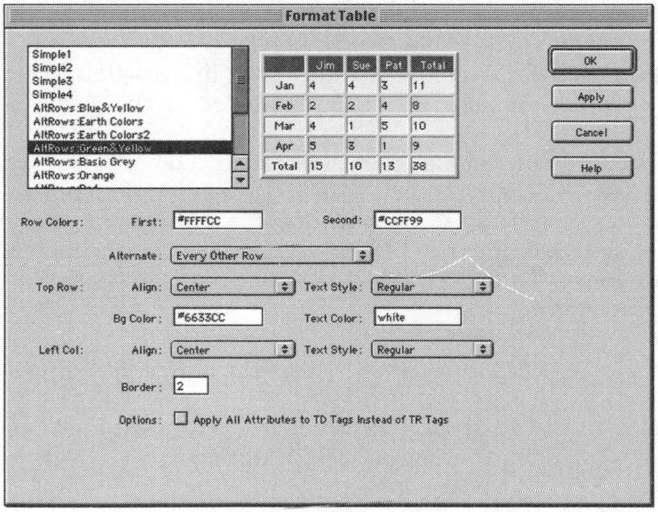

Figure 9-5:
The Dream-
weaver
Format
Table
feature
provides a
plethora of
previously
created
color
schemes to
enhance the
look of your
tables.

To use the Format Table feature, follow these steps.

1. **Select an existing table in the document.**

2. **Make sure you're in Standard View by clicking the Standard View button in the Common Objects panel.**

3. **Choose Commands⇨Format Table**

   The Format Table dialog box appears

4. **Select one of the schemes by scrolling the list or modify any of the parameters to create your own scheme.**

5. **Click OK**

   The color scheme is applied to the table.

These color schemes were created by professional designers so you can be sure they'll look good on your Web page. You can also modify any of the attributes in the Format Table dialog box and create your own interesting color schemes.

Aligning Columns in a Table

When working with lots of numbers, people use tables in word processing programs and spreadsheets because they can easily align the contents of columns to ensure that numbers line up properly. You don't have as much control in HTML as you have in a program such as Excel, in which you can align numbers on a decimal point. Still, you can align the content of columns left, right, or center.

If you want to convert a table that you created in a program such as Word or Excel, see the next section, "Importing Table Data from Other Programs."

In the following steps, I show you how to create a table of financial data in Standard View and align all the data cells on the right so that the numbers align. You can also use these steps to align the contents of table cells to the left, center, or top. In these steps, I insert the data into the table after I create it in Dreamweaver. If you've converted a table and just want to align the cells, go directly to Step 7.

To create a table of financial data and align the data, follow these steps:

1. **Make sure you're in Standard View (the Standard View icon in the Custom Objects panel should be clicked).**

2. **Click to place your cursor where you want to create a table.**

3. **Click the Insert Table icon from the Objects panel.**

   Alternatively, you can choose Insert⇨Table. The Insert Table dialog box appears.

4. **In the appropriate boxes, type the number of columns and rows you want to include in your table.**

   For this example, I specified four rows and four columns.

5. **Specify the width and choose pixels or percent; then click OK.**

   I set my table to 75 percent so that it doesn't fill the entire page. You can set the width to whatever is most appropriate for your design. The table automatically appears on the page.

6. **Click to place your cursor in a cell, and then type the data that you want in each cell.**

   As you can see in Figure 9-6, I entered the heading information across the top row of cells. Then I listed several camera models and entered the data for each camera in the rest of the table.

7. **Select the column or row for which you want to change the alignment.**

   Place your cursor in the first cell in the column or row that you want to align; then click and drag your mouse to highlight the other columns or rows that need to be changed.

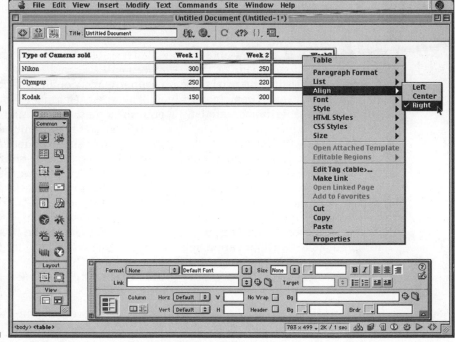

Figure 9-6:
You can
access
many
formatting
options by
right-
clicking
(Windows)
or Control +
clicking
(Mac)
selected
cells.

8. Right-click (in Windows) or Control + click (for Mac) on any cell in the highlighted column or row.

A pop-up menu appears (refer to Figure 9-6). Alternatively, you can also use the Property Inspector to change selected items.

9. From the pop-up menu, choose Alignment Left, Center, or Right.

This option enables you to change the alignment of all the highlighted cells in the column or row at once. If you're working with financial data, the Align Right option often produces the best alignment for numbers.

If you want to align one cell in a column or row differently than the others, click to place your cursor in that cell and then click one of the Alignment icons in the Property Inspector. You can also choose to align multiple cells that aren't contiguous (don't touch each other) by pressing and holding down the Ctrl key in Windows while you click the cells that you want to select. On the Mac, you press and hold down the Command key (⌘) while you click to select particular cells. Any options that you change in the pop-up menu or in the Table Inspector are applied to all the currently selected cells.

Importing Table Data from Other Programs

Manually converting financial data or other spreadsheet information can be tedious. Fortunately, Dreamweaver includes a special feature that enables you to insert table data created in other applications such as Microsoft Word or Excel. To use this feature, the table data must be saved from the other program in a *delimited* format, which means that the columns of data are separated by either tabs, commas, colons, semicolons, or other delimiters. Most spreadsheet and database applications, as well as Microsoft Word, enable you to save data in a delimited format. Consult the documentation for the application you are using to find out how to do this.

To import table data into Dreamweaver after it has been saved in a delimited format in its native application, follow these steps:

1. **Choose File⇨Import⇨Import Tablular Data or choose Insert⇨ Tabular Data.**

   Both of these commands do the same thing. Depending on which command sequence you choose, the Import Table Data or Insert Tabular Data dialog box appears. These dialog boxes are identical except for their titles (see Figure 9-7).

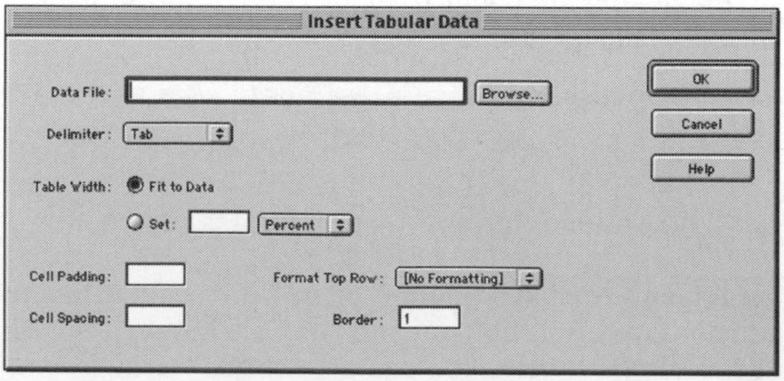

Figure 9-7: You can import tab-delimited data from other programs right into a Dreamweaver table.

2. **In the Data File text box, type the name of the file that you want to import or use the Browse button to locate it.**

3. **From the Delimiter drop-down list, select the delimiter format you used when you saved your file in the other application.**

   The delimiter options are Tab, Comma, Semicolon, Colon, and Other. You must select the correct option in order for your data to import correctly.

4. **Type or select the appropriate table formatting options for width, cell padding, cell spacing, top row formatting, and border size.**

5. **Click OK to insert the table.**

Using Tables for Spacing and Alignment

As you get more adept at creating Web pages, you may find that HTML tables are a crucial part of creating almost any design that requires more than basic alignment of elements on a page. Using tables, you can get around many of the limitations of basic HTML and accomplish some of the following design feats:

- Evenly spaced graphic bullets (little GIFs that can take the place of bullets) next to text
- Text boxes and fields properly aligned in a form
- Images placed side by side, spaced as far apart as you want them
- Columns of text that don't span the entire page
- Intricate layouts that are impossible to accomplish with HTML alone

In the rest of this chapter, I show you how to use tables to create a variety of page designs, including a few of the ones I just listed.

Any time that you want to use a table to create a great design but don't want the table itself to show, you can turn off the table border. You do that by typing **0** in the Border text box of the Table Property Inspector while the table is selected. If the Inspector isn't open, choose <u>W</u>indow⇨<u>P</u>roperties and then select the table to display its properties.

For really complex page layouts, or when you need to use precise pixel placement of elements in your designs, use the Layers to Table conversion feature described in Chapter 12. Using this feature enables you to design your layout with layer objects — as if you were working in a page layout program without the normal limits of HTML — and automatically convert the layers into tables with the click of a button.

Using tables to design forms

Creating text boxes and pull-down menus for HTML forms is easy in Dreamweaver, but you need to use tables to make them look good. In Chapter 16, you can find lots of information about creating forms; but for now, I assume that you've already created a form and that you want to align the text boxes evenly. I use a guest book form — a common, yet simple, form — as an example, but you can use this technique to align other form elements.

To use a table to align text boxes evenly on your form, follow these steps:

1. **Open a page that has an HTML form on it (or create an HTML form using the steps provided in Chapter 16).**

2. **Click to place your cursor where you want to start formatting your form.**

3. **Choose Insert⇨Table.**

   The Insert Table dialog box appears.

4. **Type the number of columns and rows you want in your table.**

   I set the table to two columns and five rows.

5. **Set the Width to whatever is most appropriate for your design and click OK.**

   I set the width to 100 percent. When you click OK, the table automatically appears on the page.

6. **Now you need to copy the data from your form into the table. Using the Copy and Paste commands from the Edit menu, copy the text preceding the form's first text field and paste it into the cell at the top-left corner of the table.**

   Alternatively, you can click and drag the text into the table cell.

   In my example in Figure 9-8, this means copying the words First Name and pasting them into the first table cell.

7. **Select the first text field (the empty box where the user would type his name) and copy and paste (or click and drag) it into the top-right cell of the table.**

8. **Repeat Steps 6 and 7 for the rest of the form until you've moved all of the form elements into table cells.**

9. **Click the vertical column divider line between the first and second columns and drag it to the left until the left column is just a few pixels wider than the widest line of text.**

10. **Select the table by clicking the border. When the Property Inspector opens, set the border to 0.**

    When you set the border to 0, the edges of your table change from solid lines to dotted lines so that you can still see where the borders are while you're working in Dreamweaver. When you view the page in a browser, as shown in Figure 9-9, the border of the table is invisible.

You can keep the Property Inspector visible at all times, or you can close it by clicking the small box with an X in Windows or the box in the top-left corner on a Mac. To open the Property Inspector, choose Window⇨ Properties.

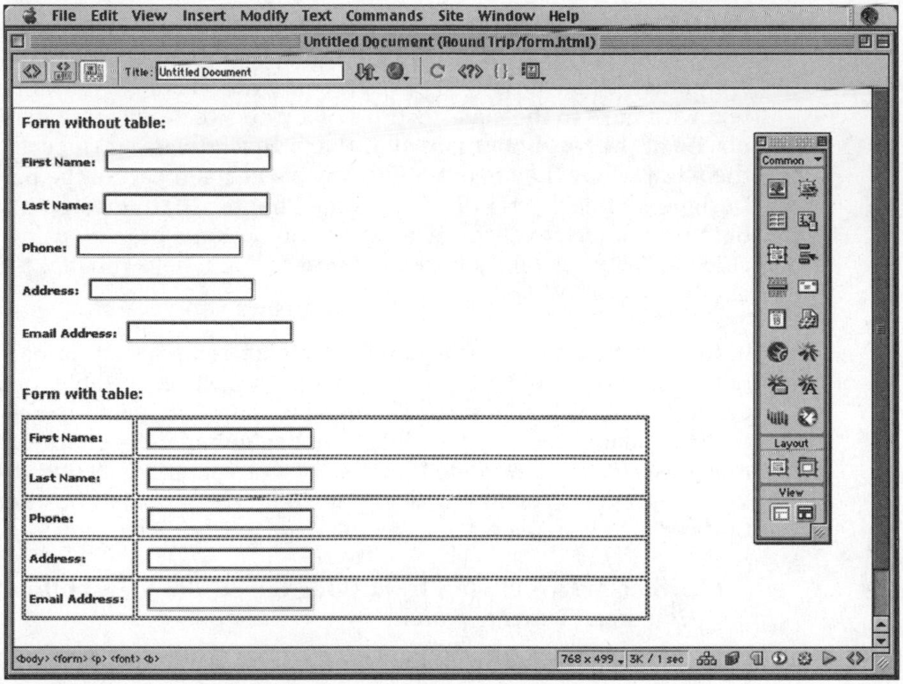

Figure 9-8:
You can use
a table to
present
form data in
a more
attractive
way.

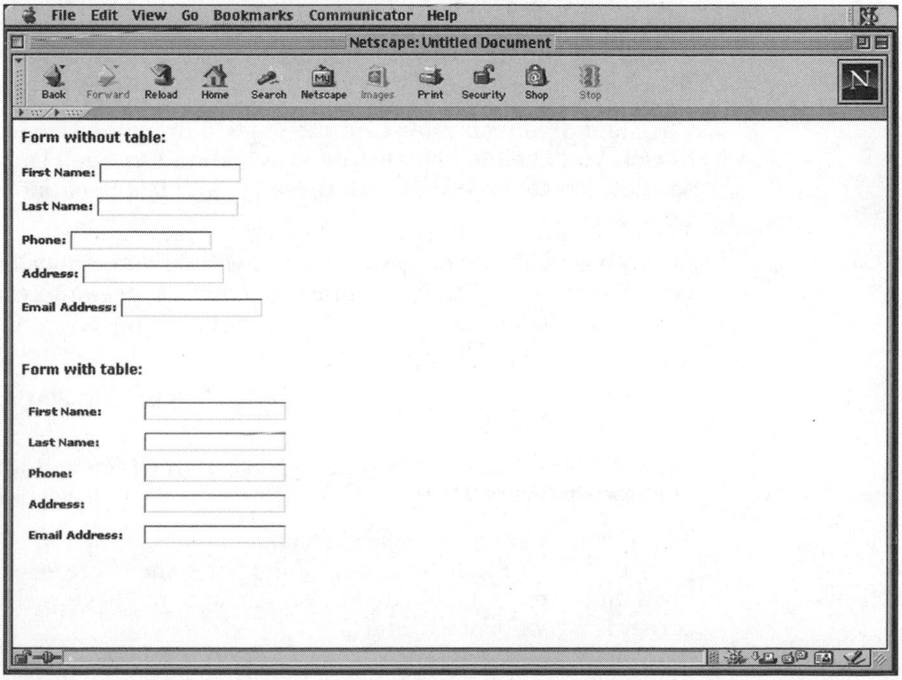

Figure 9-9:
When
displayed in
the browser,
the form
fields line up
evenly with
no visible
border.

Aligning a navigation bar

A common element on Web pages is a *navigation bar* — a row of images or text with links to the main sections of a Web site. Navigation bars are usually placed at the top, bottom, or side of a page where users can easily access them but where they're out of the way of the main part of the page design. Designers often use HTML frames (see Chapter 10) to insert a navigation bar, but you can effectively place a navigation bar on a page by using tables. The sidebar "Why use tables instead of frames?" can help you make the right choice for your Web site.

In the last example, in the section "Using tables to design forms," I show you how to create a table in Standard View with the regular table tools. In this example, I show you how to use the table tools in Layout View to build a table, similar to the way you did at the beginning of the chapter. You can really use either view mode for creating a table, but you'll find that Layout View often times makes it a lot easier. To create a table to position a navigation bar on a Web page using Layout View, follow these steps:

1. **Switch to Layout View by clicking the Layout View button in the Common Elements panel.**

2. **Click the Draw Layout Cell button to select the tool for drawing table cells.**

   Keep in mind how you want your table to be structured as you begin drawing cells in the next step. The structure is dictated by the shape and size of your navigation bar and other elements that need to be on the page.

3. **Click and drag your mouse on the page to draw the size and shape of cells you need to contain your navigation bar. See Figure 9-10 to see how I created a table with three large cells to contain my navigation bar.**

   Even while you're drawing cells, Dreamweaver automatically creates a table to enclose the cells you draw. To continue drawing cells without having to go back each time and reselect the Draw Layout Cell tool, hold down the Ctrl key (⌘ on Mac) while you draw cells to retain the tool.

4. **When you're done setting up the table, click the Standard View icon to return to Standard View.**

5. **Click to place your cursor in the table cell in which you want to insert your navigation bar.**

   To provide an example, I place a navigation bar in the top-left corner of a page. Even if you want your navigation bar somewhere else, you probably want to create a table that covers most of the page, so the top-left corner is a good place to start.

6. **Choose Insert➪Image and use the Browse button to locate the image that you want to insert into the table cell.**

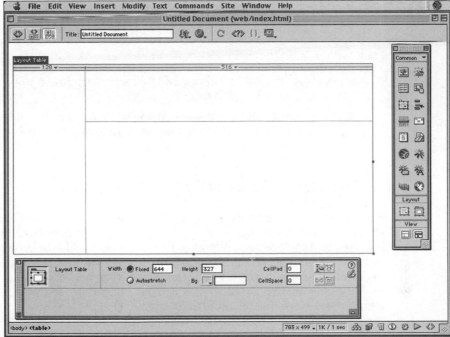

Figure 9-10:
Using
Layout View
to create a
basic table
for a
navigation
bar.

Why use tables instead of frames?

Some people don't like frames because they can be difficult to create and confusing for users to navigate, and some older browsers can't display frames. So tables provide a more universally accessible design element.

Frames can save a little time because the entire page doesn't have to reload every time a user clicks a link; only the new frame has to load, not the frame containing the link. With a navigation bar, the images and text of the navigation bar stay in their own frame while new material appears in another frame. If you design your page carefully, the download time can be minimal. If you just use text links, they load so

quickly that it doesn't matter. And if you use the same graphics on every page (as most people do in a navigation bar), the linked images reload quickly because they're *cached* (stored in temporary memory on the visitor's computer) the first time the user visits the page.

You can create very similar designs using tables or frames, so you should make your choice based on your goals and your audience. If you want to make sure that the largest possible audience can see your page, use tables; if you want to change only part of a page and keep your page elements visible at all times, use frames.

7. **Double-click the filename of the image.**

   The image automatically appears in the table cell. Repeat this step to insert multiple images.

   As you can see in Figure 9-11, I am using a series of images that I insert one beneath the other, separated by breaks, to create a row of buttons that runs down the left side of the page.

8. **Select the table and set Border to 0 in the Property Inspector. This makes your table invisible because the border lines won't show.**

Merging and splitting table cells

Sometimes the easiest way to modify the number of cells in a table is to *merge* cells (combine two or more cells into one) or *split* cells (split one cell into two or more rows or columns). This technique makes it possible to vary the space in table sections and customize their structure. For example, you may want a long cell space across the top of your table for a banner and then multiple cells underneath it so that you can control the spacing between columns of text or images. The following two sets of steps show you how to merge and split cells in a table:

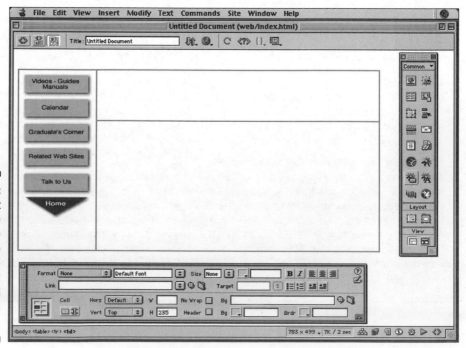

Figure 9-11:
Tables let you use separate images to create vertical and horizontal navigation bars.

Merging and splitting cells can be done only in Standard View.

To merge cells, follow these steps:

1. **Highlight two or more adjacent cells by clicking and dragging the mouse from the first cell to the last**

   Merged cells must be adjacent to one another.

2. **Click the Merge Selected Cells icon in the Property Inspector to merge the selected cells into a single cell (see Figure 9-12).**

   The cells are merged into a single cell using the span attribute. The *span attribute* is an HTML attribute that makes a single cell merge with adjacent cells by spanning extra rows or columns in the table.

Figure 9-12:
These two icons enable you to merge and split selected cells in a table.

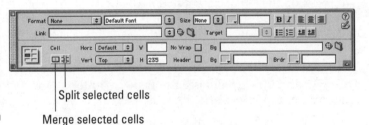

Split selected cells

Merge selected cells

To split a cell, follow these steps:

1. **Click to place your cursor inside the cell you want to split.**

2. **Click the Split Selected Cell icon in the Property Inspector.**

   The Split Cell dialog box appears.

3. **Select Rows or Columns in the dialog box, depending on how you want the cell to be divided.**

   A cell can be split into however many new rows or columns you want.

4. **Type the number of rows or columns you want to create.**

   The selected cell is split into the number of rows or columns you indicated.

Placing images and text side by side

You can apply the steps in the previous section to many designs. After you understand how to merge and split cells in a table, you can use that capability to create a variety of image and text combinations, gaining much more control over the layout of your pages.

This section takes the navigation row placement a step farther by inserting a banner graphic at the top of the page and then inserting text in the body of the page. Referring to Figure 9-11, this means that you insert content into the two remaining empty cells. With designs as specific and complex as these, walking you through every possible combination is impossible. Instead, follow these steps as an example of what's possible. You can use these steps to create exactly this design, or you can change the variables — such as the number of columns and rows or how many cells are merged — to create your own designs.

To insert a banner graphic at the top-right corner of a page when you have a navigation row on the left and want text in the body of the page, follow these steps. (Note that these steps pick up where the steps in the earlier section "Aligning a navigation bar" leave off. Refer to Figures 9-11 and 9-12.

1. **Click to place your cursor in the top-right cell of the table.**

2. **Choose Insert⇨Image and use the Browse button to locate the image that you want to insert into the table cell.**

3. **Double-click the filename of the image and click OK.**

   The image automatically appears in the table cell. Repeat this step to insert multiple images.

4. **Place your cursor in the cell beneath the cell with the banner and type the text you want displayed.**

   You can also copy and paste text from another source, such as a word processing program. Using cells next to each other like this enables you to better control the placement of elements. The steps in the next section can help you align the cell contents.

Aligning cell contents vertically and horizontally

When you insert elements of different sizes in adjacent table cells, the contents often move to the middle of the cell, creating an uneven design. You can counter this by specifying the vertical or horizontal alignment of the cell.

To align cell contents vertically or horizontally, follow these steps:

1. **Click to place your cursor in the cell that you want to align.**

   Remember that you are aligning the contents of the cell, not the cell itself.

2. **In the Property Inspector, choose the alignment option that you want from either the Horz (horizontal) or Vert (vertical) drop-down list box (see Figure 9-13).**

3. **Click OK.**

   The cell contents automatically align to according to the option you chose.

Using nested tables: Tables within tables

Placing tables within tables, called *nested tables,* can help you create the most complex designs. You create nested tables by inserting a table within a cell of another table. In the days when you had to write your own code, this was a daunting task. Today, Dreamweaver makes nesting tables easy, enabling you to create complex designs without ever looking at the HTML code.

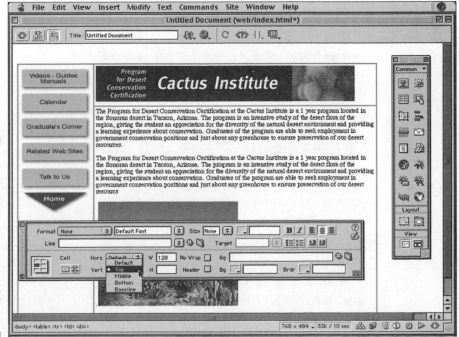

Figure 9-13:
Setting the vertical alignment of the left cell to Top keeps the navigation row at the top-left corner of the page.

Nested tables can get pretty messy. As with all design tricks, don't get carried away and overuse nested tables just because Dreamweaver makes them easy to create. The best Web designs are those that communicate the information to your audience in the most elegant and understandable way. Overuse of certain design elements, including nested tables, can actually get in the way of communicating your message. Make sure that when you use complicated designs, such as nested tables, your end result is truly the best way to display your information.

Try to avoid nesting your tables too many levels deep. A table within a table within a table is nested three levels deep. Anything more than that gets a bit hairy. Pages that use nested tables take longer to download because browsers have to interpret each table individually before rendering the page. For some designs, the slightly longer download time is worth it; but in most cases, you're better off adding or merging cells in one table, as I explain in the section "Merging and splitting table cells" earlier in this chapter.

One situation that makes a nested table worth the added download time is when you want to place a table of financial or other data in the midst of a complex page design.

To place a table inside another table, follow these steps:

1. **Click to place your cursor where you want to create the first table.**

2. **Choose Insert⇨Table.**

   The Insert Table dialog box appears.

3. **Type the number of columns and rows that you need for your design.**

   In this case, I created two columns and three rows.

4. **Set the Width to whatever is appropriate for your design, and click OK.**

   The table is automatically sized to the width you set. I used 80 percent.

5. **Use this table to create your primary design. When you're ready to create the nested table, click to place your cursor in the cell in which you want to place the second table.**

6. **Repeat Steps 2 through 4, specifying the number of columns and rows that you want and the width of the table.**

   The new table appears inside the cell of the first table.

7. **Type the information that you want in the nested table cells.**

   Figure 9-14 shows an example of a nested table that you can create by following these steps.

Figure 9-14:
By placing a table within a table, you can create columnar designs within a table, such as the acting experience displayed on this actor's Web page.

Chapter 10

Framing Your Pages

• •

• •

*N*o one wants to be "framed," whether that means being falsely accused of a crime or trapped in the HTML frameset of a Web site with no escape. That's why it's important to appreciate not only the best way to create frames, but the best way to use them to enhance site navigation and not leave viewers feeling trapped.

To help you make the most of this HTML design feature, I demonstrate not only how to build HTML framesets in Dreamweaver, but also discuss when frames are most useful and when they should be avoided. Frames add a wide range of design possibilities, but they can also create confusing navigation systems and can be very frustrating to viewers. As you go through this chapter, consider not only how to create frames, but also if they are really the best solution for your Web site project.

Appreciating HTML Frames

Frames add innovative navigation control because they enable you to display multiple HTML pages in one browser window and control the contents of each framed area individually. Designers commonly use frames to create a page with two or more sections and then place links in one section that, when selected, display information in another section of the same browser window.

Web pages that use frames, such as the one shown in Figure 10-1, are split into separate sections — or individual *frames*. All the frames together make up a *frameset*. Behind the scenes, each frame of the frameset is a separate HTML file, which makes a page with frames a little complicated to create, even with Dreamweaver. If you choose to create your frame files in a text editor, you have to juggle multiple pages, working on each frame one at a time, and you can see what you're creating only when you preview your work in a browser. The visual editor in Dreamweaver makes creating frames a lot easier because you can view all the HTML files that make up the frameset at the same time and can edit them while they are displayed in the way in which they appear in a browser.

As a navigational feature, frames enable you to keep some information constant, while changing other information on the same page. For example, you can keep a list of links visible in one frame and display the information each link brings up in another frame. The site shown in Figure 10-1 uses frames to show viewers a list of categories in the left frame that, when selected, displays listings in the right frame. The nice thing about this layout is that the navigation info is always present, and the only part of the page that needs to refresh is the content area.

Frames look great to many designers, but they're also very controversial. Although frames give you some great navigational features, they also open up a range of design problems and aren't always the best way to organize your site.

Figure 10-1:
Noted Web author Lynda Weinman created this frames based page to link to other well-designed frames sites.

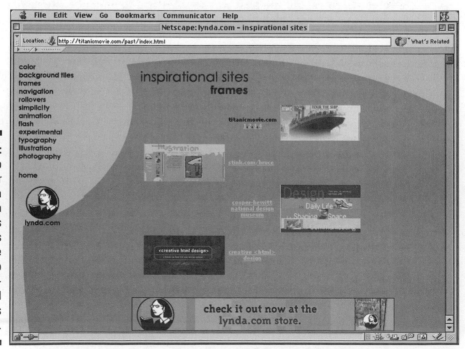

For example, you can create as many frames as you want within a browser window. Unfortunately, some people overuse them and create designs that are so complex and broken up that they're neither aesthetically appealing nor easily navigable. Putting too many frames on one page can also make a site hard to read because the individual windows are too small. This has led many Web surfers to passionately hate frames. And some sites that rushed to implement frames when they were first introduced have either abandoned them or minimized their use.

A more problematic aspect of frames is that they're not backward compatible for very old or purely text-based browsers, which means that if visitors use an older browser that doesn't support frames, they won't see anything — that's right, they get a blank page — unless you use a special tag called the <NOFRAMES> tag to create an alternative page to supplement your framed page. Fortunately, Dreamweaver automatically inserts a <NOFRAMES> tag in all frameset pages and makes it very easy to add the alternative content for viewers with browsers that don't support frames. I show you how to do this in the "Creating Alternative Designs for Older Browsers" section at the end of this chapter.

Here's a list of guidelines to follow when using frames:

- **Don't use frames just for the sake of using frames.** If you have a compelling reason to use frames, then create an elegant and easy-to-follow frameset. But don't do it just because Dreamweaver makes it easy.

- **Limit the use of frames and keep files small.** Remember that each frame you create represents another HTML file. Thus, a frameset with three frames requires a browser to display three Web pages, and that can dramatically increase download time.

- **Turn off frame borders.** Newer browsers support the capability to turn off the border that divides frames in a frameset. If the section has to be scrollable, the border is visible no matter what. But if you can turn the borders off, your pages look cleaner. Frame borders are thick and an ugly gray in color, and they can break up a nice design. Use them only when you feel that they're really necessary. I show you how to turn off frame borders in the "Changing Frame Properties" section toward the end of this chapter.

- **Don't use frames when tables are better.** Tables are often easier to create than frames and can provide a more elegant solution to your design needs because they're less intrusive to the design. I include lots of information on creating tables in Chapter 9.

- **Don't place frames within frames.** The windows get too darned small to be useful for much of anything, and the screen looks horribly complicated. You can also run into problems when your framed site links to another site that's displayed in your frameset. The sidebar "Resist using frames when you link to other people's Web sites" later in this chapter provides many more reasons to limit using frames inside of frames.

✔ **Put in alternate** <NOFRAMES> **content.** The number of users surfing the Web with browsers that don't support frames becomes smaller every day. Still, it's a good idea to show them something other than a blank page. I usually put in a line that says "This site uses frames and requires a frames-capable browser to view."

Understanding How Frames Work

Frames are a bit complicated, but Dreamweaver helps to make the whole process somewhat easier. When you create a Web page with frames in Dreamweaver, you need to remember that each frame area is a separate HTML file, and you need to save each frame area as a separate page. You also want to keep track of which file is displayed in which section of the frame so that you can set links.

Figure 10-2 shows a simple frameset example with three frames, each containing a different HTML page and different text *(Page 1, Page 2,* and *Page 3)* so that I can clearly refer to them in the numbered steps that follow.

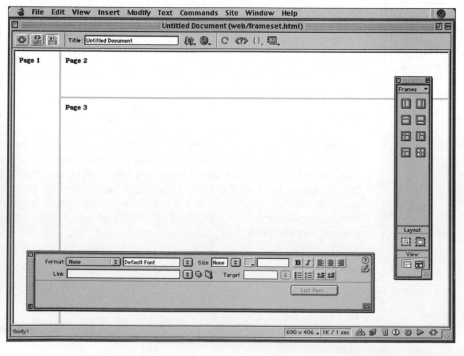

Figure 10-2:
This three frame frameset is comprised of four different HTML files: frameset. html, page1.html, page2.html, and page3.html.

Resist using frames when you link to other people's Web sites

I understand that most people don't want to lose viewers to another site when they set a link, but that's the nature of the Web. If your site is designed well, you shouldn't have to worry about losing people. Instead, you should guide them around your informative site and then politely help them to other resources that they may find of interest — and let them go. Frames keep users captive and usually leave them annoyed with you for taking up part of their browser area with your site. By displaying content from other sites within one or more of the frames in your site you do yourself more harm than good in trying to keep them.

If you insist on using frames when you link to another site, do so discretely by placing a small, narrow frame across the bottom of the screen or the left side — not a wide band across the top, and certainly not more than one frame that still contains information from your site. Not only

is this rude and ugly, but it's gotten a few Web sites sued because the people they linked to felt that the designers were making it look like their content belonged to the site using the frames.

An additional reason not to use frames when you link to another site is that many other sites use frames, too. You can quickly create a mass of frames within frames that makes it difficult for users to find their way through information. Not everyone realizes that you can get out of frames. If you haven't figured it out yet as a user, within the browser, you can always right-click on the frame in Windows or click and hold on the frame on a Mac. Then, in the pop-up menu that appears, you can choose the option to open the frame in a separate window. Now that you know this trick, you can get out of a framed situation — but don't count on your users knowing how to do this if they get annoyed.

In addition to the files that display in each frame, a separate HTML file needs to be created to generate the frameset. This page isn't visible in the browser, but it describes the frames and instructs the browser how and where to display them. This gets a little complicated, but don't worry. Dreamweaver creates these pages for you. I just want to give you a general understanding of all the files that you're creating so that the steps that follow make more sense.

To help you understand how this works, take a look at the example in Figure 10-2. In this document, you see three frames, each displaying a different HTML page. The fourth HTML file that makes up the frame page *contains* the other frames but doesn't show up in the browser, even though you see it in the title bar (it's called frameset.html). This file is the frameset file, and it describes how the frames should be displayed, whether they should be on the left side of the page or the right, and how large they should be. The frameset file also contains other information, such as the <NOFRAMES> tag I mention earlier and the names assigned to each frame section. The name of each frame is used to set links so that you can specify which frame a new HTML file should *target*, or open into. I cover more about linking frames in the "Setting Targets and Links in Frames" section later in this chapter.

Creating a frame in Dreamweaver

When you create a frame page in Dreamweaver, it's important to realize that the file you are starting with is the *frameset* file — the file that doesn't show up in the browser but merely instructs the browser how to display the rest of the frames and which pages to use as content for each frame. When you edit the *content* of any of the frames in the frameset, you're not actually editing the frameset file, but the files that populate the framed regions within the frameset. Normally you'd have to edit the files separately, but Dreamweaver makes it a lot easier to design with frames by letting you edit the content of each frame in the *context* of the frameset as it looks in a browser. If you can grasp this concept, you've come a long way in understanding how frames work and how to use Dreamweaver to create and edit them. If it hasn't sunk in yet, read on, and it will.

Creating a frame by using the Split Frame command

You can create frames in two ways in Dreamweaver. The first way is achieved by splitting a single HTML file into two sections, which then become individual frames. When you do that, Dreamweaver automatically generates an untitled page with the <FRAMESET> tag and then additional untitled pages that are displayed in each of the frames within the frameset. Suddenly you're managing several pages, not just one. This is important to understand because you have to save and name each of these pages as a separate file, even though Dreamweaver makes it look like you're working on only one page that's broken into sections.

You should always save your HTML files first before inserting anything into them; however, the opposite is true when you are working with frame files in Dreamweaver. Wait until after you've created all the frames in your frameset and then save them; otherwise, it gets a bit too complicated and confusing to track your files. I explain more in the next section, "Saving Files in a Frameset"; but first, I show you how to create a simple framed page.

To create a simple frameset in Dreamweaver, such as the one shown in Figure 10-2, follow these steps:

1. **Choose File➪New.**

   A new page opens.

2. **Choose Modify➪Frameset➪Split Frame Left.**

   The page splits into two sections. You can also choose Split Frame Right, Up, or Down. Split Frame Left or Right divides the page vertically. Split Frame Up or Down divides the page horizontally.

3. **Click inside the right frame area to make it active.**

4. **Choose Modify➪Frameset➪Split Frame Up, Down, Left, or Right to divide the page again.**

   I chose Split Frame Up. The right frame divides into two sections.

5. **Click on any of the bars dividing the frames to select the bar and drag it until the page is divided the way you want.**

6. **To edit each section of the frameset, click inside the frame that you want to work on.**

   You can type, insert images, create tables, and add any other features just as you would to any other page.

   If you want to save your file at this point, refer to the instructions in the section "Saving files in a frameset," a little later in this chapter. If you don't care about saving this frameset, see Step 7.

7. **If you were following along with these steps for practice and don't want to save your frameset at this point, choose File➪Close to close the file. When asked if you want to save the changes, choose No.**

Creating a frame by using the Frames Objects panel

The Frames Objects panel displays frames pertinent tools within the Objects panel. You can create a frameset in Dreamweaver simply by clicking icons or dragging and dropping graphic representations of different frames from the Frames Objects panel into your document. Figure 10-3 shows the Frames Objects panel, which provides icons for different types of framesets you can use. If the Frames Objects panel window isn't visible on your screen, you can bring it into view by choosing Window➪Objects. Then click the small arrow at the top-right corner of the panel and choose Frames from the drop-down list. The icons shown in Figure 10-3 are displayed.

Figure 10-3:
The Frames panel contains predefined framesets that you can drag-and-drop onto your page.

To create a framed page using the icons in the Frames Objects panel, follow these steps:

1. **Choose File⇨New to create a new page.**

2. **From the Frames Objects panel, choose one of the frames icons that closely approximates the type of frameset you want to build and drag it onto your page (you can also click the icon once to apply it).**

   Don't worry if it isn't exactly the design you want; you can alter it later. Click the icon in the Frames Object panel and drag it to your page while holding down the mouse button. Figure 10-4 shows the results of dragging the three-frames format in the lower-left corner of the Frames Objects panel.

3. **Modify the frameset as needed.**

   You can further modify your frameset by clicking and dragging the borders of the frames to resize them, splitting frames as you did in the preceding set of steps, or dragging new frames icons into existing frames.

Next, you want to save the frameset and the corresponding frames. In the next section, "Saving files in a frameset," I tell you how to do this.

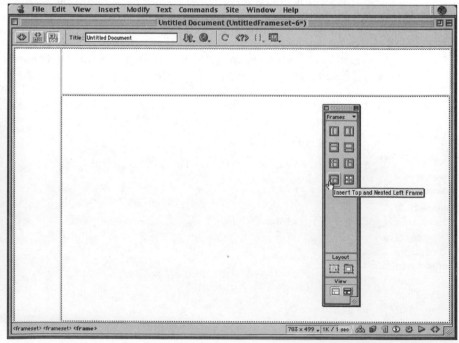

Figure 10-4: A frameset containing three frames, created by dragging one of the frames icons from the Frames Objects panel.

Saving files in a frameset

As I mention in the section "Creating a frame by using the Split Frame command," you shouldn't save your frameset file until after you've added all your frames; otherwise, keeping track of your files gets very complicated. Remember, frames in HTML consist of at least two or more HTML files, even if it appears as if you are only working on one file. When you are ready to save, Dreamweaver gives you multiple save options for saving all the files. You can either save everything all at once, or you can save each frame and frameset individually. The example in the previous section is composed of four separate HTML files, each of which needs to be named and saved to your hard drive. To save all the files in the frames document you just created, follow these steps:

1. **Choose File➪Save All Frames.**

   A Save As dialog box appears, asking you to name the file and designate a folder to save it in. This is the first of several Save As dialog boxes you are prompted with. How many dialog boxes you see depends on how many frames your document contains.

2. **Enter a name for the file.**

   Dreamweaver suggests a name, but you can choose your own. Be sure to use an .htm or .html extension. The first file you save represents the *frameset* file (the file that holds all the other frames in place). You can tell this because if you look at the Dreamweaver document window behind the Save dialog box, the entire document has a thick dotted highlight around it representing the frameset.

   Carefully name the files that you save in a way that helps you keep them in order and know which is which. When you get into setting links in the next section, you may find that the filenames you choose for your frames are crucial for the process of organizing links among framed documents.

3. **Browse your hard drive to locate the desired folder for the HTML files and click Save.**

   The frameset file is saved and a new Save dialog box appears.

4. **Type a name for the file.**

   This file represents one of the frames in your documents. You can tell which frame because Dreamweaver highlights the frame in the document window behind the Save dialog box, as shown by the highlighted border of Page 1 in Figure 10-5.

5. **Click Save.**

   The frame file is saved and a new Save dialog box appears.

6. Repeat Steps 4 and 5 until all the frames have been saved.

Remember to look at the Dreamweaver document window behind the Save dialog box in order to know which frame is being saved with which dialog box.

After you save all the frames, the Save dialog box disappears. You can continue working on your page or exit the program.

After you save and name your documents the first time, choosing Save All saves any and all of the files in your frameset without prompting you separately for each frame. Choosing Save All is a good way to make sure that all the pages in your frameset are saved whenever you edit a frames-based document.

Sometimes you may not want to save all the files at once. To save an individual frame displayed in a frameset without saving all the other frames, place your cursor in any of the frames and choose File➪Save Frame just as you would save any other individual page. Dreamweaver saves only the file for the frame in which your cursor is located.

To save only the page that defines the frameset, choose File➪Save Frameset. Remember that this page isn't displayed in any of the frames; it simply defines the entire display area, specifying which of the other pages displays in each frame, as well as the position and size of the frames.

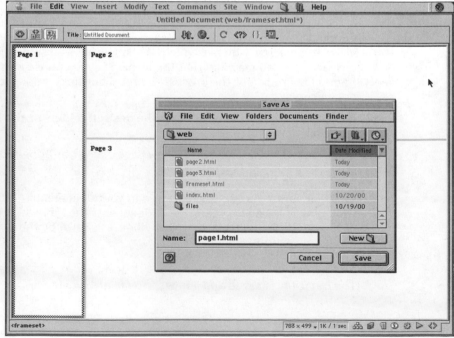

Figure 10-5:
Dream-weaver is saving the file corresponding to the frame for Page 1. Notice that the Page 1 frame is highlighted by a dotted border.

As you continue to work on your frame page, remember that whenever you make a change in one of the content frames, you're editing content in a different file from the one you started with (the frameset file). You may get confused as to which file you need to save when working in this manner. Don't worry — this is what confuses a lot of people about using frames in Dreamweaver. When you edit the content in one of the frames, make sure that your cursor is still in that frame when you choose File⇨Save Frame so that you save the page that corresponds to the frame you are working on. To be safe, you can always choose File⇨Save All Frames in order to save all changes to all files in the frameset, including the frameset file itself. Save All is also useful when you've made changes to several of the frames and want to save all the changes with just one command.

Setting Targets and Links in Frames

One of the best features of frames is that you can manipulate the contents of each frame separately within the Web browser. This feature opens a wide range of design possibilities that can improve navigation for your site. One very common way to use a frameset is to create a frame that displays a list of links to various pages of your site, and then open those links into another frame on the same page. This technique makes it possible to keep a list of links constantly visible and can make navigation a lot simpler and more intuitive.

Setting links from a file in one frame so that the pages they link to open in another frame is like linking from one page to another, and that's essentially what you're doing. What makes linking a frameset distinctive is that, in addition to indicating which page you want to open with the link, you have to specify which frame section it should *target* (open into).

But before you can set those links, you need to do a few things: First, you need to create some other pages that you can link to (if you haven't done so already). Creating new pages is easy. Choose File⇨New to create additional pages and then save them individually. If your pages already exist, you're more than halfway there; it's just a matter of linking to those pages.

The other thing you have to do before you can set links is to name each frame so that you can specify where the linked file should load. If you don't, the page will just replace the frameset altogether when someone clicks the link and defeat the purpose of using frames in the first place. Naming the *frame* is different from naming the *file* that the frame represents; the *frame name* is like a nickname that allows you to distinguish your frames from one another on a page and refer to them individually. The *filename* is the actual name of the HTML file for the frame. This makes more sense after you see how it works, as I show in the next section.

Naming frames

For the following steps, use a frameset file you previously created and saved.

1. **If you don't have a frameset file open, choose <u>F</u>ile⇨<u>O</u>pen.**

   If you saved a file in the section "Saving files in a frameset," you can open that file now. Remember, if you chose Save All, the frameset file is the first file you saved.

   The Open dialog box appears, enabling you to browse your drive for the frameset file.

2. **After you locate the frameset and highlight the file in the Open dialog box, double-click it to open it.**

   The frameset opens in Dreamweaver.

3. **Choose <u>W</u>indow⇨<u>F</u>rames to open the Frames panel.**

   The Frames panel is a miniature representation of the frames on your page that enables you to select different frames by clicking within the panel (see Figure 10-6).

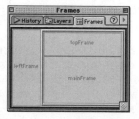

Figure 10-6:
The Frames
panel is a
miniature
represen-
tation of the
framed
page.

4. **If the Property Inspector isn't already open, choose <u>W</u>indow⇨<u>P</u>roperties.**

5. **Click to place your cursor in the area of the Frames panel that corresponds to the frame that you want to name.**

   As displayed in Figure 10-6, the frames panel displays the main document in miniature. You can click to select any of the frames in the panel, and the Property Inspector displays the properties for that particular frame. You can make any changes to the frame's properties by altering the properties in the Property Inspector after selecting the frame. You can also select the entire frameset by clicking the border around all the frames in the Frames panel window. The Frames panel allows you to select only one frame or frameset at a time.

6. **In the text box on the left side of the Property Inspector, type the name that you want to assign to the frame.**

   Dreamweaver assigns names automatically for you if you created the frames using Dreamweaver. In this example, Dreamweaver assigned the names leftFrame, topFrame, and mainFrame. You can leave these names as is or change them to something else in the Property Inspector. I recommend naming frames with descriptive words such as Top, Left, Nav, Content, and so on, so that you can easily tell which frame is which by its name.

7. **Save each file.**

   You can either save each frame individually or choose the Save All Frames command. Refer to the "Saving files in a frameset" section earlier in this chapter for more information on saving frames.

I like to save my work on a regular basis so that I never lose more than a few minutes of work if my system crashes or the power goes out. Beware, however, that when you work with frames, you need to save each page separately. Simply choosing File⇨Save Frame saves only the frame that the cursor is currently located in. Choose File⇨Save All Frames to save all the files in the frameset.

Setting links to a target frame

Setting links in a frameset requires some preliminary work. If you jumped to this section without having created a frameset or named your frames, you may want to refer to the sections earlier in this chapter. If you already have a frameset, have named the frames, and just want to get better at setting links, this section is where you want to be. Setting links in a frameset is like setting any other links between pages, except that you need to specify the target frame. That's why it's important that you take the time to name each frame — so that you can use those names as targets.

In the following steps, I continue to use the frameset that I used in Figures 10-2 and 10-6. I set three links in the left frame (Page 1) that open Pages 4 through 6 in the main frame (Page 3) area of the frameset. If this seems confusing, don't fret. It's easier to understand after you try the following steps:

To set links in one frame and have the pages open in another frame, follow these steps:

1. **Click to place the cursor inside the frame in which you want to create your links.**

   As you can see in Figure 10-7, I added text for links to Pages 4, 5, and 6 within the left frame.

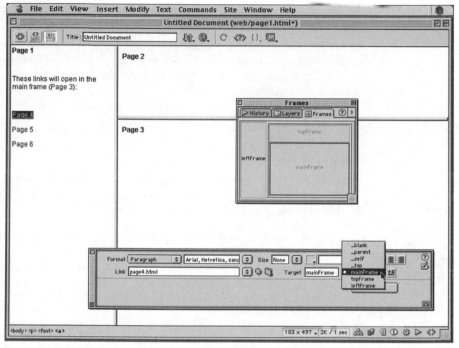

Figure 10-7:
Making a
link target to
another
frame in
Dream-
weaver is
easy.

2. **Highlight the text or image that you want to link.**

3. **In the Property Inspector, click the folder icon next to the Link field.**

   The Select File dialog box appears.

4. **Use the Browse button to find the file to which you want to link.**

5. **Click to select the file and then click the Select button.**

   The name of the file appears in the Link field in the Property Inspector.

6. **From the drop-down list next to Target in the Property Inspector, choose the name of the frame that you want the link to open into.**

   Notice that Dreamweaver conveniently lists all the frames you named in your document in this drop-down list. As you can see in Figure 10-7, I chose mainFrame.

   The result, as shown in Figure 10-8, is that when you click the linked text for Page 4 that appears in the left frame, the contents of the page4.html file are then displayed in the frame called mainFrame.

   If the numbers in the frames seem confusing, just go back and review Figures 10-2 through 10-8 and follow the steps outlined in this and the preceding sections. After you understand the process, you can adapt it to any type of frameset that you may want to create.

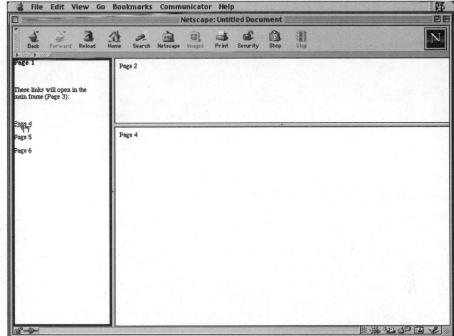

Figure 10-8:
Clicking the
Page 4 link
in the left
frame
causes
Page 4 to
open up in
the main
frame.

Comparing target options

You have many options when you target links in a frameset. As shown in the
preceding section, "Setting links to a target frame," you can specify that a
linked page open in another frame within your frameset. In addition, you can
set linked pages to open in the same frame as the page with the link, to open
a completely new page, and even to open a second browser window. Table
10-1 provides a list of target options and what they mean. You can find all of
these options in the Target drop-down list of the Property Inspector.

The Target drop-down list in the Property Inspector is activated only when
you select a linked image or section of text.

Table 10-1	Understanding Frame Target Options
Target Name	*Action*
_blank	Opens the linked document into a new browser window.
_parent	Opens the linked document into the parent frameset of the page that has the link. (The *parent* is the window that contains the frameset.)

(continued)

Table 10-1 *(continued)*

Target Name	Action
_self	Opens the linked document in the same frame as the original link, replacing the current content of the frame.
_top	Opens the linked document into the outermost frameset, replacing the entire contents of the browser window.

Changing Frame Properties

As you get more sophisticated in using frames, you may want to further refine your frames by changing properties, which enables you to turn off frame borders, change the frame or border colors, limit scrolling, and so on. To access these options in Dreamweaver, choose Window⇨Frames, click inside the Frames panel in the area that corresponds to the frame that you want to change, and then use the Property Inspector to access the options I describe in the following four sections. Figure 10-9 shows the Property Inspector as it appears when you select a frame in the Frames panel.

If you don't see the margin height and width options, make sure that you click the expander arrow in the bottom-right corner of the Property Inspector. Clicking this arrow causes all available properties to be displayed for the selected item.

Changing frame borders

I think that the best thing that you can do with a frame border is to turn it off. In the example from Lynda Weinman's site in Figure 10-1, the site appears like a single document because the frame borders have been turned off. You can do the same by choosing *No* from the Borders drop-down list in the Property Inspector for either the frameset or any of the individual frames in the frameset. Your other options include *Yes,* which forces the borders to be visible, and *Default,* which usually means Yes. In case of individual frames, however, the Default option defaults to the settings for the parent frameset.

You can make global border settings by using the Property Inspector and applying the settings to the frameset. To select the frameset so that its properties are visible in the Inspector, click on the border that encloses the frameset in the Frames panel. Figure 10-10 shows a frameset selected in the Frames panel and its corresponding properties displayed in the Property Inspector.

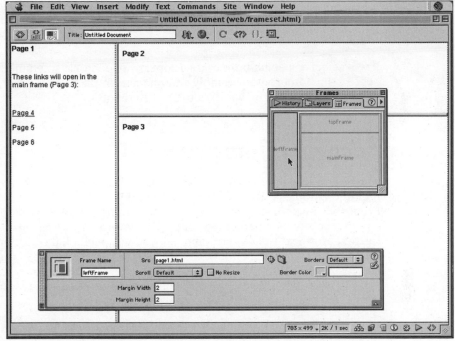

Figure 10-9:
Use the Frames panel to select frames or framesets so that their properties are visible in the Property Inspector.

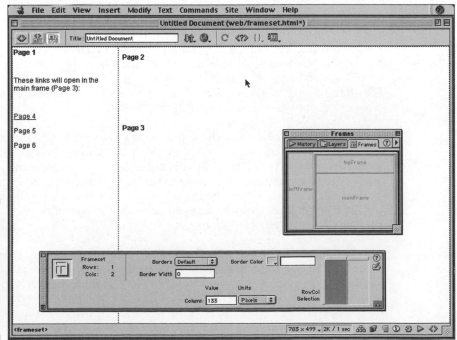

Figure 10-10:
Changing the border settings on a frameset to make the borders invisible.

If you choose to keep your borders visible, you may want to customize the color by clicking the Border Color square and then choosing a color from the Dreamweaver palette.

If you select a specific border, the Property Inspector also enables you to specify the border width. Simply enter a value in pixels in the Border Width text field to change the width of the selected border.

Changing frame sizes

The easiest way to change the size of a frame is to select the border and drag it until the frame is the size that you want. When you select the border, the Property Inspector displays the size of the frame, enabling you to change the size in pixels or as a percentage of the display area by entering a number in the text area next to Row or Column. If you've specified 0 width for your frame borders, you may not be able to see them on the page in order to drag and resize them. If this is the case, you can view the borders by choosing View⇨Visual Aids⇨Frame Borders, and Dreamweaver indicates the borders with a thin gray line so that you can easily select them.

Changing scrolling and resizing options

Scrolling options control whether a viewer can scroll up and down or left and right in a frame area. As shown in Figure 10-11, the scrolling options for frames are Yes, No, Auto, and Default. As a general rule, I recommend leaving the scroll option set to Auto because a visitor's browser can then turn scrolling on if necessary. That is, if the viewer's display area is too small to see all the contents of the frame, the frame becomes scrollable. If all the contents are visible, the scroll arrows aren't visible.

If you set this option to Yes, the scroll arrows are visible whether they're needed or not. If you set it to No, they won't be visible, even if that means your viewer can't see all the contents of the frame — a sometimes dangerous proposition because there's no way to scroll. Default leaves it up to the browser. In most browsers, the Default option results in the same display as the Auto option, but Default can yield unpredictable results, so it's best to use one of the other two options.

Also notice the No Resize option in Figure 10-11. If you place a check mark in this box, a visitor to your site can't change the size of the frames. If you leave this box unchecked, your user can select the border and drag it to make the frame area small or larger, just as you can when you develop your frames in Dreamweaver. Generally, I like to give viewers control, but I often check the No Resize option because I want to ensure that my viewers don't alter the design, especially because some viewers may do so accidentally.

Figure 10-11:
Use this list
to control
frame-
scrolling
options.

Setting margin height and width

The Margin Width and Margin Height options enable you to specify the amount of margin space around a frame. Normally in a browser window, there's always a small margin between the edge of the window and any content such as images or text. That's why you can't normally place an image on your page that is flush against the edge of the browser. With frames, though, you can actually control the size of the margin or even eliminate the margin altogether. I generally recommend that you set the margin to at least 2 pixels and make it larger if you want to create more space around your content. If you want to get rid of the margin altogether, set it to 0 and any images or text in the frame will appear flush against the edge of the frame or browser window if the frame touches the edge of the browser. If the frame touches another frame, you can use this technique to create the impression of seamless images across frames, like Lynda Weinman's site pictured in Figure 10-1.

Creating Alternative Designs for Older Browsers

Frames provide some great navigational options, but they can also provide the worst possible navigation nightmare. Navigation problems exist because frames are not *backward compatible*. For example, if you create a frameset on your site and visitors try to access your page with an old browser that doesn't support frames, they won't see the contents of any of your frames. In fact, if you don't provide an alternative, they won't see anything at all.

So what's the alternative? It's called the <NOFRAMES> tag, and Dreamweaver makes it easy to create this option for low-end users. The <NOFRAMES> tag enables you to create an alternative page that displays in browsers that don't support frames. The contents of the <NOFRAMES> tag are stored in the frameset file — that invisible file that describes how your frames look, but never shows up in the browser. A browser that supports frames ignores the contents of the alternative page because it knows not to display anything that appears in the <NOFRAMES> tag. A browser that doesn't support frames ignores the contents of the frameset because it doesn't understand the pointers within the <FRAMES> tag and displays all the content contained within the <NOFRAMES> tag instead.

If this all sounds a bit complicated, don't worry; it works like a charm. Fortunately, you don't have to know much about how it works; you just need to know that you should add the alternative content in Dreamweaver if you want to ensure that your pages look okay to people with older browsers.

To create an alternative page for older browsers by using the <NOFRAMES> tag, open any document that uses frames and follow these steps:

1. **Choose Modify⇨Frameset⇨Edit NoFrames Content.**

   A new Document window opens with NoFrames Content displayed at the top.

2. **Edit this page as you would any other page in Dreamweaver by inserting images, typing text, creating tables, and adding any other features that you want (except frames, of course).**

   Your goal is to create an alternative page that can be viewed by people using older browsers. The alternative page can be as simple as instructions for how viewers can get a newer copy of Microsoft Internet Explorer or Netscape Navigator or as complex as a copy of the page you created in frames that you've re-created as well as you can without frames.

   You can find information about adding images and formatting text in Chapter 2.

3. **To close the window and return to your frameset, choose Modify⇨ Frameset⇨Edit NoFrames Content again.**

   The check box next to the Edit NoFrames Content option disappears and the frames page replaces the NoFrames Content page in the document window.

If you create an alternative page, don't forget to update it when you make changes to your frameset.

Chapter 11

Cascading Style Sheets

● ●

● ●

Cascading Style Sheets *(CSS)* — just the name can send chills down the spine of anyone with a graphics design background. If you're not familiar with the concept of style sheets, you're sure to appreciate the benefits. Cascading Style Sheets is a kind of extended HTML that provides a way to gain greater control over the look of the type in your Web page. CSS goes a long way in giving you real typographic control and a consistent look and feel throughout a Web site, as well as saving time in designing your Web page.

In Chapter 7, I discuss HTML styles, which are a little bit like Cascading Style Sheets. HTML styles are much more limited than CSS, however, and you'll find that the real power in controlling page design comes through CSS.

Like many such time-savers, unfortunately, Cascading Style Sheets are much more complex to create than basic HTML. Fortunately, Dreamweaver takes care of creating the code for CSS, providing an intuitive interface that lets you choose fonts, colors, styles, and other formatting without worrying about the programming code that makes it all work. Later in this chapter, I introduce you to CSS and walk you step-by-step through creating and applying style sheets in Dreamweaver. In Chapter 12, you can find lots more information about using Dreamweaver to create CSS layers, a technology that enables you to achieve precise positioning of graphics on a page. Later, in Chapter 14, I show you how to use timelines to animate those layers over time.

Appreciating Cascading Style Sheets

Whereas HTML is extremely limited in the way it enables designers to control the look and layout of a page, CSS gives a whole new level of control over page design. CSS also makes it possible to do fancy stuff with Dynamic HTML, but for now I just discuss how CSS relates to controlling the look of text. By using CSS, Web page designers can gain control over such things as font type, sizing, spacing, and even exact positioning of page elements, in a way that is much more consistent across computer platforms. So if CSS is so great, why would anybody not use it? Well for one thing, CSS a lot more complicated to create and it works only in newer browsers. And unless you use Dreamweaver, you practically need a Ph.D. to use it. Still, if you want to learn how to do some really cool stuff with type, read on.

A Cascading Style Sheet is basically a list of rules defined in HTML. HTML already contains a bunch of rules of behavior, but you can neither see them (unless you read a very technical HTML manual) nor alter them — they're kind of like the grammar rules in a language. CSS, however, lets you create your own rules and override the rules of HTML, which are very limited in terms of page design. These new rules determine how the browser renders certain page elements. Imagine if you could invent a bunch of new words and grammar rules for the English language. Now imagine that everyone else can do that, too. What keeps the communication from breaking down is that every time you invent these new rules, you include a dictionary and a grammar guide to go along with each document. That's what CSS is all about.

The term *cascading* refers to the way in which the general CSS rules within a style are overridden by local rules. With CSS, you can create general rules or local rules. Because local rules override the general rules, they are referred to as cascading. This definition becomes clearer as you read on and become more familiar with how CSS operates.

Cascading Style Sheets are actually just one component of Dynamic HTML, which I talk about in Chapters 12 and 13. Cascading Style sheets are a set of technologies that gives you enhanced capabilities over standard HTML, bringing a whole new level of interactivity and design control to Web page design, even beyond just typographic control. Dynamic HTML is made possible through scripting languages that utilize the Document Object Model to create dynamic effects and global styles. Think of Cascading Style Sheets as kind of like HTML on steroids. If this still seems a little confusing, don't worry. It makes more sense as you find out what you can do with these powerful new HTML features. For more on the Document Object Model, see the sidebar "What is the Document Object Model?" In this chapter, I talk only about CSS as it refers to controlling typographic layout.

Have you ever used a style sheet in a word processor or desktop publishing application? If so, you can appreciate how style sheets make life easier. CSS is a powerful tool because with it, you can define a set of formatting attributes and then apply them to as many elements on a page or throughout a Web site as you want. For example, you can define a Headline style as bold, blue, and centered, and then you can easily apply that style to every headline in your Web page. This method saves you time because instead of formatting every headline with three steps — making it bold, blue, and centered — you can apply the redefined Headline style and all three changes occur at once.

TECHNICAL STUFF

What is the Document Object Model?

If you want to impress your geek friends, start talking about the DOM (rhymes with *mom*). But first you may want to know a bit more about what it actually means. The Document Object Model (DOM), part of the World Wide Web Consortium's HTML 4.0 specification, strives to make every element on a page an identifiable object. The properties of that object are then readable and writeable, meaning that you can use a scripting language such as JavaScript to change, hide, or move the object's attributes. So for example, if the image on a page is an object, you can say "Take object #2 and move it over here." The DOM provides a method to refer to and control objects in your document.

By defining a standard DOM, a consistent method for interacting with page elements can be achieved across platforms and browsers. This capability makes most of the DHTML effects, such as dynamically changing text and images, possible.

Unfortunately, as with many standards in the world of HTML, there is still a great divergence in the way that the major browsers implement the DOM. This inconsistency has had the effect of limiting the practical usefulness of DHTML until the major browsers can more fully support the World Wide Web Consortium (W3C) standards. Still, the foundation is there for some very powerful additions to the current limited capabilities of HTML.

You can save even more time if you decide to change one of the style attributes. If, one fine day, you decide that all your headlines should be purple rather than blue, you can change the style definition for Headline and all the text on your page or site that you formatted with the Headline style changes from blue to purple. One simple change to the style can save you hours, even days, if you ever find yourself in a redesign (and believe me, every good site goes through periodic redesigns).

Understanding Style Sheet Differences in Web Browsers

The differences in the way that Netscape Navigator and Internet Explorer support Cascading Style Sheets can be extremely frustrating, to say nothing of the differences between different versions of the same browsers. The good news is that style sheets are great for design consistency and for making fast changes throughout a page and even an entire site. The bad news is that style sheets are one of the newer additions to HTML, and some older browsers don't support them. The worse news is that style sheets aren't *backward compatible*, meaning that if you use this cool new design feature and visitors view your site using an older browser, such as Netscape Navigator 3.0, they won't be able to see any of the formatting that you created with a style sheet. They will be able to see the text — and it'll just look like plain old HTML text.

Now for even worse news: Even if your viewers use the latest browser, they won't necessarily see the same formatting because Netscape and Microsoft haven't agreed on how to implement and support style sheets.

For example, in Internet Explorer 4 and 5, you can use JavaScript to change attributes, such as font color and size, after a page has loaded. This feature can add powerful effects to your site, such as changing the color of a link when a user moves the cursor over it. But this feature doesn't work the same way in Navigator because Navigator 4.0 doesn't support changes to attributes, though Navigator 6, the latest version from Netscape, does offer support. On the other hand, Version 3.0 and above of both Internet Explorer and Netscape Navigator enable you to swap images, so you could create a similar effect by using two images of different colors. Fortunately, you don't have to know what browser supports what features. Dreamweaver takes care of that for you by enabling you to target browsers and limit design options to features supported by target browsers.

Dreamweaver works hard to try to solve these problems with browser differences. When you work with Dynamic HTML, Dreamweaver creates complex code in the background that is designed to take best advantage of the features supported by each browser. If you look at the code, it may look a bit more complex than necessary sometimes, but that's because Dreamweaver creates these tags in ways that both browsers can interpret them. And this is true not only for DHTML. As I explain in Chapter 15, the best way to insert many multimedia files, such as Shockwave and Flash, is to use a combination of code that's designed to compensate for the differences between browsers.

Creating Cascading Style Sheets in Dreamweaver

When you get into creating and using Cascading Style Sheets, you use one of the most complex and advanced features of Dreamweaver. Consequently, creating style sheets takes a little more time to grasp than applying basic HTML tags or using HTML styles. Still, Dreamweaver makes it much easier to define style sheets than to write them by hand — a task that is a lot closer to writing programming code than to creating HTML tags.

To help you get the hang of using Dreamweaver to create style sheets, I first walk you through the screens that define styles and give you an overview of your options as you create styles. After the following sections on each aspect of style sheet creation, you find specific numbered steps that walk you through the process of creating and applying your own CSS styles.

Understanding CSS style types

You can create two types of style sheets with CSS and Dreamweaver: internal style sheets and external style sheets. An *internal style sheet* stores its data within the HTML code of a page and applies styles to only that page. An *external style sheet* is a text file that you create and store outside of your HTML page. You then reference it as a link, much like you do any other HTML page on the Web. In this way, you can apply style sheets to an entire Web site or to any page that links to the external style sheet, which also means that you can have many different pages referencing the same style sheet. For most of this chapter, I discuss internal style sheets, but most of the material also applies to external style sheets. At the end of the chapter, I discuss how you can use what you've learned to create external style sheets.

You can define two different kinds of CSS styles to use in either an internal or external style sheet: custom styles and redefined HTML tag styles. The difference is that a custom style is a completely new set of formatting attributes that you can apply to any text selection. Custom styles in CSS are referred to as *classes*. Don't worry about this too much because I get into it in more detail later in the chapter. For now, just know that when you define a custom style, you give it a class name and then you use that name to apply the style to any text block on the page. So you can call a custom style anything you want, you can create a new custom style any time you want, and the new style doesn't necessarily affect anything else on the page. Creating a custom style is a little bit like making up your own HTML tag, with formatting rules that you can define yourself.

In contrast, you create redefined HTML tag styles by redefining how *existing* HTML tags are rendered by the browser; you are changing existing rules instead of creating new ones. This means that you change how common HTML tags format text throughout your page — or throughout your Web site if you want to define it that way. The result is that if you redefine a tag, such as the <BLOCKQUOTE> tag, all the text already formatted with the <BLOCK-QUOTE> tag automatically changes to reflect your new style definition.

Suppose that you define the <BLOCKQUOTE> tag to render text in blue at 12-point italic. Normally, *blockquoted text* simply creates an indent on the right and left margins — great for setting off quoted text on a page. Because you've redefined the <BLOCKQUOTE> tag, it's going to also add the new attributes of blue and 12-point italic. But there's more. Because style sheets are cascading, any styles applied to tags within the <BLOCKQUOTE> tag override the <BLOCKQUOTE> tags that enclose it. So, if you placed a set of <B> tags (that normally indicate bold text) inside the <BLOCKQUOTE> tag and defined the <B> tag as red text, any text falling inside the <B> tags would be red instead of blue, in addition to bold. The <B> tag would override the enclosing <BLOCKQUOTE> tags. This is true for any tag that you modify using CSS.

Using the Edit Style Sheet dialog box

To create either redefined HTML tag styles or custom styles, open any HTML document and choose Window⇨CSS Styles to open the CSS Styles panel. In the lower-right corner of this panel you can see four small icons. From left to right, these icons represent Attach Style Sheet, New Style, Edit Style Sheet, and Delete Style (resembles a trash can). Click the Edit Style Sheet icon (third from the right) to open the Edit Style Sheet dialog box (see Figure 11-1).

Figure 11-1:
The CSS Styles panel and Edit Style Sheet dialog box.

The Edit Style Sheet dialog box includes the following options:

- ✔ **Link:** Enables you to link to or import an external style sheet (a separate text file that defines a style) so that you can apply it to the page or even to the entire site that you're working on. You can find more information on external styles in the section "Using External Style Sheets" later in this chapter.

- ✔ **New:** Enables you to define one of three types of style sheets. You can find these explained in detail in the section "Defining styles" later in the chapter.

- ✔ **Edit:** Enables you to change an existing style. For more information, see the section "Editing an Existing Style" later in the chapter.

- ✔ **Duplicate:** Creates a copy of a selected style that you can then redefine as any one of the three style options.

- ✔ **Remove:** Enables you to delete a defined style.

The Undo feature doesn't work with the Remove option in the Edit Style Sheet dialog box. Before you select the Remove button, make sure that you really want to get rid of the style.

Understanding New Style options

If you choose the New button in the Edit Style Sheet dialog box, the New Style
dialog box shown in Figure 11-2 opens, giving you the following options:

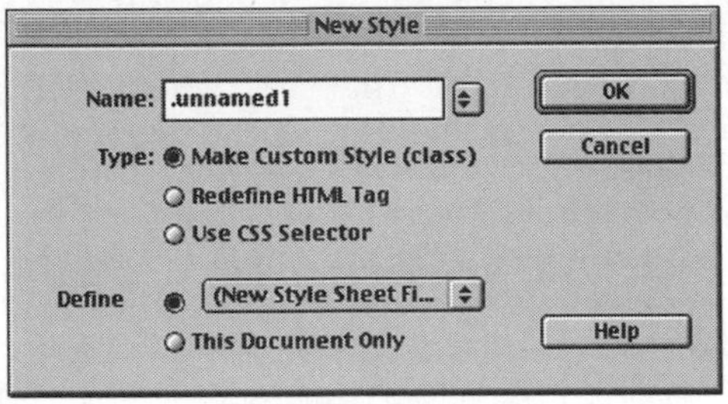

Figure 11-2:
The New
Style dialog
box.

```
┌──────────────────────── New Style ────────────────────────┐
│                                                            │
│    Name:  [.unnamed1          ] [≑]    [    OK    ]        │
│                                                            │
│    Type: ● Make Custom Style (class)   [  Cancel  ]        │
│          ○ Redefine HTML Tag                               │
│          ○ Use CSS Selector                                │
│                                                            │
│  Define  ●  [(New Style Sheet Fi... ≑]                     │
│          ○ This Document Only          [   Help   ]        │
│                                                            │
└────────────────────────────────────────────────────────────┘
```

✔ **Name:** Although the first field in this box is titled Name when you first
   bring it up, its title actually changes depending on which of the CSS
   types you select using the three radio buttons beneath it. Read the
   description for each of the CSS types in the following three bullets to see
   how to fill out this field.

✔ **Make Custom Style (class):** Enables you to define a new style that you
   can apply to any section of text on a page by using the class attribute.
   When you select this option, the first field asks for a name. All custom
   style names must begin with a period, which Dreamweaver automatically inserts as you name the style. This kind of style is also referred to
   as a *class*. If you choose this option, after clicking OK another dialog box
   appears, allowing you to define the different options for the style, which
   I explain in the section "Creating a custom style" later in this chapter.

✔ **Redefine HTML Tag:** Enables you to create a style that changes the formatting associated with an existing HTML tag. When you select this
   option, the first field asks for a tag name. Clicking the pop-up menu next
   to the tag field allows you to select from a huge list of HTML tags (the
   default one is the <BODY> tag). For more information on this option, see
   "Redefining HTML tags" later in this chapter.

✔ **Use CSS Selector:** Enables you to define a kind of pseudoclass that com-
   bines a custom style with a redefined HTML tag. CSS Selector styles
   apply only to the <A> tag and enable you to do things such as change the
   color of a link when the mouse hovers over it. When you select this
   option, the first field asks for the Selector name. Choices in the pop-up
   list are a:active, a:hover, a:link, and a:visited.

   • A:active affects an active link, which is triggered while someone
     is actually clicking on the link.

   • A:hover is triggered while the mouse is directly over the link.

- A:link is applied to any text link.

- A:visited affects links that have already been visited by the user.

  Please note that CSS Selector styles work only in Internet Explorer 4 and above browsers.

✔ **Define:** This option lets you choose whether your style sheet exists within the current page or in a separate file. When you select a new style sheet file you're creating an external style sheet. If you select This Document Only you're creating an internal style sheet. (Refer to the internal and external style sheets I mention at the beginning of this section for a refresher, if needed.)

Defining styles

When you choose to make a new style and select one of the three style options in the New Style dialog box, the Style Definition dialog box opens. This is where you decide how you want your style to look by selecting the attribute options. This dialog box includes eight categories, each with multiple options that you can use to define various style elements. In this section, I discuss each of these eight categories.

You don't have to make selections for all the options in each category. Any options that you leave blank remain at the browser's default. For example, if you don't specify a text color, the text is displayed as black or whatever the page's default color is.

Don't be frustrated by options in these categories that Dreamweaver doesn't display. If they don't display in Dreamweaver, they almost certainly won't work in any of the current browsers. The good news is that Macromedia is looking ahead and building these options into Dreamweaver so that they'll be ready when these features are supported. Keep an eye on the Macromedia Web site at www.macromedia.com and Macromedia's DHTML information site at www.dhtmlzone.com for changes and updates to Dreamweaver, as well as for news about changing standards and support for these CSS features. Right now, Microsoft Internet Explorer 5 supports the most complete CSS.

The Type category

When you choose Type from the Category panel of the Style Definition dialog box, the Type page opens (see Figure 11-3) and offers the following formatting options:

✔ **Font:** Specifies a font, font family, or series of families. You can add fonts to the list by selecting Edit Font List from the drop-down list.

✔ **Size:** Defines the size of the text. You can choose a specific point size or use a relative size, expressed as small, extra small, and so on.

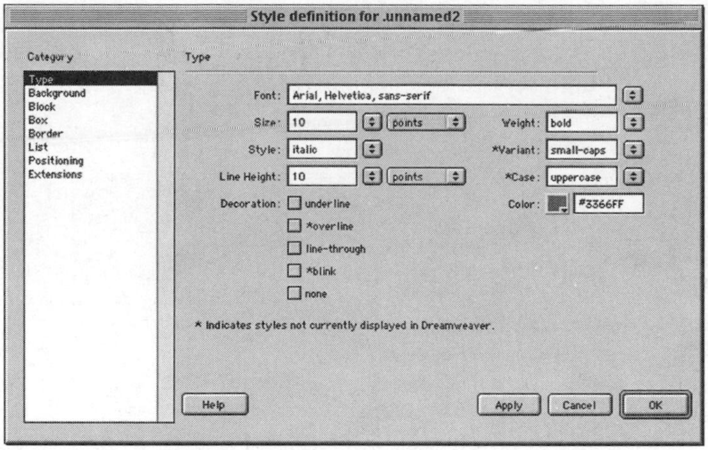

Figure 11-3:
The Type page of the Style Definition dialog box.

✓ **Style:** Enables you to choose whether the text appears as Normal, Italic, or Oblique.

✓ **Line Height:** Enables you to specify the height of a line that the text is placed on (graphic designers usually call this *leading*). The 4.0 browsers don't support this feature, and it can cause problems in older browsers. So, for now, you should probably avoid this one.

✓ **Decoration:** Enables you to specify whether text is underlined, overlined (the line appears over the text instead of under it), or displayed with a strikethrough. You can also choose blink, which makes the text flash on and off.

Use the Decoration options sparingly, if at all. Links are automatically underlined, so if you underline text that isn't a link, you risk confusing viewers. Overlined and strikethrough text can be hard to read. So use these options only if they enhance your design. And, by all means, resist the blink option; it's distracting and can make the screen difficult to read. (Overline and blink do not yet display in Dreamweaver.)

✓ **Weight:** Enables you to control how bold the text is displayed by using a specific or relative boldness option.

✓ **Variant:** Enables you to select a variation of the font, such as small caps. Unfortunately, this attribute is not yet supported.

✓ **Case:** Enables you to globally change the case of selected words, making them all uppercase or lowercase or with initial caps. Unfortunately, this attribute is not yet supported.

✓ **Color:** Defines the color of the text. You can use the color square icon to open a Web-safe color palette in which you can select predefined colors or create custom colors.

The Background category

The Background category (see Figure 11-4) lets you specify a background color or image for a style. You can choose from the following options:

Figure 11-4:
The Background page of the Style Definition dialog box.

✔ **Background Color:** Specifies the background color of an element, such as a table.

✔ **Background Image:** Enables you to select a background image as part of the style definition.

✔ **Repeat:** Determines how and whether the background image tiles across and down the page. In all cases, the image is cropped if it doesn't fit behind the element.

The Repeat options are as follows:

- **No repeat:** The background is displayed once at the beginning of the element.

- **Repeat:** The background tiles repeat vertically and horizontally behind the element.

- **Repeat-x:** The background repeats horizontally, but not vertically, behind the element.

- **Repeat-y:** The background repeats vertically, but not horizontally, behind the element.

✔ **Attachment, Horizontal Position, and Vertical Position:** Not yet supported by Dreamweaver.

Some of the CSS features available in these categories don't yet display in Dreamweaver because they're not supported by browsers, even though they're part of the proposed standard. Although you can apply these features, you're best to avoid them because they won't work when your pages display in a browser. The reason they are included is for purposes of future compatibility.

The Block category

The Block category (see Figure 11-5) defines spacing and alignment settings for tags and attributes. You can choose from the following options:

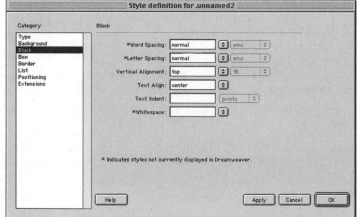

Figure 11-5:
The Block page of the Style Definition dialog box.

✔ **Word Spacing:** Not yet supported by Dreamweaver.

✔ **Letter Spacing:** Not yet supported by Dreamweaver.

✔ **Vertical Alignment:** Works only with the <IMAGE> tag in Dreamweaver. It specifies the vertical alignment of an image, usually in relation to its parent.

✔ **Text Align:** Specifies how text aligns within an element.

✔ **Text Indent:** Specifies how far the first line of text indents.

✔ **Whitespace:** Not yet supported by Dreamweaver.

The Box category

The Box category (see Figure 11-6) defines settings for tags and attributes that control the placement of elements on the page. You can choose from the following options:

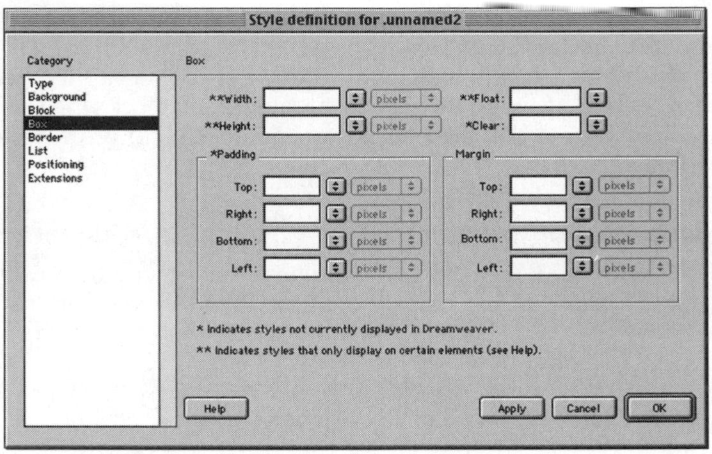

Figure 11-6:
The Box
page of the
Style
Definition
dialog box.

- **Width, Height:** Enable you to specify a width and height that you can use in styles that you apply to images or layers.

- **Float:** Enables you to align an image to the left or right so that other elements, such as text, wrap around it.

- **Clear:** Sets the side (left or right) on which layers are not allowed to be displayed next to the element. The element drops behind the layer if the layer intersects the selected side. (Doesn't currently display in Dreamweaver.)

- **Padding:** Sets the amount of space between the element and its border or margin. (Doesn't currently display in Dreamwear.)

- **Margin:** Enables you to define the amount of space between the border of the element and other elements on the page.

The Border and List categories

The Border category defines settings, such as width, color, and style, for the borders of elements on a page. The List category defines settings, such as bullet size and type, for list tags. Dreamweaver doesn't currently support any of these features because of limited browser support.

The Positioning category

The Positioning category (see Figure 11-7) enables you to change a tag or block of text into a new layer and specify its attributes. When applied, this style uses the tag specified for defining layers in the Layer preferences. The default in Dreamweaver for layers is the <DIV> tag. You can change this by editing the Layer preferences, but the <DIV> tag is the most universally supported, so you're best to stick with it. You can choose from the following options:

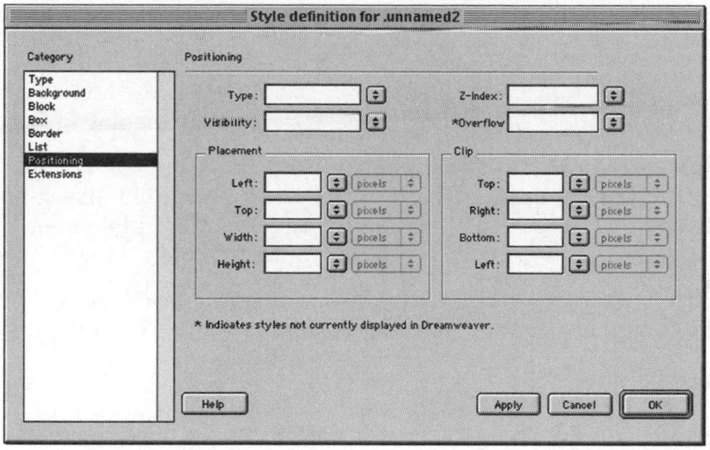

Figure 11-7:
The
Positioning
page of the
Style
Definition
dialog box.

✔ **Type:** Enables you to specify the position of a layer as absolute, relative, or static.

- **Absolute:** This positioning uses the top and left coordinates entered in the Placement text boxes on this screen to control the position of the layer relative to the top-left corner of the Web page.

- **Relative:** This positioning uses a position relative to the current position of the layer instead of the top-left corner of the page.

- **Static:** This positioning keeps the layer in the place where you insert it on the page.

✔ **Visibility:** Enables you to control whether the browser displays the layer. You can use this feature, combined with a scripting language such as JavaScript, to dynamically change the display of layers. The default on most browsers is to inherit the original layer's visibility value.

- **Inherit:** The layer has the visibility of its parent.

- **Visible:** The layer is displayed.

- **Hidden:** The layer isn't displayed.

✔ **Z-Index:** Controls the position of the layer on the Z coordinate, meaning how it stacks in relation to other elements on the page. Higher-numbered layers appear above lower-numbered layers.

✔ **Overflow:** Tells the browser how to display the contents of a layer if it exceeds its size. (Doesn't currently display in Dreamweaver.)

- **Visible:** Forces the layer to increase in size to display all of its contents. The layer expands down and right.

- **Hidden:** Cuts off the contents of the layer that don't fit and doesn't provide any scroll bars.

- **Scroll:** Adds scroll bars to the layer regardless of whether the contents exceed the layer's size.

- **Auto:** Makes scroll bars appear only when the layer's contents exceed its boundaries. (Doesn't currently display in Dreamweaver.)

✔ **Placement:** Defines the size and location of a layer, in keeping with the setting for Type. The default values are measured in pixels, but you can also use pc (picas), pt (points), in (inches), mm (millimeters), cm (centimeters), or % (percentage of the parent's value).

✔ **Clip:** Enables you to specify which part of the layer is visible by controlling what part of the layer is cropped if it doesn't fit in the display area.

The Extensions category

Extensions include filters and cursor options, most of which aren't supported in any browser or are supported only in Internet Explorer 4.0 and above:

✔ **Pagebreak:** Inserts a point in a page where a printer sees a page break.

✔ **Cursor:** Defines the type of cursor that appears when a user moves the cursor over an element.

✔ **Filter:** Enables you to apply to elements special effects such as drop shadows and motion blurs.

Creating a custom style

The following steps tell you how to use Dreamweaver to create a custom style. In this example you define a style for headlines using CSS. If you want to create a style for another element, follow these same steps but change the specific attributes.

You can leave attributes unspecified if you don't want to use them. If you don't specify them, the browser uses its own default. For example, I don't recommend using any of the Decoration options other than underline because they can distract and confuse viewers.

To define a style for a headline, follow these steps:

1. **Choose Text➪CSS Styles➪Edit Style Sheet.**

   The Edit Style Sheet dialog box appears.

2. **Choose the New button.**

   The New Style dialog box appears.

3. **Select the Make Custom Style (class) option.**

   The new style is automatically called .unnamed1.

4. **In the Name text box, type a new name for the style.**

   Dreamweaver gives you a default name that begins with a period (.) because class names must begin with a period. You can name the style anything you want as long as you don't use spaces or punctuation. Dreamweaver adds the initial period to the class name if you omit it.

5. **Next to Define, select This Document Only because you're creating an internal style sheet.**

6. **Click OK.**

   The Style Definition dialog box opens.

7. **Make sure that the Type category is selected in the panel on the left side of the dialog box.**

8. **From the Font drop-down list, choose a font or font set.**

   If you want to use fonts that aren't on the list, choose the Edit Font List option from the drop-down list to create new font options.

9. **From the Size drop-down list, choose the size you want for your headline.**

   Large headlines are generally 24 or 36 point. You may prefer to choose a relative size, such as large or larger.

10. **From the Style drop-down list, choose a style.**

    Italic and Oblique are both good for making text stand out on a page.

11. **From the Weight drop-down list, choose Bold to make your headline thicker and darker.**

12. **Ignore Variant and Case because these attributes aren't well supported by current browsers.**

13. **Click the Color square and choose a color from the color well.**

    Sticking to the default color swatches in the color well is best because it ensures that you use a Web-safe color. You can also create a custom color by clicking the icon that looks like a rainbow-colored globe in the upper-right corner of the color well.

14. **Click OK when you're finished.**

    Your style is automatically added to the Styles list.

You can apply styles in the Styles list to any Web page or selected text block. After you create your style, it appears in the submenu under Text⇨CSS Styles. Any text that you apply it to takes on the formatting attributes you just specified. For more on how to use styles, read "Applying Styles" later in this chapter.

Redefining HTML tags

When you create a custom style, as I explained in the preceding section, you start a completely new style with its own unique name. When you redefine an HTML tag, however, you begin with an existing HTML tag, such as <B> (bold), <HR> (horizontal rule), or <TABLE> (table), and change the attributes associated with that specific tag. Any new attributes that you apply through CSS to an existing tag override the existing attributes.

To redefine a tag, you choose the tag that you want to change from the Tag drop-down list (see Figure 11-8) in the New Style dialog box (refer to Figure 11-2). Then you define how you want to change it by altering the various categories and attributes in the Style Definition dialog box. Be aware that when you redefine an existing HTML tag, any text that you've already formatted with that tag changes to reflect the new definition.

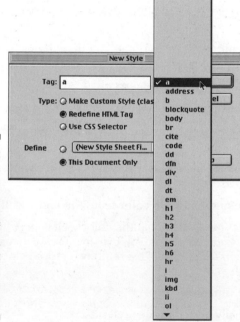

Figure 11-8:
The Redefine HTML Tag option gives you a list of the HTML tags that you can redefine using CSS.

Eliminating underlines from links

Now that you know how to redefine an HTML tag, here's your chance to put it into practice. One of the most commonly used HTML tag modifications involves disabling the underline for the anchor tag, <A>, so that hypertext links are no longer underlined in the browser. This technique works in both Netscape and Internet Explorer 4.0 (and above) browsers.

To disable underlining for hypertext links, follow these steps:

1. **Choose Text⇨CSS Styles⇨Edit Style Sheet.**

2. **In the Edit Style Sheet dialog box, choose the New button.**

   The New Style dialog box appears.

3. **Select the Redefine HTML Tag option and choose the anchor tag <A> from the drop-down list.**

4. **Next to Define, select This Document Only.**

5. **Click OK.**

   The Style Definition dialog box opens.

6. **Make sure that the Type category is selected; then check the none option under the Decoration section, as shown in Figure 11-9.**

7. **Click the OK button to apply the changes.**

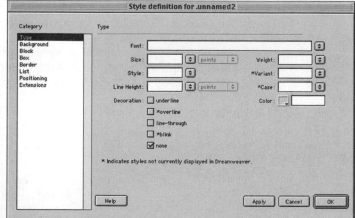

Figure 11-9:
Using CSS
to disable
underlining
of hypertext
links.

After you click OK, the underlines disappear from all the links on your page, but they will still function as normal links. You can go back and make more modifications to the <A> tag in this manner, or you can apply the same principles to any of the other HTML tags available in the New Style dialog box. Remember, any time you redefine an HTML tag using CSS, the changes are visible in your page only if those tags are actually used.

Conflicting styles

Be careful when you apply more than one style to the same text (something that is easier to do than you may realize). The styles may conflict, and because browsers aren't all consistent in the way in which they display styles, the results can be inconsistent and unexpected.

For the most part, Netscape Navigator 4.0 and above and Internet Explorer 4.0 and above display all the attributes applied to an element, even if they're from different styles, as long as the styles don't conflict. If they do conflict, browsers prioritize styles depending on how they're defined.

Here's an example to help you get the idea. You define a custom style called `.headline` as red and centered, and you apply it to a selection of text. Then you decide that you want that text to be bold, so you apply the bold tag independently by selecting it from the Property Inspector. You have now used two different types of styles. Because they don't conflict, all of them take effect and your text becomes bold, centered, and red. If, however, you decide that you want this text aligned left, instead of centered, and you apply left alignment directly from the Property Inspector, you have a conflict.

If a direct conflict exists, custom styles overrule regular HTML tag styles. The browser also gives priority to the attribute of the style that's inserted closest to the text. This can get really hard to juggle if you're applying defined styles, trying to keep track of standard HTML tags, and then trying to sort out how the browser prioritizes them. It gets worse with time, too, because these styles and priorities are sure to change and evolve. Your best bet is not to apply conflicting styles. Either go back and redefine an existing style, apply regular HTML tags individually, or create a new style. Remember that you can use the Duplicate option from the Edit Style Sheet dialog box to create a new duplicate style, and then make minor alterations. (See the earlier section "Using the Edit Style Sheet dialog box" for a refresher on the options in this dialog box.)

Editing an Existing Style

You can change the attributes of any style by editing that style. This is a major advantage of Cascading Style Sheets: You can make global changes to a page or even to an entire Web site by changing a style that you applied to multiple elements. Be aware, however, that everything you defined with that style changes.

Remember that you can also create new styles by duplicating an existing style and then altering it. Then you can apply that new style without affecting elements that are already formatted on your pages with the original version of the style.

To edit an existing style, follow these steps:

1. **Choose Text➪CSS Styles➪Edit Style Sheet.**

   Alternatively, you can click the Open Style Sheet icon in the bottom-right corner of the CSS Styles panel.

2. **Select the style that you want to change in the Edit Style Sheet dialog box and click the Edit button.**

   The Style Definition dialog box for that style appears.

3. **Choose a category that you want to change, such as Type or Background, from the Category panel; then specify the style changes you want to make.**

   You can find descriptions of all the style options in the section "Defining styles" earlier in this chapter.

4. **When you've made all the changes you want, click OK.**

   The style automatically redefines to reflect your changes. At the same time, all elements that you defined with that style automatically change.

Applying Styles

Defining styles is the complicated part. Applying them after you've defined them is easy. You simply select the text that you want to affect and choose the predefined style that you want to apply.

To apply a style, follow these steps:

1. **Highlight the text to which you want to apply a style.**

2. **Choose Window➪CSS Styles.**

   The CSS Styles panel opens, as shown in Figure 11-10.

Figure 11-10: Use the CSS Styles panel to apply styles to selected text blocks.

3. **Select the style that you want to apply from the list that appears in the white area of the CSS Styles panel.**

   The style is automatically applied to the selection.

You can also apply a custom style by selecting the text that you want to change, choosing Text➪CSS Styles, and choosing a custom style from the submenu.

Using External Style Sheets

Up to now, I discuss using CSS only in the context of internal style sheets. Internal style sheet information is stored in the HTML code of the document you are working on and only applies to that document. If you want to create styles that you can share among documents, you need to use external style sheets. External style sheets enable you to create styles that you can apply to pages throughout a Web site by storing the style sheet information on a separate text page that can be linked to from any HTML document.

External style sheets are where you can realize true time savings through using CSS. You can define styles for common formatting options used throughout an entire site, such as headlines, captions, and even images, which makes applying multiple formatting options to elements faster and easier. Big news- and magazine-type Web sites often use external style sheets because they need to follow a consistent look and feel throughout the site, even when many people are working on the same site. Using external style sheets also makes global changes easier because when you change the external style sheet, you globally change every element to which you applied the style throughout the site.

Creating and Editing an External Style Sheet

You create external style sheets almost exactly the same way you create internal style sheets, except external style sheets need to be saved in separate text files. When you use Dreamweaver to create an external style sheet, Dreamweaver automatically links the style sheet to the page that you're working on. You can then link it to any other Web page in which you want to apply the style definitions.

To create an external style sheet, follow the same steps for creating an internal style sheet, except that in the New Style dialog box (refer to Figure 11-2), select New Style Sheet File instead of This Document Only. When you click OK, you're prompted to save the style sheet somewhere on your drive as an external file.

To link an existing external style sheet to the current page, follow these steps:

1. **Select Window⇨CSS Styles.**

   The CSS Styles panel appears. (You can also click the CSS Styles button on the Launcher bar.)

2. **Click the Attach Style Sheet icon in the CSS Styles panel (the first button on the bottom right).**

   The Select Style Sheet dialog box appears, prompting you to find the external style sheet to link to.

3. **After you locate the external file, click the Select button (Open button on a Mac).**

   The dialog box disappears and the external CSS file is automatically linked to your page. Any styles that you've defined in the external style sheet now appear in the CSS Styles panel. Because you've established a link on this page to the external style sheet, the styles in the external style sheet will always appear in the CSS Styles panel whenever you open this file.

4. **To apply a style on your page, select the text you want to apply the style to and click the appropriate style in the CSS Styles panel.**

Changing Style Sheet Preferences

Style sheet preferences are available by choosing Edit➪Preferences and clicking the CSS Styles category. Dreamweaver is so good at taking care of things for you, however, that you should leave style sheet preferences alone unless you really know what you're doing. The only change you can make in style sheet preferences controls whether or not Dreamweaver writes styles using shorthand (a more concise way to write the code that creates a style). If you're experienced at writing the HTML code for style sheets and prefer using shorthand, you may want to make this change because it makes editing styles manually easier. I don't recommend it, however, because some older browsers don't correctly interpret the shorthand. And Dreamweaver does such a good job of creating styles for you that you shouldn't need to edit them yourself.

Part IV
Making It Cool

The 5th Wave   By Rich Tennant

Rothman
Paint Drying Equip.
TV Test Pattern Design
Sap Buckets

"Maybe it would help our Web site if we showed our products in action."

In this part . . .

Bring your Web pages to life with the interactive features made possible by Dynamic HTML. Add animation, sound, and video by linking a wide range of multimedia files to your Web pages. And finally, use HTML forms to create search engines, online shopping systems, and so much more. This part arms you with the information you need to tackle these tasks. You also get a bonus chapter on Fireworks, Macromedia's image design program for the Web, which is fully integrated with Dreamweaver 4.

Chapter 12

Adding Interactivity with Dynamic HTML and Behaviors

Dynamic HTML *(DHTML)* has received so much hype and attention that you'd think you could do anything with it, including your laundry. Well, DHTML isn't quite powerful enough to take over your domestic duties, but it does add a range of functionality to a Web page that has been impossible with HTML alone. In fact, DHTML is kind of like HTML on steroids. You can use other technologies, such as Java, Shockwave, and Flash, to make interactive animations, but you can create DHTML animations right within Dreamweaver, without the need to learn or buy another animation program.

DHTML is really about using advanced scripting techniques to create precise positioning of elements and dynamic content, which is impossible with HTML alone. *Dynamic content* means that you can create and alter page content *after* the page has been loaded in the browser. JavaScript has been used by designers to add dynamic effects to Web pages for a while. But with DHTML, you can actually affect the attributes of HTML tags, which means that you can create many more kinds of effects and make them happen more quickly.

All in all, DHTML deserves most of its hype because it takes Web page design to another level of interactivity and multimedia without compromising download times. Like any new Web technology, however, DHTML has a few problems. The biggest one is browser compatibility. At the end of this chapter, I tell you how Dreamweaver makes designing pages that work in various browsers easier, even if you decide to use the latest features. The rest of this chapter shows you how to use layers, and later on behaviors, which are a simplified way to add complicated yet powerful scripts to your pages.

Understanding DHTML

DHTML is exciting because it adds so many possibilities to Web design — from global style formatting with Cascading Style Sheets to fast-loading animations and other interactive features made possible with the addition of layers and timelines. (Check out Chapter 11 to find out more about Cascading Style Sheets, and see Chapter 13 for more on timelines.)

One way in which DHTML brings dramatic improvements to Web design is by providing more precise design control. Using DHTML, you can actually position text blocks and images exactly where you want them on a page by specifying their distance from the top and left side of a page — something sorely missing in HTML. Dreamweaver refers to these as Top and Left, but in DHTML, they're officially called X,Y coordinates. One of the greatest limitations of HTML is the inability to stack elements on top of each other. In DHTML, a third positioning option — the Z coordinate — adds this capability.

DHTML also enables you to use a scripting language, such as JavaScript or VBScript, to control many of the elements or attributes of elements on a page. This means that you can dynamically change the size or color of text, the alignment of an image, or any other attribute of an HTML tag. When I say that you can change those dynamically, I mean that you can make those changes happen automatically, after a page loads, or you can assign the action to be triggered by an event, such as the click of a mouse. What is unique in DHTML is that the entire page doesn't have to reload for these changes to take effect; they happen right on the same page — that's what makes them dynamic.

Designers have been using JavaScript to create some of these effects for a while. For example, you've probably seen sites where images change when you move a cursor over them. That trick, called a *rollover* effect, is just one that DHTML takes a step farther by adding many more events and actions to the arsenal of design tools. DHTML is, however, much more complicated to write than regular old HTML. Even HTML frames, which are complex by many Web design standards, look relatively simple when compared to JavaScript and the kind of code that you have to write to create DHTML. This is where Dreamweaver really shines — Macromedia has successfully created a WYSIWYG (What You See Is What You Get) design environment that you can use to create these complex DHTML features without ever having to look at the code (unless you want to, of course).

Three powerful features in Dreamweaver make creating DHTML features possible: layers, behaviors, and the timeline. Layers and behaviors are covered in this chapter, and I provide step-by-step instructions for using them. I cover timelines in Chapter 13, also with detailed step-by-step instructions. But before you get into each section, it's helpful to understand what each feature accomplishes and how they can all work together to create even more advanced features.

To enable precise positioning of elements, DHTML uses what's called *layers*. Think of a layer as a container. For this example, think of the container as a ship. Then break down *behaviors* as events and actions. For example, the ship hitting an iceberg is an event the same way in which clicking on a graphic is an event. The ship sinking could be considered an action the same way in which a graphic moving across a page is an action. Finally, think of a *timeline* as the ship's schedule. The ship leaves port at a certain time and passes the islands at another time, all on schedule. If you could control the ship's fate, you could determine its sinking at a certain time interval as well. The timeline in Dreamweaver enables you to control the actions and events on your page over time, giving you the power to create a precise schedule of events and actions and control the experience of your viewers.

At the Control Freak site, shown in Figure 12-1, designers use DHTML layers and effects to add interactivity and dynamism to their Web site. This is just one example of the many ways you can use DHTML to enhance your Web site. You can see more innovative examples of Dynamic HTML in action at `www.advancedinnovation.com/controlfreak` or visit Macromedia's DHTML zone at `www.dhtmlzone.com`.

Working with Layers

Think of a layer as a transparent box or a container that you can use to hold images, text, and other elements. This box is handy because you can manipulate all its contents together, move them on top of another layer, or make them visible or invisible as a unit. If you're familiar with Adobe Photoshop, you might be familiar with the general concept of how layers work. DHTML layers in Dreamweaver are very similar; you can move them around to position elements exactly where you want them, use them to overlap elements on a page, or turn them on and off to control visibility. If you're new to layers, you may want to use the following numbered steps to experiment a little with creating layers, adding images and other elements, and moving them around.

By using the positioning controls, you can place layers in exact locations on a page for precise design control. You can treat each layer as if it's a separate page that can be manipulated independently and can contain anything from text to images to plug-ins to tables, and even other layers.

Creating layers

To create a layer, follow these steps:

1. **Choose Insert⇨Layer.**

   A box, representing an empty layer, appears at the top of the page.

Figure 12-1:
Control
Freak uses
DHTML
layers and
effects to
create an
innovative
navigational
system and
interactive
content.

2. **Click anywhere along the outline of the layer box to select it.**

   When you hold the mouse over the outline of the layer, the cursor turns to a four-pointed arrow (a hand on the Macintosh); clicking with this cursor selects the layer. When the layer is selected, eight tiny, black, square handles appear around the perimeter of the box, indicating that it has been selected.

3. **Click and drag any of the handles to resize the layer.**

Adding elements, resizing, and repositioning layers

Remember that layers are like containers; to make a layer useful, you have to put something inside of it. You can place pretty much anything that you can place into a document within a layer. To add images or text to a layer, follow these steps:

1. **Click to insert your cursor inside the layer.**

   A blinking cursor appears inside the layer box.

2. **Choose Insert⇨Image.**

   The Select Image Source dialog box appears.

3. **Browse your drive to locate the image file that you want to insert; after you locate the image file, click the filename of the image to highlight it.**

4. **Double-click the filename or click the Select button (Open button on Macintosh) to insert the image.**

   The image appears inside the layer.

5. **Click inside the layer again to insert your cursor and enter some text.**

   As you can see in Figure 12-2, I typed *Layers are groovy* next to an image I inserted.

6. **Highlight the text and format it by using the text formatting options in the Property Inspector or by selecting the appropriate formatting options from the Text menu.**

   Formatting text inside of layers is just like formatting text inside a regular Dreamweaver document. In this case, I chose Heading 1 for the text.

7. **Select the image and use the Property Inspector to make any desired formatting changes to it.**

   Formatting images inside of layers works the same way. In this example, I chose Align⇨Middle from the Align option in the Property Inspector to achieve the positioning shown.

8. **Click the tab that appears at the top-left of the layer area or anywhere along the border to select the layer.**

   You know that you've successfully selected the layer when you see the selection *handles* — the little black squares that appear at the corners and in the middle of each side (refer to Figure 12-2) — again.

9. **Click any handle and drag to resize the layer.**

   As a general rule, always size a layer so that its contents just fit within its boundaries, which makes positioning the layer on the page easier.

10. **To move a layer, click the little tab that appears at the top-left of the layer when it is selected and use it to drag the layer to any place on the page.**

    Because layers use exact positioning, you can move them to any precise location on a page, and they display in that exact location in browsers that support DHTML, such as Navigator 4 and Internet Explorer 4 and above.

    If you refer to Figure 12-2, you can see that the Property Inspector displays the Layer coordinates in pixels when the layer is selected: L (for left), T (for top), W (for width), and H (for height). In addition to using the click-and-drag method to move a layer, you can change a layer's position by entering a number in the position boxes, L (number of pixels from the left edge of the page) and T (number of pixels from the top of the page). Likewise, you can resize the layer by typing in new coordinates for width and height directly into the Property Inspector. The Property Inspector displays these options only when the layer is selected.

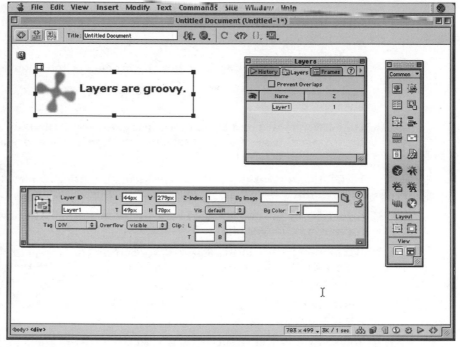

Figure 12-2:
You can
insert
images and
text inside
of layers
just like you
would insert
them inside
a document.

11. **Name your layer by typing a name in the Layer ID text box in the top-left corner of the Property Inspector.**

    When you create a new layer, Dreamweaver automatically names your layers for you, starting with Layer1, Layer2, and so on. It's a good idea to change the name to something more descriptive by entering a new name in the Layer ID field. This is especially true if you're working with a lot of layers on a page. Keeping track of them by name makes them much easier to manage. Remember that you must select the layer first in order for its properties to appear in the Property Inspector.

Stacking layers and changing visibility

A powerful feature of layers is their maneuverability — you can stack them on top of each other and make them visible or invisible. Later in this chapter, in the section on adding behaviors, I show you how to use these features in combination with behaviors to create animations and other effects. Here, I help you get the hang of moving layers and changing layer visibility.

To stack layers, simply drag one layer on top of another. Unlike images, layers give you complete layout control on the page by including the ability to overlap one another. To overlap images, simply place each image within a separate layer like in the previous exercise and then move one layer so that it overlaps the other one. To control the order in which layers overlap, Dreamweaver provides two options: the Z index, available from the Property Inspector, and the Layers panel, shown in Figure 12-3, which you can access by choosing Window⇨Layers.

To stack layers and change their order and visibility, follow these steps:

1. **Select the layer by clicking anywhere on the border outline of the layer.**

2. **Click the small tab in the top-left corner of the layer and drag the layer to reposition it.**

   You can use drag-and-drop to move the layer anywhere on the page, including on top of another layer. When the layer is where you want it, release the mouse button.

   Using the 4-sided arrow cursor (or hand cursor on the Macintosh) that appears when you hover your cursor over the selected Layer's border, you can click and drag the layer anywhere else on the page without having to click the tab at the top left of the layer.

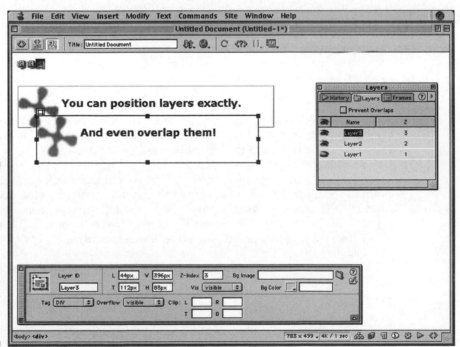

Figure 12-3:
Use the Layers panel to change the visibility and stacking order of your document's layers.

3. **Choose Window⇨Layers to open the Layers panel.**

   The Layers panel lists any layers that appear on your page. If you're familiar with layers in Adobe Photoshop or Macromedia Fireworks, you may find some similarities here, such as the eye icon to control layer visibility and the ability to drag layers around in the panel to reposition them.

4. **Reposition the layers by clicking on the layer name in the Layers panel and dragging it up or down.**

   The layer order changes in the Layers panel.

   Layers are automatically named Layer1, Layer2, and so on, as they're created. You can rename a layer by double-clicking the name to select it, using the Delete key to remove it, and then typing a new name in its place.

5. **Click on the eye icon to the left of any layer in the Layers panel to turn the layer visibility on or off (refer to Figure 12-3).**

   If no eye appears, then the visibility is set to default, which usually means on, except in the case of nested layers. (I cover nested layers in the next section.) Click in the visibility column to view the eye icon. If the eye is open, a layer is on, meaning that it's visible on the screen and in the browser. Click until the eye icon appears closed to turn a layer off and make it invisible — it's still there; it just doesn't display on screen or in the browser. Click again to remove the eye icon.

Nesting layers: One happy family

Another way to position layers on a page is by nesting them. A *nested layer* is essentially a layer that's invisibly tied to another layer, where the layers maintain a kind of parent-child relationship. The first layer becomes the parent while the layer nested within it becomes the child layer. The child layer then uses the upper-left corner of the parent layer as its orientation point for positioning instead of using the upper-left corner of the document because it is nested *within* the parent layer. Even if the layers are on different areas of the page, they still retain this parent-child relationship. When you move the first layer around on the page, the nested layer moves along with it. You can also think of this scenario as an owner walking his dog on a leash — where the owner goes, the dog has to follow, even though the dog can still move independently of its owner within the confines of the length of the leash.

If you were to nest another layer into the child layer, that would then make the child layer both a parent and a child. The new layer then uses the upper-left corner of its parent layer (in this case both a parent and a child) as its orientation point. The first layer in the nested chain still retains control over all the child layers, meaning that they will move when you move the parent.

Dreamweaver enables you to manage large numbers of layers in a document by nesting — in fact, this is one of the best reasons to use nested layers. Instead of trying to keep track of loads of different layers scattered all over your page, you can group them into more easily manageable "family units." Then, you can easily move a whole family around as one unit.

Furthermore, you can make a whole family visible or invisible by clicking the eye icon of the parent layer in the Layers panel if the child layer's visibility has been set to default (no eye icon in the Layers panel). When the child layer's visibility is set to default, it inherits the visibility of its parent layer, enabling you to show and hide whole families at a time. As you experiment with layers and start using a lot of them on your page, this becomes almost essential. Be aware, though, that when a child layer is set to either visible (eye icon on) or invisible (eye icon off) in the Layers panel, the child layer will be unaffected by the visibility setting of its parent layer. The child layer must be set to default to inherit the visibility properties of its parent.

To create a nested layer, follow these steps:

1. **Choose Insert⇨Layer.**

   A box representing the layer appears at the top of the page. Dreamweaver automatically names this Layer1.

2. **Move the cursor into the Document window and drag any of the corners of the box to resize the layer.**

3. **Repeat Steps 1 and 2 to create a second layer.**

4. **Position the second layer anywhere on the page by dragging the small tab on the top left of the layer box or clicking and dragging anywhere on the layer's border.**

   Nested layers do not need to physically reside inside of their parent layer; they can be placed anywhere else on the page or they can be stacked on top of each other.

5. **Choose Window⇨Layers to open the Layers panel.**

   The Layers panel lists each layer separately. Dreamweaver automatically names them Layer1 and Layer2.

6. **Click Layer2 in the Layers panel, press and hold down the Ctrl key (the Command key on the Mac), and then drag Layer2 over Layer1 until you see an outline appear around Layer1 in the Layers panel. Release the mouse.**

   The outline disappears and Layer2 now becomes a child of Layer1. The Layers panel changes to display Layer2 indented under Layer1 to reflect the nested relationship (see Figure 12-4). Although the layers still appear separate in the document window, the child layer moves when you move the parent layer.

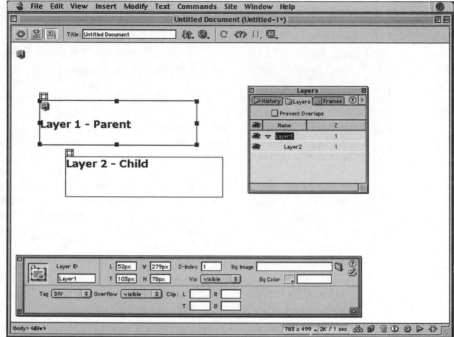

Figure 12-4:
Dream-
weaver lets
you nest
layers
together, a
useful way
to manage
multiple
layers in a
document.

Another way to create a nested layer is to simply place your cursor inside any layer and choose Insert➪Layer. When you do this, the new layer becomes a child of the first layer. You can then reposition the child layer as needed by dragging it elsewhere on the page.

Setting layer options

Like other HTML elements, layers come with many options, such as height and width. Dreamweaver makes these options available in the Property Inspector when you select a layer (see Figure 12-5).

The following list describes the layer options and what they control:

- ✔ **Layer ID:** In the top-left corner of the Property Inspector, an unmarked text box lies just under the words Layer ID where you can enter a name to identify the layer. Use only standard alphanumeric characters for a layer name (no special characters, such as spaces, hyphens, slashes, or periods).

- ✔ **L (Left):** This value specifies the distance of the layer from the left side of the page or parent (outer) layer. Dreamweaver automatically enters a pixel value when you create or move a layer with drag-and-drop. You can also enter a numeric value (positive or negative) to control the positioning.

Figure 12-5:
Select a
layer, and
the Property
Inspector
reveals the
options for
the layer.

✔ **T (Top):** This value specifies the distance of the layer from the top of the page or parent (or outer) layer. Dreamweaver automatically enters a pixel value when you create or move a layer with drag-and-drop. You can also enter a numeric value (positive or negative) to control the positioning.

✔ **W (Width):** Dreamweaver automatically specifies the width when you create a layer on a page. You also have the option of entering a numeric value to specify the height. In addition, you can change the default measurement of px (pixels) to any of the follwing: pc (picas), pt (points), in (inches), mm (millimeters), cm (centimeters), or % (percentage of the parent's value). Don't put any spaces between the number and the measurement abbreviation.

✔ **H (Height):** Dreamweaver automatically specifies the height when you create a layer on a page. You also have the option of entering a numeric value to specify the height. In addition, you can change the default measurement of px (pixels) to any of the following: pc (picas), pt (points), in (inches), mm (millimeters), cm (centimeters), or % (percentage of the parent's value). Don't put any spaces between the number and the measurement abbreviation.

✔ **Z-Index:** This option determines the position of a layer in relation to other layers when layers are stacked. Higher-numbered layers appear on top of lower-numbered layers, and values can be positive or negative.

Changing the stacking order of layers is easier to do by using the Layers panel than by entering specific Z-index values. For more on using the Layers panel to change the order of layers, see "Stacking layers and changing visibility" earlier in the chapter.

✔ **Vis:** This visibility setting controls whether a layer is visible or invisible. You can use this setting with a scripting language, such as JavaScript, to dynamically change the display of layers.

You can choose from the following visibility options:

- **Default:** The default option in most browsers is the same visibility property as the parent's value.

- **Inherit:** This option always uses the visibility property of the layer's parent.

- **Visible:** This option always displays the layer, regardless of the parent's value.

- **Hidden:** This option always makes the layer transparent (invisible), regardless of the parent's value. Hidden layers take up the same space as visible layers.

You can dynamically control visibility by using the JavaScript behaviors covered in "Attaching behaviors" later in this chapter.

✔ **Bg Image:** With this option, you can select a background image for the layer in the same way that you would select a background image for a Web page. Click the folder icon to select an image or enter the name and path in the text box.

✔ **Bg Color:** Use this option to fill the background of a layer with a solid color. Click the color square to open a color palette, from which you can select a color. If you want the layer background to be transparent, leave it blank.

✔ **Tag:** This enables you to choose between using CSS layers (<DIV> or <SPAN> tags) or Netscape layers (<LAYER> or <ILAYER> tags). As a general rule, you should use CSS layers (Dreamweaver uses the <DIV> tag as the default setting). To find out more about the difference, see the sidebar "Netscape layers versus CSS layers."

✔ **Overflow:** These options determine how the contents of a layer are displayed if they exceed the size of the layer. (Note that this option only applies to CSS layers.)

You can choose from the following Overflow options:

- **Visible:** This option forces the layer size to increase so that all its contents are visible. The layer expands down and to the right.

- **Hidden:** This option clips off the edges of content that doesn't fit within the specified size of a layer. Be careful with this option; it doesn't provide any scroll bars.

- **Scroll:** This option adds scroll bars to the sides of a layer regardless of whether the contents exceed the layer's size or not. The advantage of this option is that scroll bars don't appear and disappear in a dynamic environment.

- **Auto:** If you select this option, scroll bars appear only if the layer's contents don't fit within the layer's boundaries.

✔ **Clip:** This option controls what section of the contents of a layer are cropped if the layer isn't large enough to display all the contents. You should specify the distance from the L (Left), T (Top), R (Right), and B (Bottom). You can enter values in px (pixels), pc (picas), pt (points), in (inches), mm (millimeters), cm (centimeters), or % (a percentage of the parent's value). Don't add any spaces between the number and the measurement abbreviation.

TIP

Netscape layers versus CSS layers

Netscape was the first to bring layers to the Web. However, it pushed the limits on its own and didn't wait for a standard. Unfortunately for Netscape (and for those of us sorting out DHTML), the result is that today you have two different ways to create layers — the Netscape layer tag, which consists of the <LAYER> and <ILAYER> tags, and the CSS positioning option *(CSS-P)*. In this chapter I really only cover CSS positioning, though below you do see some of the options for working with Netscape layers in the event that you want to use them in Dreamweaver.

I recommend (as do many others, including Macromedia) that you avoid Netscape's <LAYER> and <ILAYER> tags because the W3C (the committee that officially sets standards for the Web) and Microsoft Internet Explorer don't support them. Fortunately, Netscape did agree to adopt the standard proposed in the HTML 4.0 specification from the W3C, so some semblance of a standard is now emerging. If you use the <DIV> and <SPAN> tags, you can reach a broader audience because both Navigator 4 and Internet Explorer 4 and above support these tags. If you use Dreamweaver, you don't have to worry about this. The <DIV> tag is the default, although you can change it in Preferences.

If, for some reason, you choose to use the <LAYER> tag, you see additional options in the lower-right corner of the Property Inspector when you select the layer.

The following options apply only to Netscape layers and appear only if you select LAYER or ILAYER from the Tag option. To find out more about the difference between Netscape layers and CSS layers, see the sidebar "Netscape layers versus CSS layers."

- **Top, Left or PageX, PageY:** Use these options for positioning the layer.
- **Source:** This option enables you to display another HTML document within a layer. Type the path of the document or click the folder icon to browse and select the document. Note that Dreamweaver doesn't display this property in the Document window.
- **A/B:** This option specifies the position of layers on the Z index, which controls the stacking of layers.

Converting layers to tables: Precise positioning for older browsers

If you want to achieve precise pixel-perfect positioning of elements on a Web page, layers are the only way to go. As I show you in this chapter, you can achieve any kind of precision layout using layers in a way that can't be done with regular HTML. Unfortunately, layers work only in Version 4.0 and above browsers. What if you want to use the precision layout features allowed by layers but want to support a wider audience of pre-4.0 browser users? Or perhaps you like the ease of using layers for layout but prefer using tables instead for your final design. You're in luck. Dreamweaver includes a great feature that enables you to easily convert a layout you created using layers to the same exact layout using tables. By building a layout using layers and then converting it to tables, you can easily (with a single command) create a version of your page that works in older browsers.

To convert a page that uses layers to a page that uses tables only, yet maintains the same page layout, choose Modify➪Convert➪ Layers to Table. Dreamweaver rebuilds the page with a table structure that mimics the layers' layout using table cells to control positioning.

Suppose, for example, that you need to go back later and alter the layout — editing a table for exact positioning is not an easy task! Don't worry, converting the table to layers, which can be easily edited for exact positioning, is also just a command away. Choose Modify➪Convert➪ Tables to Layers and the table layout converts to a layers layout where you can easily reposition elements with pixel level precision. After you're done, convert to tables again and voilà! — you've achieved exact positioning without requiring a 4.0 or above browser.

Working with Behaviors

Some of the coolest features used on the Web today are created by using Dreamweaver behaviors, which use a scripting language called JavaScript. These behaviors are really just built-in scripts — some of which use DHTML and some of which don't — that provide an easy way to add interactivity to your Web pages. You can apply behaviors to many elements on an HTML page, and even to the entire page itself. Writing JavaScript is more complex than writing HTML code, but not as difficult as writing in a programming language such as C, C++, or Java. (No, Java and JavaScript are not the same. Read Chapter 15 for more on Java applets and how they differ from JavaScript.) Dreamweaver takes all the difficulty out of writing JavaScript behaviors by giving you an easy and intuitive interface that doesn't require you to ever touch the complicated code behind the scenes.

In this section, I show you how surprisingly easy Dreamweaver makes it to apply a whole range of behaviors that you can use to create dynamic effects. Using the behaviors options, you can make images change when viewers pass their cursors over them (swapping images), and you can create animations that start when a visitor clicks an image or other element on a page. Combining the power of behaviors with layers opens up a range of tricks that look great on a page and load very fast. Add to that the power of the timeline, described in the next chapter, and you can make this happen automatically. The timeline enables you to trigger behaviors after a specified amount of time and to set one behavior to happen before another.

Attaching behaviors

If you've always wanted to add cool interactive features, such as making something flash or pop up when users move their cursors over an image or click a link, you're going to love the *behavior* feature in Dreamweaver. To fully appreciate what Dreamweaver can do for you, you may want to open the HTML Source window (available under the Window menu) before and after attaching a behavior just to see the complex code required to create behaviors. If you don't like what you see, don't worry; you can close the HTML Source window and just let Dreamweaver take care of the code for you.

When you use behaviors in Dreamweaver, you don't have to write any code at all. Instead, you use a couple of dialog boxes, and with a few clicks of your mouse, you get interactive effects. You can attach behaviors to a page, a link, an image, or almost any other element on a page simply by selecting the element, specifying the action or event that triggers the behavior, and then choosing the behavior from the Behaviors panel.

The following steps show you how to apply a behavior to an element, such as an image. Behaviors add lots of interesting capabilities to your pages. The one I demonstrate here opens a new browser window with a new Web page when the user clicks the image.

To add a behavior to an element on a page, follow these steps:

1. **Select an image on a page by clicking it.**

   You can select any image, text, or layer on a page to apply a behavior to.

   To attach a behavior to the entire page, click the <BODY> tag in the tag selector at the left end of the Status Bar at the bottom of the document window.

2. **Choose Window⇨Behaviors to open the Behaviors panel.**

   You can also click the Behavior button on the Launcher bar to open the panel.

3. **At the top left side of the Behaviors panel, click the plus sign (+) and choose the Open Browser Window behavior from the pop-up menu (see Figure 12-6).**

   The Open Browser Window dialog box appears, enabling you to specify the parameters for the new browser window.

   You can choose any of the behaviors listed on the pop-up menu. If an action is grayed out on the list in the pop-up menu, it means that the action won't work with the file or element that you selected. The Control Shockwave Action, for example, works only if you select a Shockwave file. After selecting the behavior, a dialog box specific to the behavior always appears enabling you to specify the parameters for each behavior.

Adding new behaviors to Dreamweaver

If you know how to write JavaScript, you can also add your own behaviors to the list of choices in Dreamweaver. You can find instructions for creating and adding new actions in the Dreamweaver Exchange section of Macromedia's site at www.macromedia.com/exchange/dreamweaver. You can also find new behaviors created by Macromedia, as well as other developers, that you can download free of charge and then add to Dreamweaver.

To automatically go to this site to get new behaviors, click the plus sign in the Behaviors panel and select the Get More Behaviors option at the bottom of the drop-down menu. This launches your default Web browser and connects you to the Dreamweaver Exchange section of the Macromedia Web site if you are online.

Figure 12-6:
Selecting a behavior from the Behaviors panel.

4. **In the dialog box associated with the action, specify the parameter options to control how you want the behavior to work.**

   Each behavior allows you to enter specific parameters to define how the behavior acts. In Figure 12-7, I set the Open Browser Window so that it opens the file ball.html into a new browser window. The new window's display area is only 150 pixels wide by 350 pixels high when it opens. You can choose any pixel dimensions you like by entering the height and width in the appropriate fields in this dialog box. The other parameters for this behavior control which elements of the browser such as the navigation bar, title bar, menu bar, and so on, are present in the new window when it opens. You can use this behavior to completely customize the new window that opens up when the behavior is executed.

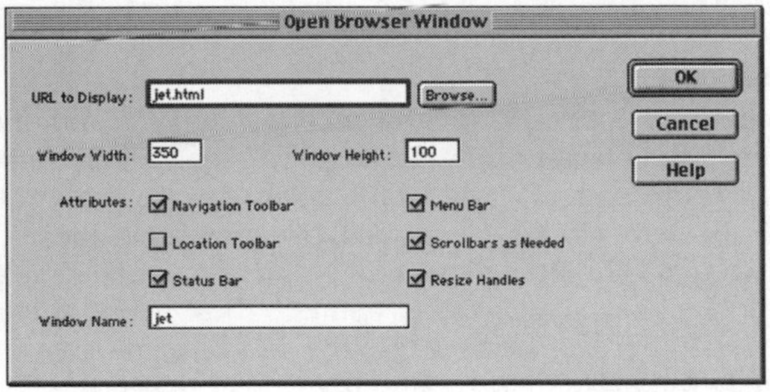

Figure 12-7:
Select
an action
from the
Behaviors
panel and a
dialog box
offers you
different
options for
controlling
the
behavior.

5. **After you have specified the parameters for the behavior, click OK.**

   The dialog box goes away and the Open Browser Window behavior now appears in the Behaviors panel under the Actions category.

6. **To change the event that triggers your behavior, click the small downward-pointing triangle to the right of the Events category in the Behaviors panel.**

   This opens the Events drop-down list, from which you can select various events to trigger the behavior. I selected the onClick event, which causes the behavior to execute when the user clicks the image.

   An *event* is an action that a user takes on your Web page to trigger the behavior that you insert. Dreamweaver lists various events based on the target browsers that you selected for your behavior. For more information about events and what each one accomplishes, see the section, "About Events," later in this chapter.

7. **To test the action, choose File⇨Preview in Browser, and then select the browser that you want to test your work in.**

   This opens the page in whatever browser you choose so that you can see how it really looks in that browser. The result, shown in Figure 12-8, is that a small browser window opens when you click the image, displaying the contents of the page I've specified in the URL field (in this case a bouncing ball).

   Unfortunately, most of these actions only work in Internet Explorer 4.0 or later. See the sidebar "Choosing a target browser" for more about actions and browser differences.

   If you get an error message from your browser about a filename after you try and preview the page, you need to go back and enter a name in the Name field of the Property Inspector for the page element you applied the behavior to (for example, image, layer, and so on). Click the element to display its properties in the Property Inspector and enter the name in the Name field and try again. Giving the element a "name" is usually necessary before the behavior can work properly.

Many event options, such as onMouseDown, onMouseOver, and onMouseOut, are available only if the element is linked to a URL. Dreamweaver helps you get around this by automatically adding the link tag when you choose one of these events for an element that isn't linked. Dreamweaver doesn't link the element to an external URL, though; instead, it places a hash sign in place of a filename or URL. The hash sign specifies a link to the current document instead of another document. This makes kind of a fake link, one that doesn't really go anywhere but allows you to attach an event that normally requires a link. Make sure that you don't delete the hash mark (#) from the Property Inspector or the HTML code. This is how it looks:

```
<a href="#">
```

You can replace the hash mark with a URL if you want the element to open another page. If you leave it as a hash mark, the event triggers the action, without opening a new URL.

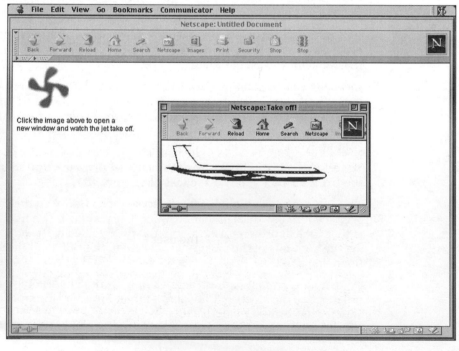

Figure 12-8: Using a Dreamweaver behavior, a new, customizable browser window opens when the image on the main page is clicked.

About Events

Events in interactive Web-speak are things that a user does to interact with your Web page. Clicking an image is an event, as is loading a page in the browser or pressing a key on the keyboard. There are many more events available as well when you define your behaviors. Different browser versions support different events (and the more recent the browser version, the more events available), so based on which browser version you have selected as your target browser in the Behaviors panel, different events will be displayed in the events pop-up menu. To see the list of available events for specific browsers, click on the plus sign (+) in the Behaviors panel to select a behavior. After selecting the behavior, the event appears in the Behaviors panel below it under the Events column. To the right of the event is a small triangle, which reveals a list of available events for that behavior when clicked. Notice that if you scroll to the bottom of the list of events, the final option says Show Events For. Use this submenu to select which browser version you want to design for, which increases or decreases the number of events you can select from the list. Remember to try and target the widest possible audience when you design behaviors; this usually means selecting either 3.0 and later browsers or 4.0 and later browsers.

The following list describes some of the more commonly used events, ones that can be experienced by the majority of Web users (4.0 and above browsers, Netscape and Internet Explorer).

- ✔ **onAbort:** Triggered when the user stops the browser from completely loading an image (for example, when the user clicks the browser's Stop button while an image is loading).

- ✔ **onBlur:** Triggered when the specified element stops being the focus of user interaction. For example, when a user clicks outside a text field after clicking in the text field, the browser generates an onBlur event for the text field. OnBlur is the opposite of onFocus.

- ✔ **onChange:** Triggered when the user changes a value on the page, such as selecting an item from a pop-up menu, or when the user changes the value of a text field and then clicks elsewhere on the page.

- ✔ **onClick:** Triggered when the user clicks an element, such as a link, button, or image map.

- ✔ **onDblClick:** Triggered when the user double-clicks the specified element.

- ✔ **onError:** Triggered when a browser error occurs while a page or image is loading. This can be caused, for example, by an image or URL not being found on the server.

- ✔ **onFocus:** Triggered when the specified element becomes the focus of user interaction. For example, clicking in a text field of a form generates an onFocus event.

- ✔ **onKeyDown:** Triggered as soon as the user presses any key on the keyboard. (The user does not have to release the key for this event to be generated.)

- ✔ **onKeyPress:** Triggered when the user presses and releases any key on the keyboard; this event is like a combination of the onKeyDown and onKeyUp events.

- ✔ **onKeyUp:** Triggered when the user releases a key on the keyboard after pressing it.

- ✔ **onLoad:** Triggered when an image or page finishes loading.

- ✔ **onMouseDown:** Triggered when the user presses the mouse button. (The user does not have to release the mouse button to generate this event.)

- ✔ **onMouseMove:** Triggered when the user moves the mouse while pointing to the specified element and the pointer does not move away from element (stays within its boundaries).

- ✔ **onMouseOut:** Triggered when the pointer moves off the specified element (usually a link).

- ✔ **onMouseOver:** Triggered when the mouse pointer first moves over the specified element.

- ✔ **onMouseUp:** Triggered when a mouse button that has been pressed is released.

- ✔ **onMove:** Triggered when a window or frame is moved.

- ✔ **onReset:** Triggered when a form is reset to its default values, usually by clicking the Reset button.

- ✔ **onResize:** Triggered when the user resizes the browser window or a frame.

- ✔ **onScroll:** Triggered when the user scrolls up or down in the browser.

- ✔ **onSelect:** Triggered when the user selects text in a text field by highlighting it with the cursor.

- ✔ **onSubmit:** Triggered when the user submits a form, usually by clicking the Submit button.

- ✔ **onUnload:** Triggered when the user leaves the page, either by closing it or focusing on another browser window.

Adding a rollover image behavior to swap images

Rollover images are some of the most commonly used interactive elements on Web sites today. With rollovers, you can swap an image on the page when the mouse passes over it, giving users visible feedback when they interact with your site. You've seen this effect on Web site navigation menus in which moving your mouse over a menu choice makes it appear highlighted. In the past, creating a rollover image required that you know how to code in JavaScript, and even then took lots of time to do. With Dreamweaver behaviors, the same JavaScript code is generated automatically behind the scenes far more easily and in only a fraction of the time.

To create a rollover (swapping) image in Dreamweaver, follow these steps:

1. **Place an image into your document and click to select it.**

   Rollover effects require at least two images of the same exact dimensions, one for the initial state and one for the rollover state. You'll probably want to make a special set of images to use with your rollover behavior.

2. **Name your image in the Name field of the Image Inspector panel.**

   In order to apply a behavior to an element, such as an image, the element must have a name so that the behavior script can reference it. Names also enable you to swap images in other locations on the page by using their names as a reference ID.

3. **Choose <u>Window</u>⇨<u>B</u>ehaviors to open the Behaviors panel.**

   The Behaviors panel appears. You can also click the Behaviors button in the Launcher bar to open the Behaviors panel.

4. **Click the plus sign in the Behaviors panel to access the drop-down list of behaviors. Choose the Swap Image option from this menu list.**

   The Swap Image behavior dialog box appears, as shown in Figure 12-9.

5. **In the Swap Image dialog box, select the image that you want to swap out.**

   The name of the image appears in the list of images.

   In this example, I swap out an image named *airplane,* which is the same one that is rolled over initially to trigger the effect. If you have multiple images on your page, you can swap out any of them when you roll over the first image, and their names will appear in the Images list provided they have been given a name in the Property Inspector.

Figure 12-9:
In the Swap
Image
behavior,
one image
replaces
another
during a
mouseover
event.

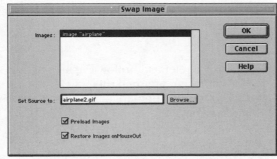

6. **Select the replacement image by clicking the browse button or by typing the path of the image in the Set Source to text box.**

Make sure that the new image has the same width and height pixel dimensions as the first one. The browser always renders the second image at the same size as the first image in a rollover action, regardless of its original size. If the second image is a different size to begin with, it appears distorted when resized.

7. **Click to select the Preload Images and Restore Images onMouseOut check boxes.**

   Selecting the Preload Images check box loads the rollover image into the browser's cache when the page loads. This ensures that there is no delay in downloading the new image the first time that the rollover is executed. Selecting the Restore Images onMouseOut check box restores the image source to its original state when the mouse leaves the area of the rollover image.

8. **Click OK.**

   The behavior is applied to the image and the Swap Image and Swap Image Restore actions appear in the Behavior Inspector window.

9. **Test the rollover by choosing File⇨Preview in Browser.**

You can also automatically generate rollover images in Fireworks and easily import the code into Dreamweaver. For more on creating rollovers in Fireworks and adding them to your Dreamweaver documents, see Chapter 14.

Attaching multiple behaviors

You can attach multiple behaviors to the same element on a page (as long as they don't conflict, of course). For example, you can attach one action that is triggered when users click an image and another when they move their cursor over the image. You can also trigger the same action by more than one event. For example, you can play the same sound when a user triggers any number of events. You can't, however, attach multiple actions to one event — meaning that you can't open a browser window and play a sound when the same image is selected.

To attach additional behaviors to an element, follow the same steps in "Attaching behaviors" earlier in this chapter and then click the plus sign again and select another option from the pop-up menu to add another behavior. Repeat this as many times as you want.

Editing a behavior

You can always go back and edit a behavior after you create it. You can choose a different event to trigger the behavior, choose a different action, and add or remove behaviors. You can also change the parameters that you have specified.

Choosing a target browser

Because behaviors are a newer development on the Web, only the latest browser versions support the majority of the events and actions available in the Behaviors Inspector. But Dreamweaver offers a couple of ways to accommodate browser differences. You can choose to limit yourself to the most basic behaviors by selecting Netscape Navigator 3, or you can choose the browser with the most options (Internet Explorer 5). These choices ensure that your pages work in the browsers that you've chosen. (If you choose one of the most advanced browsers, such as Internet Explorer 5.0, your pages may not work at all in other browsers.)

To edit a behavior, follow these steps:

1. **Select an object with a behavior attached.**

2. **Choose <u>W</u>indow⇨<u>B</u>ehaviors to open the Behaviors panel.**

   You can also click the Behaviors button in the Launcher bar.

   Here are some options that you can choose from in the Behaviors panel:

   - To change an event, choose a different one from the Events drop-down menu in the Behaviors panel while the action is selected.

   - To remove an action, click the action in the Behaviors panel to select it and then click the minus sign located at the top of the pane. The action disappears.

   - To change parameters for an action, double-click the action, change the parameters that you want to affect in the Parameters dialog box, and then click OK.

   - To change the order of actions when multiple actions have been set, select an action, and then click the Up or Down buttons to move it to a different position in the list of actions.

Browser issues

Figuring out which browser to target when you start working with behaviors can be frustrating — the most powerful behaviors work only in Internet Explorer 5, but not everyone has access to that browser. Dreamweaver provides an alternative that strives to give you the best of both worlds. To take advantage of it, design your pages for Internet Explorer 5 and then convert them to a copy that works in 3.0 browsers when you're done. You then have two pages to which you can direct viewers. Dreamweaver can easily convert your pages for you and includes a script that can automatically direct viewers to the correct page based on the browser that they use. You can add the script to a page by using the Check Browser behavior and selecting the onLoad event in the Behaviors panel.

Using Extensions and the Package Manager

Extensions let you easily add new features to Dreamweaver simply by downloading them from a Web site or by creating your own new extensions, which you can share with others. Extensions are kind of like Behaviors, except that they are even more powerful — you can actually alter the menu system in Dreamweaver, adding new features by adding new menu items. With extensions, you can do things like change background colors, add a list of state zip codes or country codes, instantly embed QuickTime movies, or connect to backend databases with a simple menu command. The idea behind extensions is that anyone with a little bit of scripting ability can create new ways to customize Dreamweaver and share their creations with the Dreamweaver community. The place to go to find out more about extensions and to download them (mostly for free) is the Macromedia Exchange for Dreamweaver site at www.macromedia.com/exchange/dreamweaver.

After you log in to the Exchange for Dreamweaver site (membership is free), you're welcome to download and install any of the scores and scores of extensions — they grow every day as new developers are constantly creating new ones. You can search for extensions by category or simply browse the ever-growing list.

To install an extension, download it first from the Exchange site and then use the Package Manager, a utility program that comes with Dreamweaver. Extensions that you download from the site are saved as files on your computer with an .mxp extension. The Package Manager makes installing and removing these files in Dreamweaver a breeze. To run the Package Manager and install an extension:

1. **Select Commands⇨Manage Exchange Packages.**

   The utility launches.

2. **Select File⇨Install Package within the Package Manager; then browse your drive to select the Extension you downloaded from the Exchange site.**

   After installing, you see brief instructions on how to use the extension.

3. **Simply switch back to Dreamweaver, and you're ready to use your new extension.**

Chapter 13

Creating Advanced DHTML Features

*I*f you read Chapter 12 before you turned to this chapter, you found out how to work with layers to achieve absolute positioning and add interactive elements to your site with behaviors. In terms of what DHTML can do, though, you still have only scratched the surface.

By animating DHTML layers, as I show you how to do in this chapter, you can escape the world of static Web pages by adding the components of time and motion to your pages. Using a Dreamweaver feature called the *timeline,* you can create animations by changing the size, position, visibility, and stacking order of layers and their contents over time, frame by frame. For example, you can put a logo on your page that comes in from off-screen and scrolls across the page when viewers first load your page. Then, when they click your logo, it spins around and shoots off the page. Timelines let you build this kind of interactivity into your site without having to hand-edit the complex code that makes it all work.

Although the code for creating animated layers is quite complex, Dreamweaver simplifies it all with a very easy to use and intuitive interface. In addition, timelines can easily be integrated with behaviors, allowing for some really cutting-edge effects to further enhance the interactivity of your pages.

Using a Timeline

As the name implies, a timeline enables you to control actions over time, making it possible to create animations and automatically trigger behaviors.

If you're familiar with other animation programs, such as the Macromedia products Flash or Director, you can figure out the timeline feature in Dreamweaver without much trouble. If you're completely new to timelines, you may find this a bit confusing at first. But hang in there; it's not that tough.

The steps in this section introduce you to the timeline options and explain the features that you can create. To work with timelines, you need to have a basic understanding of how DHTML layers work. If you don't, you may want to go back and read the section on layers in Chapter 12.

Only Dynamic HTML provides the functionality that makes a timeline necessary, so you can use timelines only if you're designing DHTML features (which means that the animations and effects you create with the timeline work only in 4.0 or later browsers because they support DHTML).

Timelines work by defining a series of frames that change over time. The elements in the frames (such as images or layers) can change in a variety of ways — from moving to a new location to being replaced by another layer or image. Thus, you can use timelines to create animations or to trigger other actions, such as starting a behavior when a page loads or after a series of other actions occur. You create timelines using the Timelines panel (see Figure 13-1), which is basically a grid showing *channels* (running vertically) and *frames* (running horizontally). If you look closely at Figure 13-1, you can see that an object named Layer 1 occupies the first channel and that it has a duration of 22 frames.

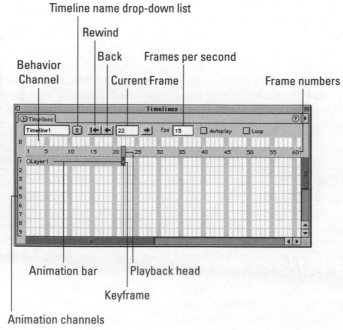

Figure 13-1: Using frames to represent time, the Timelines panel allows you to control objects and events over time.

Understanding the Timelines panel controls

Before you get into using the timeline, take a few minutes to review the various components of the Timelines panel. Starting at the top and going from left to right, the Timelines panel features these controls and options:

- ✔ **Timeline name drop-down list:** You can have multiple timelines on one page, and assigning each a name allows you to manage them more easily. You give a timeline a name by typing it into the first field. Though Dreamweaver automatically names the timelines for you, starting with timeline1, it's best to use a more descriptive name to make it easier to manage multiple timelines. The timeline drop-down list enables you to select which of the timelines appear in the Timelines panel.

- ✔ **Rewind:** Represented by a left-pointing arrow with a vertical line, this button returns the playback to the first frame in the timeline.

- ✔ **Back:** Represented by a left-pointing arrow, this button moves the playback to the left one frame at a time. You can click and hold the Back button to play the frames backward continuously.

- ✔ **Current frame indicator:** Represented by a number field between the Back and Play buttons. The number listed in this field represents the frame that the playback head is currently located in.

- ✔ **Play:** Represented by a right-pointing arrow, the Play button moves the playback to the right one frame at a time. You can click and hold the Play button to play the frames forward continuously. When you reach the last frame, the playback loops and continues at the beginning of the timeline.

- ✔ **FPS:** This field represents the number of frames per second *(fps)* that play in the timeline. The default setting of 15 frames per second is a good rate for most browsers on Windows and Macintosh systems. Browsers always play every frame, even if they can't achieve the frame rate that you specify.

- ✔ **Autoplay:** Checking this box causes a timeline to begin playing automatically when the page loads in the browser. (Otherwise, the timeline can be triggered only by an event, such as a mouseclick, for example.)

- ✔ **Loop:** Checking this box causes the timeline to repeat while the page displays in the browser window. When you check the Loop box, the Go To Timeline Frame action is added. If you want to control the number of loops, you need to double-click the marker that is added to the Behavior channel (as I explain in the next bullet). This action opens the Behavior Inspector, where you can edit the parameters to define the number of loops.

- **Behavior channel:** Just below the controls across the top of the Timelines panel, the Behavior channel has a B to the left of it and displays behaviors that should execute at a particular frame in the timeline. See the section later on in this chapter called "Inserting behaviors into a timeline to trigger actions" to see how this works.

- **Frame numbers:** The numbers (listed in increments of 5) along the bar that separates the Behavior channel from the Animation channels indicate how many frames each bar occupies. The number of the current frame is displayed between the Back and Play buttons at the top of the Timelines panel.

- **Animation channels:** This area is where the animation bars appear. In Figure 13-1, they are represented by Rows 1-9. Each row represents a different channel, which is kind of like a layer. You can create multiple animations by using multiple channels.

- **Playback head:** Indicated by a red vertical marker, which shows the active frame in the timeline (the one that currently displays on the page). In Figure 13-1, it is located at Frame 22.

- **Animation bars:** These blue bars appear in the timeline when you add an object. Each bar shows the duration of an object in number of frames over time. You can have multiple animation bars and control multiple objects in one timeline. In Figure 13-1, the animation bar is indicated by the horizontal bar titled Layer1.

- **Keyframes:** Represented by a circle within the animation bar, keyframes are frames in an animation that indicate properties, such as the position of an image on a page. In Figure 13-1, Layer1 has only two keyframes, a start frame and an end frame, each represented by circles at the beginning and end of the animation bar.

The best way to understand timelines is to compare them to frames in a cartoon animation. A cartoon animator creates an animation by drawing many versions of a single image that change slightly over time, frame by frame. In the same way, the timeline gives you frames to work with, in which objects move over time. The more frames your animation uses, the smoother it plays and the longer it takes to play through.

One of the advantages of timelines is that they can help automate the animation process. By using keyframes, Dreamweaver can automatically fill in intermediate frames between a starting and ending frame by calculating intermediate values. For example, if you set a keyframe for an image positioned at the top of a page and then set a second keyframe for the same image positioned lower on the page, the timeline draws the image moving from the first keyframe to the last automatically, saving you the time of having to draw each frame individually. For this reason, working with timelines saves an enormous amount of time when building DHTML animated effects. For instructions on setting keyframes and an example of how this works, try the step-by-step example in the next section, "Creating timelines."

You can use the HTML Source window to view the JavaScript code that Dreamweaver creates when you use a timeline. You can find the code in the MM_initTimelines function, inside a <SCRIPT> tag in the <HEAD> of the document. If you choose to edit the HTML source of a document that uses timelines, be careful not to change anything controlled by the timeline. Just make sure you don't change anything between the opening tag:

```
<script language="JavaScript">
```

and the closing tag:

```
</script>
```

unless you are really familiar with how to write and edit JavaScript.

Creating timelines

In the following steps, I create a timeline that causes two layers to automatically move into position when a page loads and demonstrate how keyframes work.

To create a timeline with keyframes, follow these steps:

1. **Start by creating a layer and filling it with either text or an image.**

   Creating and positioning layers is covered in detail in Chapter 12.

2. **Position the layer where you want the animation sequence to begin by selecting it and then clicking the layer marker (the small box in the top-left corner of the layer) to drag it around on the page to the correct position for the beginning of the sequence.**

   If you're using multiple layers and want to change the position of other layers on the page in your animation, you can get them into their starting positions for the beginning frame of the animation as well.

   If you want to position a layer off the visible page, it's impossible to manually drag it completely off. However, you can still move it off the page by typing a negative number in the text boxes marked L (for left) or T (for top) in the Property Inspector for the layer. This is a great trick when you want to have a layer start off-screen and then slide into position as part of the animation sequence. Controlling the position of a layer by changing these numbers, rather than by using the drag-and-drop technique, also provides greater control over precise positioning.

3. **Choose Window⇨Timelines.**

   The Timelines panel opens.

4. **Click the layer that you want to add to the timeline to select it and choose Modify⇨Timeline⇨Add Object to Timeline.**

   You can also just click and drag the layer (or a selected image) from the document window into the Timelines panel to create a new animation bar.

   A bar appears in the first channel of the timeline. The name of the layer or image appears in the bar (like the bar in Figure 13-1 labeled Layer1).

5. **Click to select the blue dot that represents the ending keyframe at the right end of the animation bar.**

   Dots on the timeline represent keyframes. All objects in the timeline have a beginning and ending keyframe.

6. **With the keyframe still selected, go back and select the layer in the main document window and move it to a different position by clicking and dragging it to another location on the page.**

   The position of the layer on the page is now different in the final keyframe than it is in the first keyframe. By changing the physical location of the layer in the final keyframe, Dreamweaver automatically creates an animated sequence of frames to fill in the gaps between the first and last keyframe layer positions. A line appears on the page between the new location of the layer and its original location in Keyframe 1, indicating the path of the layer over time, as shown in Figure 13-2. By clicking the Rewind or Play buttons at the top of the Timelines panel, you can see how the layer moves along this path frame by frame.

7. **To increase the duration of the animation, click the keyframe circle in the Timeline panel and drag it farther to the right, or drag it to the left to shorten it.**

   This lengthens and shortens the animation bar and controls the amount of time that elapses while the timeline moves the element from the first keyframe to the second.

8. **If you want to add a bend or curve to the animation motion, you just need to add another keyframe and change the layer position associated with the new keyframe. Click on any frame in the middle of the animation bar so that the playback head moves to that frame and choose Modify⇨Timeline⇨Add Keyframe.**

   A new keyframe circle appears in the frame you selected. You can add as many keyframes as you like and use them to control the location or other features of the element. In the example in Figure 13-3, I added a new keyframe at frame 10.

9. **After adding the keyframe, it is automatically selected in the animation bar. With the new keyframe circle still selected, move the layer on the page to the position that you want it to be in at that particular point in the animation sequence.**

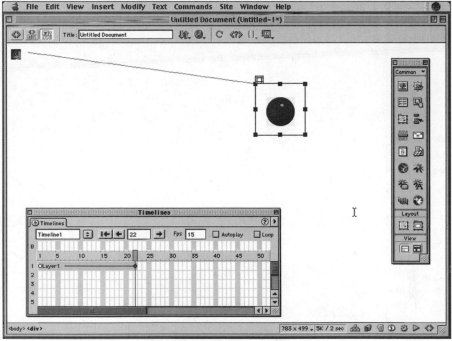

Figure 13-2:
The diagonal line indicates the layer's path of motion over time from frame 1 to frame 22.

For example, if you wanted a layer to move across the page on a curved path instead of a straight one, you could add a keyframe like the one in Step 8. Then position it, as shown in Figure 13-3, in a place on the page that would cause the motion of the layer to move to a third location as it progresses from the first keyframe to the last one.

10. **Click to place a check mark in the Autoplay option in the Timelines panel.**

    Clicking the Autoplay option ensures that the animation begins right after the page loads. Otherwise, the animation won't take place until you define another event to trigger it. (See the section later in this chapter called "Using a behavior to trigger a timeline animation" for information on other ways to trigger the animation.)

11. **To preview the animation, click and hold down the Play button or select File⇨Preview in Browser.**

    By pressing the Play button, you can get a preview of how the animation runs. The Preview in Browser command shows you how the rest of the world will see the animation.

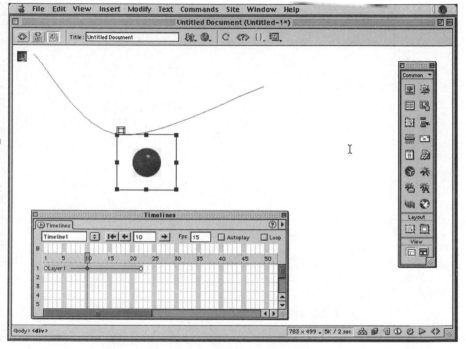

Figure 13-3:
By adding a
keyframe at
frame 10 and
repositioning
the layer in
that frame,
the motion
path is
modified to
a curved
path.

By following these same steps, you can add additional layers to the timeline causing simultaneous actions. You can also click and drag the animation bars to stagger frame sequences. In Figure 13-4, you see two layers, each represented by a different animation bar in the timeline. Notice that the two animation bars are staggered and that, as the layers move across the page, one progresses ahead of the other. In this example, Layer1 stops animating at Frame 22 while Layer2 continues until the last frame.

Recording a layer's path

In the steps in the preceding section, you see how to use keyframes to allow Dreamweaver to automatically generate in-between frames for an animated sequence by changing the position of the layer at each keyframe. Another way to create animations is to record a layer's path on the page simply by dragging it around manually. Suppose that you want your logo to circle around some text as it moves across the page or maybe follow a particular path that requires too many keyframes to generate. The Record Path of Layer feature can help you accomplish this.

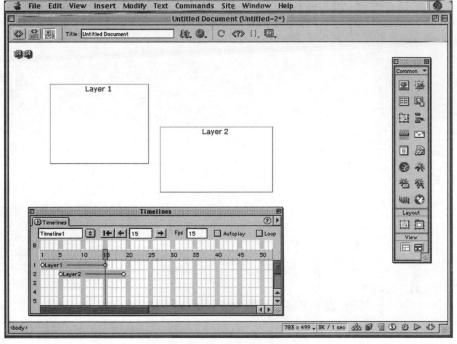

Figure 13-4:
Controlling
multiple
layers is
easy; each
bar in the
timeline
controls a
different
layer.

To record a layer's path, follow these steps:

1. **Select the layer whose movement you want to record, then click and drag it to the position where you'd like the animation to begin.**

2. **With the layer still highlighted, choose Modify⇨Timeline⇨Record Path of Layer.**

   If not already visible, the Timelines panel appears.

3. **Click and carefully drag the layer onscreen to define the animation path that you want it to take from beginning to end.**

   As you drag the mouse around, a gray line appears onscreen indicating the path of the layer. The timeline also automatically generates new keyframes represented by dots on the timeline. The slower you draw, the closer the keyframes (see Figure 13-5).

4. **When you're finished drawing, release the mouse button. The path has now been recorded and the keyframes generated automatically.**

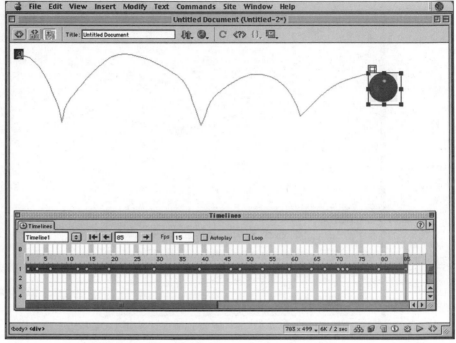

Playing your animations

When you create time-based animations, it's important that you control the time that these animations occur — right after the page loads for instance, or perhaps only after a certain event occurs.

When you create a timeline in Dreamweaver, you create an action that will occur, but you still need an event to trigger it — to define *when* it will occur. In order for the timeline to execute automatically after the page loads, you need to check the Autoplay option in the Timelines panel. Checking the Autoplay option adds an Onload event handler in the <BODY> tag of your HTML. This tells the browser to begin playing the animation immediately after the page loads. After checking the Autoplay option, you can preview your animation in the browser by choosing File⇨Preview in Browser. You can also instruct the timeline to continue playing by selecting the Loop option. The Loop option tells the animation to continue to play over and over, rather than to stop after it has reached the last frame of the animation.

A note about frame rates and animation speed

You can increase the speed of your animation by increasing the frame rate in the *fps* (frames per second) indicator in the Timelines panel. Fps settings, however, can be deceiving. They are more dependent on the speed of the computer being used to view the page and the Internet connection speed than they are on an accurate frame rate per second.

The browser always plays every frame regardless of the fps setting, so speed can vary widely. For this reason, it's often best to stick with the default frame rate of 15 fps or at least stay close to it.

In order to increase or decrease the speed of your animation, it's more effective to lengthen or shorten the number of frames in your animation by dragging the last frame in the timeline in or out. To slow the animation, add more frames by dragging right; to speed up the animation, decrease the number of frames by dragging left.

You can also make your animations appear smoother by increasing the number of frames in the timeline rather than by increasing the frame rate.

In the event that you don't want to play your animation directly after the page loads — for example, if you want to have it play only if the user clicks a certain button — leave the Autoplay button unchecked. You can then add a behavior that instructs the timeline to begin whenever you specify. In the next section, you see how to use timelines and behaviors together in this manner.

Using behaviors with a timeline

Just as you can attach behaviors to text and images, you can also insert behaviors into a timeline for even greater interactivity on your pages (for more about behaviors, see Chapter 12). You can use behaviors to trigger animations, meaning that you can start, stop, or even jump to any frame in a timeline by linking it to a behavior, or you can also execute behaviors anywhere along the timeline. This means that the behavior can be attached to any element, such as text, images, or even other layers, to control when and how the timeline animation occurs or to generate other interactive elements at a given point in time.

Using a behavior to trigger a timeline animation

Sometimes you don't want an animation to occur immediately when a page loads, but only after the user does something, such as clicking a logo. These steps show you how to start a timeline animation using a behavior.

To trigger the timeline that you just created by clicking on an image link, follow these steps (these steps assume that you've already created a timeline on your page, as I describe earlier in the "Creating timelines" section):

1. **First, insert and position the image on your page that you want to trigger the timeline action.**

2. **Select Window⇨Behaviors to bring up the Behaviors panel.**

3. **With the image selected in the document window, click the plus sign (+) in the Behaviors panel to access the Behaviors pop-up list.**

   The list of available behaviors appears for this object.

4. **Click the plus sign in the Behaviors panel to display the list of actions. Scroll down to Timeline and select Play Timeline from the submenu.**

   The Play Timeline dialog box appears (see Figure 13-6) with a drop-down list box containing the available timelines on your page. The names appearing in this list reflect the names applied to various timelines in the name text box of the Timelines panel. If you haven't already created a timeline on your page, the drop-down list will be empty.

Figure 13-6:
You can add
a behavior
to play a
timeline.

Play Timeline
Play Timeline: [Timeline1]   OK   Cancel   Help

5. **Select the appropriate timeline from the drop-down list.**

   The Play Timeline action now appears in the Actions column of the Behaviors panel and the default onClick in the Events column is chosen as the trigger, as shown in Figure 13-7.

Figure 13-7:
This
behavior
will play the
timeline
when the
mouse is
clicked.

With this action now linked to the image with an onClick event handler, clicking the image triggers the action, initiating the timeline animation. You may want to turn off the Autoplay option by unchecking it in the Timelines panel so that the animation plays only when the image is clicked, not when the page loads.

Besides using a behavior to start an animation, you can also have it stop the animation or jump to a specific frame in the animation. Both of these actions are available as submenus of the Timeline action in the Actions pop-up list (available by clicking the plus sign) in the Behaviors panel.

Inserting behaviors into a timeline to trigger actions

You can also add behaviors to keyframes, triggering actions from within a timeline animation, or add behaviors to a specific frame in the Behaviors channel in the Timelines panel. These kinds of behaviors are triggered when the animation reaches a certain frame in the timeline rather than requiring an external event such as a mouse click. So far, I've been animating a bouncing ball in this chapter. But to make this animation more realistic, I want to make it look like the ball gets a little squished at the top and bottom when it bounces. I can get this effect by *swapping* the round ball image with a second image that shows the same ball with a little squish on each side at the appropriate frame, and this is accomplished by adding a behavior to the timeline that swaps the ball image at a certain keyframe. You can create similar effects by swapping any images at any point in a timeline sequence.

To add a swap image action to the timeline, follow these steps:

1. **Click to select the image inside the layer (select only the image, not the layer, by carefully clicking the image itself) and drag the image into the Timelines panel to create a second animation bar like the one you see in Figure 13-8.**

   This animation bar is labeled with the word Image instead of Layer.

2. **Create a new keyframe at the point where you want the images to swap.**

   To do so, click anywhere in the image animation bar and choose Modify⇨Timeline⇨Add Keyframe. In this example, I add two keyframes because the image swaps twice, first to the squished ball, and then back to the normal ball. Notice where I've placed the keyframes in Figure 13-8. Their positions, at the middle of the animation bar, are in the right place to cause the image to change at the bottom of the motion path, as the ball hits the imaginary ground and then back again as it bounces up.

3. **With a keyframe circle selected in the image animation bar, use the Property Inspector to change the image source.**

   You can type in the name of another image or click the folder icon to browse for an image. In my sample, I change the round ball to an image of a squished ball.

4. **Select the next keyframe and change the image source again.**

   In this case, I change it back to the round ball image.

5. **Repeat Steps 2 and 3 if you want to change the image at any other keyframe.**

6. **To preview the animation, click and hold down the Play button.**

7. **When you're finished, you can choose Window⇨Timelines to close the Timelines panel.**

Another way to add a behavior to the timeline is to click any frame in the Behavior channel of the Timelines panel (the row at the top of the Timelines panel labeled with a B) and select a behavior from the Actions list in the Behaviors panel. This causes the behavior to execute when the playback head of the timeline reaches the frame that the behavior has been applied to.

Time-based layer animations are made possible by DHTML, and Dreamweaver makes it easy for anybody to animate layers by using the timeline. You can do an endless number of things with a timeline, from scrolling credits and flying logos to elements that come in off-screen and appear when needed. Use your imagination and have fun with the timelines in Dreamweaver. And be sure to check out www.dhtmlzone.com, Macromedia's Web site for DHTML tips and information, for more ideas on how to work with DHTML on your Web pages.

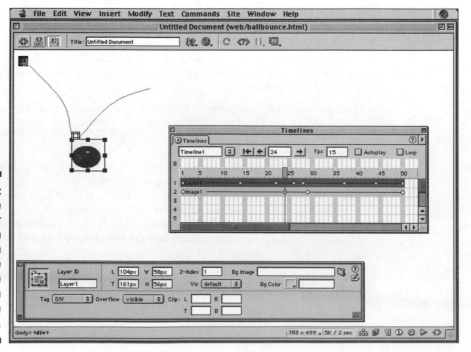

Figure 13-8:
Making the ball appear to squish with each bounce makes the animation more realistic.

Don't overestimate your viewer's browser

Too many Web designers overestimate their audiences. Most of us who build Web sites are quick to upgrade, downloading new browser versions and installing plug-ins as soon as they're released. But many people on the Web don't know how to upgrade their browsers, or they just can't or don't bother.

Employees at big corporations are usually on networks where upgrading a browser means upgrading the entire system. Technical support staff are often slow to do the upgrade because they're busy with so many other tasks. Home users are often intimidated by the prospect of downloading anything off the Internet, so they're likely to stick with whatever browser they got when they first set up their connection to the Net.

Slowly, things are improving. Users are getting more sophisticated and software is getting easier to use. But for now, if you want to reach the broad audience on the Web, you need to design a Web site that works in a variety of browsers. Fortunately, Macromedia understood that problem when it developed Dreamweaver and included a number of features to help make it easier to design your site so that it takes advantage of high-end browsers, while still being accessible to older browsers. Make sure that you take advantage of these features, such as the Target Browser options, Browser Check features, and the 3.0 Conversion features that enable you to easily create a second page that works in older browsers. You can find out more about all of these options in "Ensuring That Your Pages Work in Older Browsers" in this chapter.

Ensuring That Your Pages Work in Older Browsers

You may love all the Dreamweaver features described in this chapter and in Chapter 12 because they make creating dynamic, interactive elements for your Web pages easy. Unfortunately, most of these features can be viewed only by the latest browsers, and many people on the Internet still use older browsers. By "older browsers," I mean any version of Microsoft Internet Explorer or Netscape Navigator earlier than Version 4.0 (and even the latest version of Netscape 4 doesn't offer as many options as Internet Explorer 5 and above).

So that you can easily compensate for browser differences as you design your Web pages in Dreamweaver, the folks at Macromedia included features for targeting different browsers. When you choose a target browser in the Behaviors Inspector, you get a list of behavior options that work only in the browser that you select. This list allows you to know which behaviors work with which browsers. To expand your options, Dreamweaver includes a number of other features for targeting different browsers.

The Check Browser action

One way to deal with the problem of browser incompatibilities is to create two or more different versions of your site. To decide which browser sees which site, you can use the Check Browser action in the Actions list of the Behaviors panel, as shown in Figure 13-9. This action automatically sends users to different URLs depending on the version of browser they are using, so you can create a fancy version of your site for new browsers and a simpler version for older browsers. This action even allows you to send Netscape and Internet Explorer users to different URLs, so you can design different pages for each browser's capabilities. The best way to use this action is to select the <BODY> tag using the HTML tag selector in the document's status bar and then choose the Check Browser action in the Behaviors panel (click the plus sign to access the list of actions). Applying this behavior to your page causes a browser-detect script to determine the type of browser that your visitor uses when the page first loads. After loading, the visitor is either directed to a different URL based on that detection or kept on the same page. For example, you can send all visitors using Netscape 3 or lower to one page in your site and users of Internet Explorer 5 to another page. To ensure that the oldest browsers see the simple page instead of trying to interpret fancy code that they don't understand, it's best to insert this behavior in the basic version of the page and then redirect the newest browsers to the alternate fancy pages. Of course the only problem with this solution is that you have to create more than one site, one for older browsers and one or more for the newer browsers, and that can turn into a lot more work.

The Convert to 3.0 Browser Compatible command

Because Web designers often have to create alternate versions of their fancy pages for older browsers, Macromedia added another feature when they developed Dreamweaver. The Convert to 3.0 Browser Compatible command automates creating a second page that can display in older browsers. The 3.0-level browser is considered by most Web designers as a minimal target that virtually everyone surfing on the Web will be able to view. Here's how it works: You create a page by using all the latest features that you want, such as layers and Cascading Style Sheets, and then run the conversion option. Dreamweaver automatically creates a second page that works in 3.0 browsers yet looks largely the same.

This isn't a perfect solution, but it's a great step toward making maintenance of dual sites easier. The problem is that you can't have the same features in the 3.0 version that work in the 4.0 and later version, and advanced features don't all convert down to less advanced features gracefully. For example, if you have an animated timeline that moves your buttons across the page, you lose the animation in the 3.0 conversion, but at least you can see your buttons. Still, you may have to tweak the converted page a little to get the buttons to the best location on a static page.

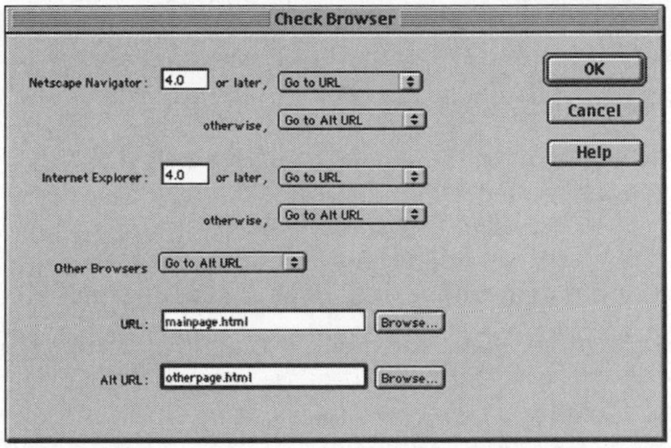

Figure 13-9:
The Check Browser dialog box lets you direct users to different URLs based on which browser they are using.

The 3.0-conversion process does the best job it can and works well for most CSS *(Cascading Style Sheets)* options because it converts applied styles back to individual formatting options. For example, if you've applied a headline style that is Helvetica, bold, and centered, Dreamweaver changes the formatting from the headline style to the individual tags for those three formatting options.

When you convert a file to 3.0-compatible using the Convert to 3.0 Browser Compatible command, Dreamweaver creates a copy of the original file and changes the code, often altering the design. Here are some of the changes that you can expect:

- Layers change to tables in an effort to preserve positioning. The table displays the layers in their original locations.
- HTML character styles replace CSS markup.
- Any CSS markup that can't be converted to HTML is removed.
- Timeline code that animates layers is removed.
- Timeline code that doesn't use layers, such as behaviors or changes to the image source, is preserved.
- The timeline is automatically rewound to Frame 1 and all elements are placed in a static position on the page in the location specified in the first frame of the timeline.

You may have to reposition some of your elements after this conversion to ensure that they look good on a static page.

To convert a file that you designed with 4.0 or higher browser options to be 3.0 browser–compatible, follow these steps:

1. **Choose File⇨Convert⇨3.0 Browser Compatible.**

   The Convert to 3.0 Browser Compatible dialog box appears.

2. **Choose the conversions options that you want.**

   You can convert layers to tables or CSS styles to HTML markup. I recommend that you do both.

3. **Click Continue.**

   Dreamweaver opens the converted file in a new, untitled window.

4. **Choose File⇨Save and save the page with a new name.**

Dreamweaver also includes a Layer to Tables option that automates the process of converting a 4.0-compatible file that uses layers to a 3.0-compatible file with the same positioning offered by layers and DHTML. See Chapter 12 for more information on how this works.

I like to keep all of these pages in their own folder so that I can easily keep track of them and they don't clutter the rest of my Web site structure.

If you maintain a site with two sets of pages (one for 4.0 browsers and another for 3.0 and older), don't forget that you have to update both sets every time you make a change.

Designing for multiple browsers is a key element to good Web design. Dreamweaver makes it easy to create lots of features that don't work in older browsers. Make sure that you also take advantage of the features that can help you ensure that your pages reach as broad an audience as possible.

Chapter 14

Roundtrip Integration: Fireworks and Dreamweaver

In This Chapter

▶ Fireworks as an image-editing program

▶ Roundtrip graphics editing

▶ Using other image editors besides Fireworks

▶ Inserting and editing Fireworks HTML

In this chapter, I discuss some of the special features in Dreamweaver that integrate with Fireworks, Macromedia's image creation and editing program. If you're not familiar with Fireworks, you may want to have a look at *Fireworks 4 For Dummies,* published by IDG Books Worldwide, Inc., to find out more about this excellent program. If you don't own or have access to Fireworks, you may just want to skim through this chapter as most of it is specific to using Fireworks and Dreamweaver together as a pair, but there's still relevant info for integrating other image editors with Dreamweaver.

Unlike Dreamweaver, Fireworks is primarily a graphics tool. Because Dreamweaver doesn't have any native graphics capabilities, Fireworks (or programs like it — see Chapter 8) enables you to create images from scratch and edit them, or work with existing images and prepare them for usage on the Web. However, Fireworks goes a lot further than most graphics programs because it's one of the very first image-editing programs designed specifically for the special needs of the Web. Using Fireworks, you can automate your workflow, *optimize* graphics (compress and prepare them for Web use), create sophisticated animations, fancy *rollovers* (images that change when you hover the mouse pointer over them), and special effects in a fraction of the time that it used to take. Fireworks can even generate HTML and output Web pages all by itself! But more importantly for you, Fireworks integrates especially well with Dreamweaver, allowing roundtrip graphics editing back and forth between the two programs. Normally when you work with Dreamweaver and another graphics editor, it takes many steps to create and edit images back and forth between the two programs — one of the most time-consuming parts of building and maintaining a Web site. *Roundtrip graphics editing* simply gives you a lot of shortcuts, making the trips back and forth between the two programs a whole lot quicker and easier.

Dreamweaver to Fireworks: Image Editing

Suppose that you've got a logo on your Web page and your client suddenly wants it in a different color. Normally this would mean launching another image-editing program, tracking down the logo, opening it, editing it, saving it, switching back to Dreamweaver, and then re-importing the logo onto your page. Whew, that's a lot of steps. Using the special integration features between Dreamweaver and Fireworks, though, greatly simplifies the entire process — a few clicks of the mouse can replace all of those other time consuming tasks.

The following steps show you how to select an image in Dreamweaver, automatically open it in Fireworks, edit it, and update the image back into Dreamweaver with just a few mouse clicks.

To launch Fireworks directly from Dreamweaver and edit an existing image, follow these steps:

1. **In Dreamweaver, select the image you want to edit and make the Properties Inspector visible by choosing Window➪Properties.**

2. **In the Properties Inspector, click the Edit button as shown in Figure 14-1.**

   The Find Source dialog box appears asking if you want to edit an existing document for the source of the file that you selected.

3. **Click one of the options in the Find Source for Editing dialog box.**

   Clicking Yes lets you select a different file from the actual optimized image file on your page. For example, you can select a PNG version of the optimized graphic (which may have been the original file from which you exported the optimized Web version of the graphic on your page). Clicking No opens the source file that you selected in Dreamweaver (the actual GIF or JPEG file that's linked on the page).

   If you click No, Fireworks launches with the GIF or JPEG image that you selected. If you click Yes, Fireworks allows you to pick an alternate image and launches by opening the alternate image in a new document. Most likely, the alternate image will be a PNG file. (PNG is the Fireworks native file format. For more information, take a look at the sidebar in this chapter on PNG files.)

Figure 14-1:
The
Properties
Inspector
displays an
edit button
whenever
an image is
selected.
Click this
button to
launch your
image editor
of choice.

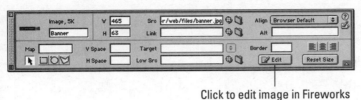

Click to edit image in Fireworks

Because the source file of the image used on your Web page was probably optimized earlier, editing an optimized GIF or JPEG image usually doesn't give you the best image quality results after you edit, re-optimize, and re-export it back into Dreamweaver. It's kind of like reheating leftovers: Each time you heat it up again you lose taste, but if you can start with a fresh cooked meal, you always get the best taste. Going back to the original, pre-optimized version of the graphic gives you that option to start again from scratch. By clicking Yes in the Find Source for Editing dialog box, you can select a different file from the optimized source graphic. If you exported the image from a PNG file, you can select the PNG instead, edit a higher quality version of the file, and export it without suffering extra image degradation.

After clicking Yes or No, the image document opens in Fireworks.

4. **Make the edits that you need to make to the image within Fireworks.**

   You can make any changes or edits to the image using any of the tools in Fireworks as well as using the Optimize panel to change the optimization settings for the file.

5. **When you're finished editing the image, click the Done button in the Fireworks document window (Figure 14-2).**

   After clicking the Done button, the Fireworks document fades to the background, and the Dreamweaver document automatically comes into view. The image automatically updates on the page, reflecting the recent edits without requiring any other action on your part other than saving the document.

After you press the Done button in Fireworks, you can't undo any changes you make to the image files by selecting the Undo command. The changes are permanent.

Click to update in Dreamweaver

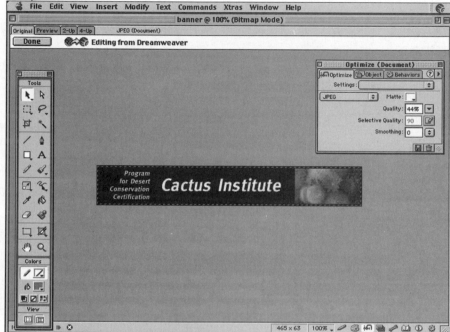

Figure 14-2:
Clicking the
Done button
in Fireworks
automati-
cally
updates the
image in
Dream-
weaver
without any
further
steps.

Using an Image Editor
Other Than Fireworks

When you click the edit button in the Properties Inspector (as in Step 2 in the previous example), Dreamweaver tries to launch Fireworks as the default editing application. But what if you don't use Fireworks or don't own a copy? Fear not, you can achieve a somewhat less-automated workflow with most any other graphics editor. You just need to change the preferences in Dreamweaver to specify which program you prefer to use instead of Fireworks.

To designate a different application as the Dreamweaver external image editor, follow these steps:

1. **In the Dreamweaver menu bar choose Edit⇨Preferences and select the File Types/Editors category.**

   The Preferences dialog box for File Types/Editors appears, as shown in Figure 14-3.

PNG: Portable Network Graphics files

Fireworks uses the PNG *(Portable Network Graphics)* format as its native file format. PNG is kind of similar to the PSD format used by Adobe Photoshop in that it retains the highest quality possible for the graphic without suffering any of the degradation in image quality that usually occurs when a GIF or JPEG is generated. The Portable Network Graphics format was actually created long before Fireworks, and it is one of the few graphics formats, in addition to the GIF and JPEG formats, that can be viewed from within a Web browser. Because the PNG format supports far more features than either GIF or JPEG formats, and allows for the many extra features that Fireworks offers, Macromedia chose it as the native format for Fireworks.

The PNG file format was originally created as a potential replacement for the GIF format because it offered far greater image quality, compression levels, and numerous other features lacking in GIFs. PNG files offer a multitude of improvements over GIF, including resolution up to 48 bits (as opposed to 8 bits in GIF), better compression, built-in *gamma correction* (the capability to adjust to the different brightness levels between PC and Mac monitors), and greater levels of transparency.

All in all, PNG is a much more modern and feature-rich file format. Although PNG files represent a marked improvement over GIF files, they haven't seen widespread use on the Web yet due to limited native browser support and a lack of tools capable of generating the PNG format.

For more information about PNG files, take a look at the PNG home page at www.libpng.org/pub/png/ or the W3C's PNG page at www.w3.org/Graphics/PNG.

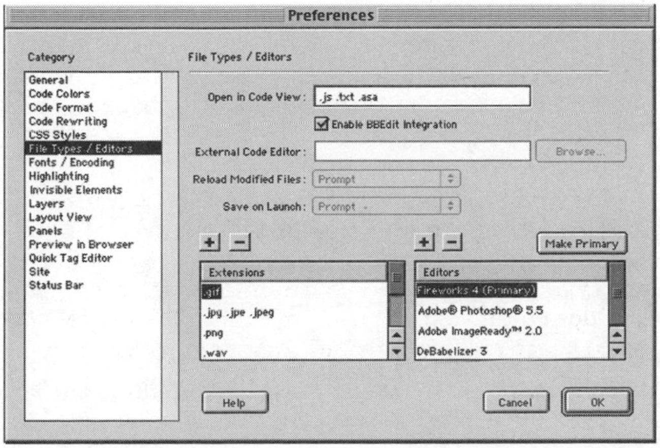

Figure 14-3:
You can specify other image editors besides Fireworks.

2. **Select the .gif format in the Extensions list on the left side of the dialog box.**

   For each file format you can specify one or more external editors, in addition to a primary editor.

3. **In the Editors list on the right, click the plus sign (+) to add an editor for all your GIF files.**

   A standard browse dialog box appears asking you to find the program to assign as the editor for this file type.

4. **Browse your drive until you locate the graphics application you want to assign; then click Open.**

   After you click Open, the application appears in the list of image editors on the right.

5. **Click the Make Primary button to make this your primary editor. You can add as many editors to the list as you want, but you can assign only one primary editor for each file type.**

6. **Repeat Steps 2 through 5 for the .jpg extension and any other extensions you want to assign to other graphics editors.**

After you've assigned your program of choice as your primary external editor, clicking the Edit button in the Properties Inspector (see Figure 14-1) whenever you select an image will now automatically launch that program instead of Fireworks. Also, any other programs that you assign as image editors but not as primary editors will appear in a pop-up menu if you right-click on an image (control-click on the Mac) as shown in Figure 14-4.

Because Fireworks is a companion tool to Dreamweaver, you can automatically update an image directly from Fireworks into Dreamweaver when you click the Done button in Fireworks. Note, though, that this won't work with any other image-editing program. You can open a file in that other program by clicking the Edit button in Dreamweaver, but you'll still need to save the edited graphic and re-import the image into Dreamweaver manually. Only Fireworks offers one-click automatic image updating back to Dreamweaver.

Dreamweaver to Fireworks: Optimizing an Image

Suppose that logo on your page looks fine, but you decide that it is taking too long to download and needs to be compressed a bit more. Earlier you learned how to easily edit a file in Fireworks from within Dreamweaver. In this example, I show you how to re-optimize an image in Fireworks from within Dreamweaver when all you need to do is change the optimization/compression settings but not make any actual alterations to the image.

To optimize an image in Fireworks from within Dreamweaver, follow these steps:

1. **Select the image in Dreamweaver.**

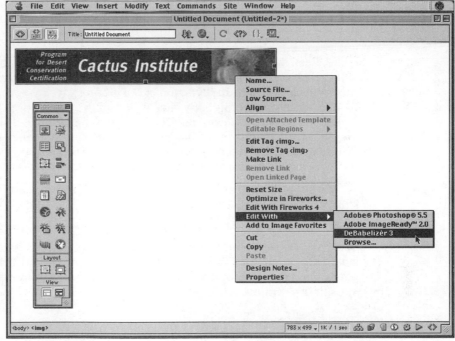

Figure 14-4:
You can add a whole lot of image editors to your preferences and they will all appear in this pop-up menu when you right-click an image.

2. **Choose Commands⇨Optimize Image in Fireworks, or right-click the image (control + click on the Mac) to access this from a pop-up menu as shown in Figure 14-4.**

   The Find Source dialog box appears asking if you want to edit an existing document for the source of the file that you selected.

   The default setting for this command is for Dreamweaver to ask if you want to open an existing file each time you launch Fireworks. You can change the default by selecting Always Use Source PNG or Never Use Source PNG from the pull-down menu in this same dialog box.

3. **Click one of the options in the Find Source dialog box.**

   Clicking Yes enables you to select a different file from the actual optimized image file on your page. For example, you can select a PNG version of the optimized graphic which may have been the original file from which you exported the optimized Web version of the graphic on your page. Clicking No opens the source file that you selected in Dreamweaver (the actual GIF or JPEG file that is linked on the page).

   If you click No, Fireworks launches with the GIF or JPEG image that you selected and displays the optimization dialog box within Fireworks. If you click Yes, Fireworks allows you to pick an alternate image and launches by opening the alternate image into the optimization dialog box within Fireworks.

Because the source file of the image used on your Web page was probably optimized earlier, editing an optimized GIF or JPEG image usually doesn't give you the best image quality results after you edit, re-optimize, and re-export it back into Dreamweaver. It's kind of like reheating leftovers. Each time you heat it up again you lose taste, but if you can start with a fresh cooked meal you'll always get the best taste. Going back to the original, pre-optimized version of the graphic gives you that option to start again from scratch. By clicking Yes in the Find Source for Editing dialog box, you can select a different file from the optimized source graphic. If you exported the image from a PNG file, you can select the PNG instead, edit a higher quality version of the file, and export it without suffering extra image degradation.

Whichever option you click, the image opens in Fireworks in the Optimize dialog box, ready to export.

 4. **Apply the new optimization settings in Fireworks Optimize panel.**

You can change the bit depth and quality settings of the file to achieve a smaller file size, and then preview the changes within Fireworks preview panel. You can also crop the image, but you can't make any other image edits in this window.

 5. **Click Update.**

The file is automatically updated in Dreamweaver with the changes that you just applied. If you selected a PNG file to edit (you clicked Yes in the dialog box), the original PNG file is not altered, only the resultant GIF or JPEG file.

After you press the Update button in Fireworks, you cannot undo any changes you make to the image files by selecting the Undo command. The changes are permanent.

Inserting Fireworks HTML

One of the great features of Fireworks is that you can automatically generate tables and HTML files when cutting up images for your Web designs. This feature is great for slicing graphics where you need to use complicated tables to hold the pieces all together. The only question is, after you generate this HTML code from Fireworks, how do you get it onto your Dreamweaver page? Before Dreamweaver 4 came along you had to copy and paste the HTML manually. Now with Dreamweaver 4, you can easily insert the HTML and associated images with just the click of a button.

To insert a Fireworks generated table with sliced images into Dreamweaver follow these steps (this example assumes you know how to use Fireworks to slice up images and generate HTML tables, and you have already output an HTML file from within Fireworks):

1. **Choose Insert⇨Interactive Images⇨Fireworks HTML.**

   The Insert Fireworks HTML dialog box appears (see Figure 14-5).

2. **Click the Browse button to select the HTML file to import; click Open when you've located it.**

   Dreamweaver inserts the table and associated images from the Fireworks document (see Figure 14-6).

Figure 14-5:
You can insert HTML code created by Fireworks directly into Dream-weaver.

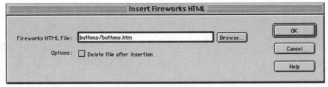

Figure 14-6:
Dream-weaver has a special Property Inspector for Fireworks-generated HTML with a visual indication of the source PNG file.

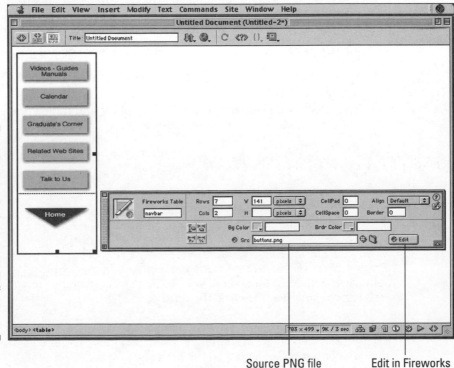

Source PNG file   Edit in Fireworks

Editing Fireworks HTML

After you insert Fireworks HTML into Dreamweaver, some special options become available in the Properties Inspector, allowing you to easily edit the images and associated code back in Fireworks. Looking at Figure 14-6, you see that the Property Inspector adds a few items that appear only when you insert a Fireworks HTML table. One is an indicator of the source PNG file for the images, in this case a navigation bar with multiple buttons, and the other is an Edit button, which lets you edit the table in Fireworks.

To edit an existing Fireworks table in Dreamweaver, follow these steps:

1. **Select the table in the Dreamweaver document.**

   Fireworks-generated HTML imported into Dreamweaver becomes kind of an "object" that you can distinguish by dotted lines representing the top-level table of the imported HTML/graphics. You must select this "object" in order to display the options in the Properties Inspector (as shown in Figure 14-6).

2. **Click the Edit button to launch Fireworks.**

   You are asked to find the original PNG file corresponding to the inserted HTML/graphics if it can't be found. After locating the PNG file, the graphic appears within a Fireworks document window.

3. **Make any edits or adjustments to the Fireworks document.**

4. **Click the Done button in the Fireworks document window (see Figure 14-7).**

   The HTML code is re-output and the graphics and table code are automatically updated in Dreamweaver!

Click to update in Dreamweaver

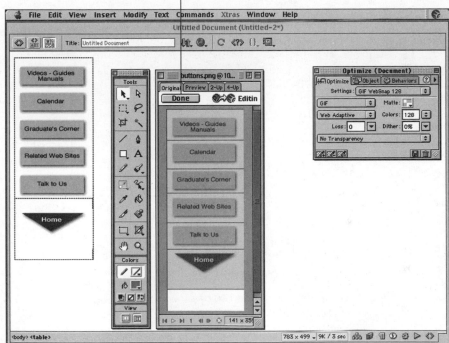

Figure 14-7:
Clicking the
Done button
in Fireworks
automat-
ically
updates the
code in
Dream-
weaver
without any
further
steps.

Chapter 15

Showing Off with Multimedia

● ●

In This Chapter

▶ Integrating multimedia into your Web pages

▶ Adding Shockwave and Flash movies

▶ Creating Flash buttons and text

▶ Getting familiar with Java and ActiveX controls

▶ Using sound, video, and other multimedia files

● ●

*T*hose who live in this multimedia world, spoiled by CD-ROMs and music videos, are still far from satisfied with flat, text-based Web sites. Most Web designers want the rich, interactive features that they know are possible, even with the limits of bandwidth. They want animation, sound, video — the features that bring life to other media. But HTML, even with the addition of Dynamic HTML features, just doesn't fulfill those desires.

That's where plug-ins come in.

Plug-ins are small programs that work in cooperation with a Web browser to play sound, video, and animation. They're called plug-ins because they're basically small applications that plug into the browser and extend its capabilities. Any company can create plug-ins for browsers to enable the browsers to display and use new technologies. Some plug-ins have become so popular that browser makers Netscape and Microsoft have built them into their latest browsers. Plug-ins that aren't so well known require viewers to download and install them on their computers to run with the browsers.

Well-known multimedia and plug-in technologies include Macromedia's Shockwave and Flash (shown in action on the CyberSlacker Web site — www.cyberslacker.com — in Figure 15-1), Real Networks' RealAudio and RealVideo, and Apple's QuickTime, to name a few. In this chapter, I tell you about the various types of multimedia technologies and how to use Dreamweaver to place these files into your Web pages or even create multimedia files, for instance with Flash, right in Dreamweaver. I also give you tips about making your pages work best in multiple browsers and how Dreamweaver makes that easy for you.

Figure 15-1: CyberSlacker is a full-length animated cartoon created entirely using quick-downloading Flash technology.

© 1998, 1999, 2000 Electronic Hollywood, Inc. Cyberslacker is a trademark of Electronic Hollywood, Inc.

Creating Multimedia for Different Browsers and Platforms

When Macromedia developed Dreamweaver, it made sure that the program creates HTML code that's universally accepted by as many Web browsers as possible. The differences between Netscape Navigator and Microsoft Internet Explorer mean that you sometimes have to use two tags to do what one should handle. For example, when you add plug-in files to a Web page, you must use both the <EMBED> and <OBJECT> tags because each browser supports a different one. Fortunately, you don't have to worry about learning how to write the code for the <OBJECT> and <EMBED> tags or even how they work together. Dreamweaver generates these tags for you. If you want to know how this works, read the "Using the <OBJECT> and <EMBED> tags together" sidebar. If you don't really care about the difference, skip the sidebar and keep reading to find out how to use Dreamweaver to add plug-in technologies and set their parameters.

Working with Macromedia Shockwave and Flash Files

Flash and Shockwave are currently among the most widely used plug-in technologies for the Web. Although there are similarities between the two, Macromedia provides a different plug-in for Shockwave and Flash media types. Anyone can download each of these plug-ins separately or get them all in one large plug-in package from the Macromedia Web site. The software that plays Shockwave and Flash is available as both a Netscape plug-in and an ActiveX control for Internet Explorer.

Dreamweaver can handle both Shockwave and Flash (I describe both in more detail later) media types as well as most other media types that use a Netscape plug-in architecture. Other plug-ins from Macromedia include the Authorware plug-in for viewing Authorware media files in the browser. Treat the other file types as you would any other technology not specifically described in this chapter. You can find more on that in the section "Working with Other Plug-In Technologies" later in this chapter.

What is Shockwave?

Macromedia Shockwave for Director enables you to display multimedia files created in Macromedia Director on a Web page. Director is the most popular program around for creating CD-ROMs and other types of multimedia titles, which means that the program has a large following and many people know how to use it. You can recognize a Shockwave file because it uses the extension .DCR. Shockwave is one of the best formats available for creating complex multimedia files, such as games, that include animation, sound, video, and other interactive features like the capability to shoot a target or drive a car. Shockwave has some very powerful capabilities, but it can also be a pretty difficult program to learn, and an even harder one to master.

Though Shockwave for Director has become one of the most popular plug-ins on the Web, there's still a problem with file sizes. Most files created for CD-ROMs are huge by Web standards, and consumers are spoiled by the quality and speed of CD-ROMs. Because of the bandwidth limitations of the Web, developers who create Shockwave files face many limitations. Even though the process of converting Director files to Shockwave results in somewhat reduced file sizes, most developers still stick to small, simple files that download quickly. Still, a few developers create large, complex Shockwave files and hope that their users have the bandwidth, or patience, to enjoy them. As always, when creating high-bandwidth multimedia files, you need to consider the audience that you're targeting and the type of Internet connections that visitors are likely to be using when you decide on file sizes. For more information on creating Shockwave for Director files, visit www.macromedia.com/software/director/.

Using the <OBJECT> and <EMBED> tags together

HTML supports plug-in file formats, such as Macromedia's Shockwave or Flash, through either the <OBJECT> or <EMBED> tag. Both accomplish the same thing, yet each one is designed only for a particular browser. If you're designing Web pages for the broader audience of the World Wide Web, your best option is to use both tags in your HTML because, unfortunately, Netscape and Microsoft have never agreed on a standard. You see, some time ago, the two largest browser makers went off in different directions, with Netscape creating the <EMBED> tag and Microsoft introducing the <OBJECT> tag to accomplish the same goal of displaying plug-in media. Today, the best way to handle the situation is to use both tags when you insert plug-in files.

You can use these HTML tags together because browsers ignore HTML tags that they don't recognize. That means that because Navigator doesn't support the <OBJECT> tag, Navigator doesn't display any file that is embedded using that tag. If there's nothing else in the code that the browser does support, it may just display ugly gray squares in place of the plug-in file — and nobody wants ugly gray squares on a Web page. By using the <OBJECT> and <EMBED> tags together, you can achieve the best designs for the most browsers. For example, you can use the <EMBED> tag options to link an alternate GIF or JPEG image that displays in place of the plug-in file if the browser doesn't support plug-ins or lacks the appropriate plug-in.

If you're writing the code yourself and want to design for optimal results in both browsers, make sure that you nest the <EMBED> tag within the <OBJECT> tag. You should write the tags in this order because browsers that support the <OBJECT> tag, such as Internet Explorer, also support the <EMBED> tag and need to see the <OBJECT> tag first. Browsers that don't support the <OBJECT> tag, such as Navigator, ignore it and read the <EMBED> tag. Here's an example of what the HTML code looks like when you use both tags in combination to embed a Macromedia Flash file:

```
<OBJECT
classid="clsid:D27CDB6E-
AE6D-11cf-96B8-
444553540000"
codebase="http://
active.macromedia.com/
flash2/cabs/
swflash.cab#version=2,0,0,0"
width=100 height=80>
<PARAM name="Movie"
value="filename.swf">
<EMBED src="filename.swf"
width=100 height=80
pluginspage="http://
www.macromedia.com/
shockwave/download/
index.cgi?P1_Prod_Version=
ShockwaveFlash"> </EMBED>
<NOEMBED> <IMG
src="imagename.gif"
width=100 height=80>
</NOEMBED>
</OBJECT>
```

Before you get too worried about how complex the code is, let me reassure you: Dreamweaver creates all of this for you. Just follow the steps in the rest of this chapter and Dreamweaver takes care of the rest. The code example here is just to show you what's happening behind the scenes and to provide an example for those of you who like to code these things by hand.

What is Flash?

You've probably heard a lot about Flash but may be wondering what exactly it is and how it differs from Shockwave. Flash utilizes something called *scaling vector graphics*. This technology means that the graphics in Flash are based on mathematical descriptions that take up far less space than bitmapped graphics like the kind Shockwave uses. Vector graphics can be scaled up or down to fill any size browser window without affecting the image quality or the size of the file that's downloaded. Because of this ability to scale, Flash is perfectly suited for usage on the Web. Flash files can be recognized by their file extension .SWF.

As a format that was designed specifically for the Web, Flash continues to win acclaim and widespread adoption because it enables users to create animations that download really fast. You can also produce scalable, interactive animations with synchronized sound. All that, and you still get smaller file sizes than with any other animation technology on the Web.

So with such great performance on the Web, why would anybody choose Shockwave over Flash? Well, Director is still a far more robust multimedia programming environment than Flash, allowing for much more complicated applications, particularly for games. If you don't have a need for a really high degree of interactive content and you don't relish the steep learning curve of Director, Flash is a better bet. For more on why Flash files download more quickly than other file types, see the sidebar "Download Flash files in a flash."

Inserting Shockwave and Flash movies

In the following section, I assume that you have already created the Shockwave or Flash movie file and that it's ready to be placed into your Web page. If you don't have any movie files to use, you can find sample Flash files on the CD-ROM accompanying this book — just look for the files with the .SWF extension. In the section following this one, I show you how to create Flash buttons and text directly within Dreamweaver.

If you need help using Shockwave or Flash, check out these books: *Shockwave For Dummies,* 2nd Edition, by Greg Harvey and *Flash 4 Bible* by Robert Reinhardt and Jon Warren Lentz (both published by IDG Books Worldwide, Inc.).

To add an existing Shockwave or Flash movie file to a Web page by using Dreamweaver, follow these steps:

1. **Click to insert the cursor where you want the Shockwave or Flash movie to be displayed on your Web page.**

2. From the Objects panel, click the button for either Insert Shockwave, or Insert Flash (see Figure 15-2).

You can also choose Insert⇨Media⇨Shockwave or Insert⇨Media⇨Flash. The Select File dialog box appears in either case.

3. In the dialog box, browse your drive to locate the appropriate movie file that you want inserted into your page.

4. Click to highlight the filename and then click the Select button.

After you click Select, the dialog box closes.

Alternatively, you can also type the name and path to the movie file in the text field under Movie Source. The Shockwave or Flash movie is automatically inserted in the page.

Figure 15-2:
You can insert many different multimedia file types into your documents by clicking the appropriate icon in the Objects panel

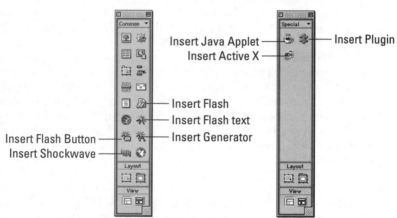

Dreamweaver doesn't display plug-in media files in the editor when first inserted. Instead, you see a small icon that represents the Shockwave or Flash movie file (refer to Figure 15-2). To preview your choice, click the green Play button on the left side of the Property Inspector (if the Inspector is not visible, click the Shockwave or Flash file icon to open it). If you preview the page in your browser, you can also see the Shockwave or Flash movie displayed in context.

5. With the Property Inspector panel visible, specify the width and height of the file in the text fields next to W and H.

You can set many options in the Property Inspector, but only the width and height are required. The next section tells you more about the other options.

Download Flash files in a flash

Flash files are dramatically faster to download because Flash images are vector-based. *Vector-based* means that the images are made up of coded instructions to draw specific geometric shapes, filled with specific colors. This takes far less space than the individual pixel data needed for bitmapped images, such as those used in animated GIFs. As a result, Flash files can be significantly smaller than other types of images and animation files. An animated GIF that's 200K and takes a minute to download on a 33K modem may only be 20K when recreated as a Flash animation. In fact, whole animated cartoon movies that are 10 minutes or more in length can be viewed in Flash over a regular 56K modem. You can find lots more information about creating Flash files at www.macromedia.com/software/flash.

Setting parameters and other options for Shockwave and Flash

Like most HTML tags, the tags that link Shockwave, Flash, and other plug-in files to Web pages have *attributes* (they're called *parameters* when used with the <OBJECT> tag). These parameters are even more important for plug-in files because you must set some of them — such as the height and width — for the file to work properly in a browser. Dreamweaver takes care of setting the height and width, but you may want to change some of the other settings. This section provides a list of attributes and parameters that you can change in the Property Inspector and what those attributes affect.

Don't worry about making sure that you specify property settings for both the <EMBED> and <OBJECT> tags. When you change options in the Property Inspector for either Shockwave or Flash, Dreamweaver automatically applies those changes to both the <EMBED> and <OBJECT> tags.

If you don't see all the options in the Property Inspector, click the expander arrow in the bottom-right corner to display the more advanced options.

Here are the Shockwave and Flash options in the Property Inspector, as shown in Figure 15-3:

> ✔ **Name field:** Use the text field in the top-left corner of the Inspector just to the right of the Shockwave icon if you want to type a name for your file. You can leave this blank or name it whatever you want. Dreamweaver won't apply a name if you leave it blank. This name only identifies the file for scripting.

✔ **W (Width):** Use this option to specify the width of the file. You can change the measurement by typing pc (picas), pt (points), in (inches), mm (millimeters), cm (centimeters), or % (percentage of the original file's value) immediately following the number. Don't put any spaces between the number and the measurement abbreviation.

✔ **H (Height):** Use this option to specify the height of the file. You can change the measurement by typing pc (picas), pt (points), in (inches), mm (millimeters), cm (centimeters), or % (percentage of the original file's value) immediately following the number. Don't put any spaces between the number and the measurement abbreviation.

✔ **File:** Use this text field to enter the name and path to the file. You can change this by typing in a new name or path, or by clicking the folder icon to browse for a file.

✔ **Align:** This option controls the alignment of the file on the page. This setting works the same for plug-in files as for images.

✔ **BgColor:** This option sets a background color that fills the area of the file. This color displays if the specified height and width are larger than the file and during periods when the movie isn't playing, either because it's loading or it has finished playing.

✔ **Play button:** Click the green Play button to preview the Shockwave or Flash file directly in Dreamweaver. This button resembles a right-pointing arrow and is located on the left side of the Property Inspector in the lower half of the window.

✔ **Parameters:** This button provides access to a dialog box where you can enter additional parameters for the Shockwave movie.

✔ **ID:** This optional parameter specifies the ActiveX ID. This parameter is used to pass information between ActiveX controls. Consult the documentation for the ActiveX control you're using to find out which parameters to use here.

✔ **Border:** This sets the width of the border around the file.

✔ **V Space (Vertical Space):** If you want blank space above or below the file, enter the number of pixels here.

✔ **H Space (Horizontal Space):** If you want blank space on either side of the file, enter the number of pixels here.

The following options are unique to Flash, so they aren't available in the Property Inspector for Shockwave files.

✔ **Reset Size:** Because Flash files can be scaled without losing any image quality, it's common to scale a Flash file on a Web page to a different size from the size it was created at. Clicking this button reverts the Flash file to the original size at which is was created.

Figure 15-3:
The
Property
Inspectors
for
Shockwave
and Flash
files let you
specify how
files are
displayed.
You can also
click play to
preview the
animation.

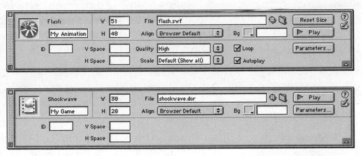

✔ **Quality:** This option enables you to prioritize the antialiasing options of your images versus the speed of playback. *Antialiasing,* which makes your files appear smoother, can slow down the rendering of each frame because the computer must first smooth the edges. The Quality parameter enables you to regulate how much the process is slowed down by letting you set priorities based on the importance of appearance versus playback speed.

You can choose from the following Quality options:

- **Low:** With this option, antialiasing is never used. Playback speed has priority over appearance.

- **High:** With this option, antialiasing is always used. Appearance has priority over playback speed.

- **Autohigh:** A somewhat more sophisticated option, Autohigh sets playback to begin with antialiasing turned on. However, if the actual frame rate supported by the user's computer drops below your specified frame rate, antialiasing automatically turns off to improve playback speed. This option emphasizes playback speed and appearance equally at first but sacrifices appearance for the sake of playback speed, if necessary.

- **Autolow:** With this option, playback begins with antialiasing turned off. If the Flash player detects that the processor can handle it, antialiasing is turned on. Use this option to emphasize speed at first but improve appearance whenever possible.

✔ **Scale:** Specify this option only if you use percentages for the Height and Width parameter. The Scale parameter enables you to define how the Flash movie displays within the boundaries of the area specified in the browser window.

Flash movies are scaleable. With the Scale option, you can specify the original dimensions in pixels or in percentages of a browser window in the W (width) and H (height) fields. This enables you to control how the Flash movie displays if a browser window is a different size from your original design. For example, if you always want your Flash movie to take up a quarter of the screen (no matter how large the screen is), set it to 25%; if you want it to always fill the screen, set it to 100%.

Because using a percentage can lead to undesired effects (such as cropping or distorting a file to make it fit), the following options in the Scale drop-down list enable you to set preferences about how a scaled Flash movie displays within the window:

- **Show all:** This option enables the entire movie to display in the specified area. The width and height proportions of the original movie are maintained and no distortion occurs, but borders may appear on two sides of the movie to fill the space.

- **No border:** This option enables you to scale a Flash movie to fill a specified area. Again, the original width and height proportions are maintained and no distortion occurs, but portions of the movie may be cropped.

- **Exact fit:** Using this option, the entire movie is visible in the specified area. However, the Flash movie may be distorted because the width and height proportions may be stretched or shrunk in order to fit the movie in the specified area.

- ✔ **Loop:** Checking this box causes the Flash file to repeat (or loop). If you don't check this box, the Flash movie stops after it reaches the last frame.

- ✔ **Autoplay:** This controls the Play parameter, enabling you to determine whether a Flash movie starts as soon as it downloads to the viewer's computer or whether a user must click a button or take another action to start the Flash movie. A check in this box causes the movie to automatically start to play as soon as the page finishes loading. If you don't check this box, whatever option you've set in the Flash file (such as onMouseOver or onMouseDown) is required to start the movie.

Creating Flash Files from within Dreamweaver

A new feature in Dreamweaver 4 is the ability to create and edit simple Flash files from within Dreamweaver, which is really great because not only can you utilize Flash in your Web site without having to buy another program, but you don't have to learn another program, either. Though you can't create any really fancy Flash animations, this feature still allows you to create graphical text objects and cool Flash buttons using the familiar Dreamweaver interface. Dreamweaver inlcudes a large library of existing Flash objects that you can use and, even better, because the Macromedia Flash Objects architecture is extensible, you can download new Flash styles from the Web or work with Flash developers to create new Flash objects for you to use in Dreamweaver.

Creating Flash text

With the Flash text object, you can create and insert a Flash (.swf) text movie into your document. Flash text movies allow you to utilize a vector-based text graphic in the font of your choice (*vector-based* means that the images are made up of coded instructions to draw specific geometric shapes). The great advantage to using Flash text is that you can utilize any fonts you want without worrying whether or not your audience has the same font on their computer. You can also set a rollover effect without the need to create separate images, and the size of the text can scale up or down without any effect on image quality or file size.

To insert a Flash text object follow these steps:

1. **Save your Dreamweaver document.**

   The document must be saved before you can insert a Flash text object.

2. **Click the Insert Flash Text icon in the Objects panel (see Figure 15-2).**

   Or you can select Insert⇨Interactive Images⇨Flash Text.

   The Flash Text dialog box appears, as pictured in Figure 15-4.

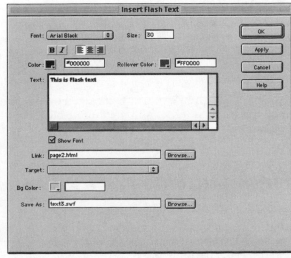

Figure 15-4: The Insert Flash Text dialog box lets you create and edit interactive Flash text within Dreamweaver.

A word about Generator

Macromedia Generator is an advanced programming application for creating dynamic Flash applications that integrate with databases. Because Generator is a pretty high-level program, I won't devote time to it in this book, but you should know that Generator files are treated just like other media files in Dreamweaver. To insert a Generator file into a Dreamweaver document, choose Insert➪Media➪Generator or click the Insert Generator button on the Common Objects panel.

---

3. **Select the desired Text options including font, style, size, color, alignment, and so on.**

    To see the text previewed in your font of choice, check the box next to Show Font. The other options are defined below.

    • **Rollover Color** indicates the color that the text should change to when the user rolls the mouse over the text. If you don't want a rollover effect, make the rollover color the same color.

    • The **Link** and **Target** can be set for the text using the appropriate fields. The link is activated when the user clicks on the text.

    • Make the **Bg Color** (background color) the same as the background color of the Web page you're placing the text on.

    • For **Save As,** always save the file with the .swf extension as you will actually be creating a Flash file. Browse your drive to indicate where you want to save the Flash file.

4. **When you're done selecting the appropriate options, click OK to insert the text.**

    You can also click Apply to see the effects in your Dreamweaver document before clicking OK.

    The dialog box closes and the Flash text is inserted on the page. To edit the text again or change any of the options, double-click the Flash text to open the dialog box.

Creating Flash buttons

Even more exciting than Flash text are Flash buttons. Flash buttons are pre-created graphics that can be customized and used as interactive buttons on your Web sites. Like Flash text, Flash buttons are made up of vector graphics and can be scaled and resized without any degradation in quality.

Dreamweaver ships with a library of over 50 button styles for you to use. You can also add styles by downloading them from the Web or creating your own in Flash.

To insert a Flash button follow these steps:

1. Save your Dreamweaver document.

The document must be saved before you can insert a Flash button object.

2. Click the Insert Flash Button icon in the Objects panel (see Figure 15-2).

Or you can select Insert⇨Interactive Images⇨Flash Button.

The Flash Button dialog box appears, as shown in Figure 15-5.

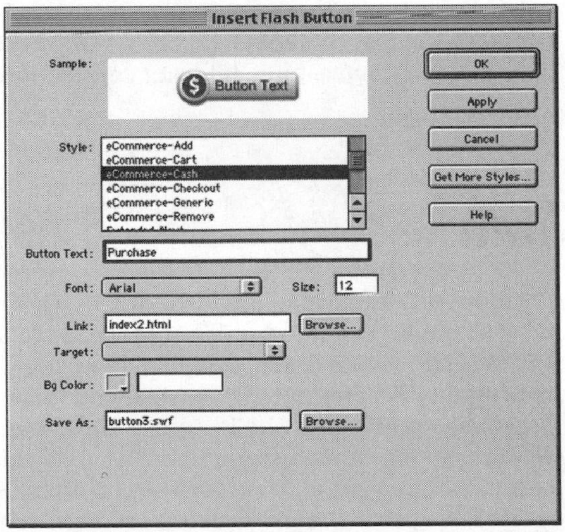

Figure 15-5:
The Insert Flash Button dialog box lets you create and edit interactive Flash button graphics within Dreamweaver.

3. In the Style field, scroll to select the type of button you want to use.

You can view the currently selected choice in the Sample field.

4. Select the appropriate options to customize your button.

Enter the text you want to use in the Button Text field or leave this blank if you don't want any text on the button. Select the other text options including font, style, size, color, alignment, and so on.

Select the link, target, and background colors in the appropriate fields if applicable.

Always save the file with the .swf extension as you will actually be creating a Flash file. Browse your drive to indicate where you want to save the Flash file.

5. When you're done setting the options, click OK to insert the button.

You can also click Apply to see the effects in your Dreamweaver document before clicking OK.

The dialog box closes and the button is inserted on the page. To edit the button again or change any of the options, double-click the button to open the dialog box.

Adding new button styles

Because the Macromedia Flash Objects architecture is extensible, you can download new Flash styles from the Web or work with Flash developers to create new Flash objects for you to use in Dreamweaver. To get more styles from the Macromedia Exchange Web site, click the "Get More Styles" button in the Insert Flash Button dialog box. Clicking this button launches your Web browser and connects you to the Macromedia Exchange site where you can download more buttons (you must have a live Internet connection for this to work).

Working with Java

Java is a programming language, like Pascal, Basic, C, or C++, that you can use to create programs that run on a computer. What makes Java special is that it can run on any computer system and it can display in your browser. Usually, if you create a program in a computer language, you have to create one version for the Macintosh, another for the PC, and a third for UNIX. But Java, created by Sun Microsystems, is platform-independent so that developers can use it to create almost any kind of program — even complex programs like word processors or spreadsheets — that work on any type of computer without having to customize the code for each platform. Normally, programs also run independently of each other. But with Java, the programs (also called *applets*) can run within a Web browser, allowing the program to interact with different elements of the page or with other pages on the Web. This has made Java very popular because it provides a way to add more sophisticated capabilities to Web browsers regardless of which operating system the Web browser is running on. You can embed Java applets in Web pages, you can use Java to generate entire Web pages, or you can run Java applications separately after they download.

To find out more about Java, check out *Java For Dummies,* 3rd Edition, by Aaron E. Walsh (published by IDG Books Worldwide, Inc.).

Inserting Java applets

To insert a Java applet in your Web page, follow these steps:

1. **Click to insert the cursor where you want the applet to display on your Web page.**

2. **From the Objects panel, click the button for Java applets (the button looks like a little coffee cup).**

   Alternatively, you can also choose Insert⇨Media⇨Applet.

   The Insert Applet dialog box appears.

3. **Use the Browse button to locate the Java applet file that you want inserted in the page.**

4. **Click to highlight the filename, click the Select button, and then click OK to close the dialog box.**

   You can also type in the name and path to the file in the text box under Java Class Source. The applet automatically links to the page.

   Dreamweaver doesn't display applets in the editor. Instead, you see a small icon that represents the applet (the icon looks like the coffee cup icon you see in the Objects panel). To view the applet on your Web page (the only way to see the applet in action), preview the page in a browser, such as Navigator 4.0 and higher or Internet Explorer 4.0 and higher, that supports applets.

5. **Double-click the Applet icon to open the Property Inspector.**

   You can set many options in the Property Inspector. If you want to know more about these options, read on.

Setting Java parameters and other options

Like other file formats that require plug-ins or advanced browser support, Java applets come with the following options (see Figure 15-6):

- ✔ **Applet Name:** Use this field in the top-left corner if you want to type a name for your applet. Dreamweaver does not apply a name if you leave this field blank. This name identifies the applet for scripting.

- ✔ **W (Width):** This option specifies the width of the applet. You can change the measurement by typing pc (picas), pt (points), in (inches), mm (millimeters), cm (centimeters), or % (percentage of the original file's value) immediately following the number. Don't put any spaces between the number and the measurement abbreviation.

✔ **H (Height):** This option specifies the height of the applet. You can change the measurement by typing pc (picas), pt (points), in (inches), mm (millimeters), cm (centimeters), or % (percentage of the original file's value) immediately following the number. Don't put any spaces between the number and the measurement abbreviation.

✔ **Code:** Dreamweaver automatically enters the code when you insert the file. Code specifies the content file of the applet. You may type in your own filename or click the folder icon to choose a file.

✔ **Base:** Automatically entered when you insert the file, Base identifies the folder that contains the applet. You may type in your own directory name.

✔ **Align:** This option determines how the object aligns on the page.

✔ **Alt:** This option enables you to specify an alternate file, such as an image that's displayed if the viewer's browser doesn't support Java. That way, the user doesn't see just a broken file icon. If you type text into this field, the viewer will see this text; Dreamweaver writes it into the code by using the Alt attribute of the Applet tag. If you use the folder icon to select an image, the viewer sees an image; Dreamweaver automatically inserts an <IMG> tag within the open and close tags of the applet.

✔ **V Space (Vertical Space):** If you want blank space above or below the applet, enter the number of pixels that you want.

✔ **H Space (Horizontal Space):** If you want blank space on either side of the applet, enter the number of pixels that you want.

✔ **Parameters:** Click this button to access a dialog box in which you can enter additional parameters for the applet.

Figure 15-6:
The
Property
Inspector
lets you
specify
options for
Java
applets.

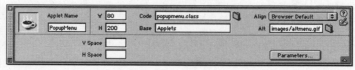

You can find lots more information on JavaScript in *JavaScript For Dummies,* 2nd Edition, by Emily A. Vander Veer (published by IDG Books Worldwide, Inc.).

Using ActiveX Objects and Controls

Microsoft ActiveX objects and controls are reusable components similar to miniature applications that can act like browser plug-ins. Because they only work in Internet Explorer on the Windows platform, they haven't been widely accepted on the Web. As a result, no clear standard for identifying ActiveX objects and controls exists. Still, Dreamweaver supports using ActiveX and provides some flexibility so that you can set the parameters for the ActiveX control that you use, should you decide to use them.

The ActiveX Property Inspector provides the following options (see Figure 15-7):

Figure 15-7:
The Property Inspector lets you specify options for ActiveX objects and controls.

✔ **Name text field:** Use the text field in the top-left corner of the Inspector just to the right of the ActiveX icon if you want to type a name for your ActiveX object. You can leave this blank or name it whatever you want. Dreamweaver does not provide a name if you leave it blank. This name identifies the ActiveX object only for scripting purposes.

✔ **W (Width):** You can specify the measurement of an ActiveX object by typing pc (picas), pt (points), in (inches), mm (millimeters), cm (centimeters), or % (percentage of the original file's value) immediately after the number. Don't put any spaces between the number and the measurement abbreviation.

✔ **H (Height):** You can specify the measurement of an ActiveX object by typing pc (picas), pt (points), in (inches), mm (millimeters), cm (centimeters), or % (percentage of the original file's value) immediately following the number. Don't put any spaces between the number and the measurement abbreviation.

✔ **ClassID:** The browser uses the ClassID to identify the ActiveX control. You can type any value or choose any of these options from the drop-down list: RealPlayer, Shockwave for Director, and Shockwave for Flash.

✔ **Embed:** Checking this box tells Dreamweaver to add an <EMBED> tag within the <OBJECT> tag. The <EMBED> tag activates a Netscape plug-in equivalent, if available, and makes your pages more accessible to Navigator users. Dreamweaver automatically sets the values that you've entered for ActiveX properties to the Embed tag for any equivalent Netscape plug-in.

✔ **Src (Source):** This option identifies the file to be associated with the <EMBED> tag and used by a Netscape plug-in.

✔ **Align:** This option specifies how the object aligns on the page.

✔ **Parameters:** Click this button to access a dialog box in which you can enter additional parameters for the ActiveX controls.

✔ **V Space (Vertical Space):** If you want blank space above or below the object, enter the number of pixels that you want.

✔ **H Space (Horizontal Space):** If you want blank space on either side of the object, enter the number of pixels that you want.

✔ **Base:** This option enables you to specify a URL for the ActiveX control so that Internet Explorer can automatically download the control if it's not installed in the user's system.

✔ **ID:** This option identifies an optional ActiveX ID parameter. Consult the documentation for the ActiveX control you're using to find out which parameters to use.

✔ **Data:** This option enables you to specify a data file for the ActiveX control to load.

✔ **Alt Img:** This option enables you to link an image that displays if the browser doesn't support the <OBJECT> tag.

JavaScript is not Java

JavaScript, a scripting language that many people often confuse with Java, has little in common with Java other than its name and some syntactic similarities in the way that the language works. To be more accurate, think of JavaScript as a much-simplified relative of Java with far fewer capabilities. Unlike Java, though, you can write JavaScript directly into HTML code to create interactive features, but you can't use it to create stand-alone applets and programs as you can in Java. You won't get the complex functionality of Java, but JavaScript is a lot easier to use and doesn't require a plug-in.

JavaScript is often used in combination with other multimedia elements on the page, such as images or sound files, to add greater levels of interactivity. Dynamic HTML also uses JavaScript and is covered in Chapters 12 and 13. In these chapters, you can read about how to use Dreamweaver to apply behaviors and other features created by using JavaScript together with HTML.

Working with Other Plug-In Technologies

So many plug-ins, so little bandwidth. You can find literally hundreds of plug-ins available for Web pages. Some of them give you fabulous results, such as sound, video, a variety of image formats, and even three-dimensional worlds and animations. But with plug-ins — perhaps more than with any other technology on the Web — you have to be very careful. Web page visitors aren't usually excited about having to download a new plug-in, even if you as a Web site creator are excited about deploying it. Indeed, many visitors are scared off by the idea and others are just plain annoyed, while others lack the hardware or software requirements to run them. Don't risk doing that to your viewers unless you have a compelling reason.

If I visited your site, I wouldn't be happy if you sent me off to get a plug-in just so I could see your logo spinning around in all its three-dimensional splendor. On the other hand, if your site features interactive games or a three-dimensional environment with chat capability targeted for users with those interests, I may be quite happy to get a plug-in that enables me to experience something as interesting as a multi-user game or interactive environment. Make sure that you let your users know what they're in for before you send them off on a plug-in adventure. You're also wise to stick to the better known plug-in technologies — such as QuickTime, RealAudio, RealVideo, and the Shockwave/Flash suite — because users are more likely to already have them or appreciate the benefit of getting them because they know that they can use them on other sites.

Inserting Netscape Navigator plug-ins

Because Netscape invented the idea of browser plug-ins, most plug-ins use Netscape's original specifications to create new browser plug-ins. In most cases, Netscape Navigator plug-ins also function in Internet Explorer. Some of the more popular plug-ins include RealAudio, RealVideo, Quicktime, and Beatnik, as well as Flash and Shockwave, which are also considered Navigator plug-ins.

To use Dreamweaver to insert a Netscape-compatible plug-in file other than Flash or Shockwave into your Web page, follow these steps:

1. **Click to insert the cursor where you want the file to display on your Web page.**

2. **From the Objects panel, click the button for Netscape Plug-Ins (the button looks like a puzzle piece).**

   You can also choose Insert⇨Media⇨Plugin.

   The Select File dialog box appears.

3. **Browse your drive to locate the plug-in media file that you want inserted in your page and click to select it.**

4. **Click the Select button and then click OK to close the dialog box.**

   You can also type in the name and path to the file in the text field under Plug-in Source. The file is automatically inserted in the page and you see a small icon that represents the file (the icon looks like the puzzle piece icon in the Objects panel).

5. **Double-click the Plug-in icon to open the Property Inspector.**

   You can set many options in the Property Inspector. If you want to know more about these options, continue reading the next section.

6. **Preview the plug-in.**

   Dreamweaver doesn't display plug-in files in the editor unless the plug-ins are installed on your computer and you click the green Play button in the Property Inspector. To view the plug-in file in Dreamweaver, click the Play button in the Property Inspector and it displays in the Document window.

Setting Netscape plug-in parameters and other options

You can specify the following settings in the Plug-In Property Inspector (see Figure 15-8):

- ✔ **Name text field:** Use the text field in the top-left corner of the Inspector just to the right of the plug-in icon if you want to type a name for your plug-in file. You can leave this blank or provide any name you want. Dreamweaver does not provide a name if you leave this field blank. This name identifies the file only for scripting purposes.

- ✔ **W (Width):** You can specify the measurement of any Netscape plug-in by typing pc (picas), pt (points), in (inches), mm (millimeters), cm (centimeters), or % (percentage of the original file's value) immediately following the number. Don't put any spaces between the number and the measurement abbreviation.

- ✔ **H (Height):** You can specify the measurement of any Netscape plug-in by typing pc (picas), pt (points), in (inches), mm (millimeters), cm (centimeters), or % (percentage of the original file's value) immediately following the number. Don't put any spaces between the number and the measurement abbreviation.

  For most plug-ins, the height and width tags are required. However, in some cases, such as sound files that don't display on a page, you can't specify height and width.

Figure 15-8:
The
Property
Inspector
lets you
specify
options for
Netscape
plug-ins.

- **Src (Source):** This option specifies the name and path to the plug-in file. You can type in a filename, or click the folder icon to browse for the file.

- **Plg URL:** This option enables you to provide a URL where viewers can download a plug-in if they don't already have it.

- **Align:** This option enables you to specify how the element aligns on the page.

- **Alt:** Here, you can provide alternate content that displays if the viewer's browser doesn't support the `<EMBED>` tag. You can link an image as an alternative or simply type text that displays in place of the plug-in file.

- **Play button:** Click the green Play button (the right-pointing arrow on the left side of the Property Inspector) to preview the media file. The media plug-in must be installed either in Dreamweaver (in the Configuration/Plugins folder) or in one of the browsers on your computer for it to preview in Dreamweaver.

- **V Space (Vertical Space):** If you want blank space above and below the plug-in, enter the number of pixels that you want.

- **H Space (Horizontal Space):** If you want blank space on either side of the plug-in, enter the number of pixels that you want.

- **Border:** This option specifies the width of the border around the file.

- **Parameters:** Click this button to access a dialog box in which you can enter additional parameters for the plug-in file. To enter a parameter, click the plus (+) button and enter the parameter name in the parameter column as well as the corresponding value in the value column. See the documentation for the plug-in media type that you're using for information on the parameters that it utilizes.

Chapter 16

Forms Follow Function

• •

• •

Many powerful and interactive Web sites are adorned with HTML forms. Whether they create a simple text box that provides the interface to a search engine or a long registration form that collects valuable consumer information from visitors, HTML forms are a crucial part of any sophisticated site these days.

The HTML tags used to create forms — from radio buttons to drop-down lists — are a different kind of tag designed to work in conjunction with more complex programming on your server. These programs are called CGI *(Common Gateway Interface)* scripts.

Whether you want to create a simple guest book or a complicated online shopping cart system, you need to know how to set up the text areas, radio buttons, and drop-down lists that make up an HTML form. Fortunately, Dreamweaver makes creating forms easy by including a special toolbar on the Objects panel to provide quick access to common form elements.

In this chapter, I introduce you to the kinds of forms commonly used on the Web and show you how to use Dreamweaver to create them. I also explain a little about the CGI scripts required to process forms, how they work, and where you can get scripts for your Web site.

Understanding how CGI scripts work

Think of CGI scripts as the engine behind an HTML form and many other automated features on a Web site. CGI (or Common Gateway Interface) scripts are programs that are usually written in a programming language, such as Perl, Java, C, or C++. These scripts are much more complex to create than HTML pages, and these languages take much longer to learn than HTML. CGI scripts reside and run on the server and are usually triggered by an action that a user makes, such as clicking the Submit button in an HTML form.

A common scenario with a script may go like this:

1. The user loads a page, such as a guest book, fills out the HTML form, and clicks the Submit button.

2. That action triggers the CGI script on the server to gather the data entered into the form, format it, place it in an e-mail message, and send it to a specified e-mail address.

In Dreamweaver, you can easily create HTML forms and the Submit buttons that go with them — you can even use the new code editor in Dreamweaver 4 to write CGI scripts — but you have to know a programming language to do so. If you know Perl, JAVA, C, or C++, writing most simple CGI scripts isn't that hard. But if you

don't know one of these programming languages, you're probably better off hiring someone else to do it for you or downloading ready-made scripts from the Web. If you search the Web for CGI scripts, you can find that many programmers write them and then give them away for free. Be aware, however, that you still have to install these scripts on your server and almost always have to alter the programming code at least a little to tailor them to work with your unique system. You may also need to contact your Internet Service Provider *(ISP)* to help you load the script on the server because many commercial service providers won't give you access to do it yourself.

Many ISPs make basic CGI scripts (such as guest-book forms and simple shopping-cart systems) available to their customers as part of membership. This is an easy way to get scripts for your Web site and may even be worth changing ISPs for if your current ISP doesn't offer the scripts you want. Most ISPs that offer CGI scripts provide instructions for using them on their Web sites. These instructions include the location of the script on the server. You must include this information in your HTML form so that the Submit button triggers the proper script. You can find more information about setting your HTML form to work with a script in the section "Creating HTML Forms" later in this chapter.

Appreciating What HTML Forms Can Do for You

Forms follow function, to paraphrase the old saying. On the Web, forms are an integral part of the function of many interactive features. By using forms, Web designers can collect information about users — information that they can then use in a variety of ways. Here are a few of the common forms that you might want to create for your Web site.

Signing in with a guest book

The most common form on the Web is the simple *guest book*. Guest books usually include a few fields to collect basic contact information, such as name, e-mail address, and comments or feedback about the Web site. Once collected, this information can be sent via e-mail to the Web site administrator or anyone else who wants to collect it, or it can be stored on the server or added to a database. The CGI script that makes a guest book work is usually a basic e-mail script, meaning that the script collects the data and e-mails the data to a specified address. More-complex guest book systems may automatically add comments to a Web page, generating a list of messages from viewers that can be read by other viewers.

Gathering information using surveys and feedback forms

Using the same kind of CGI scripts as guest books, *feedback forms* and *surveys* collect information from users. Feedback forms and surveys differ from guest books in that they generally include a list of questions designed to gather specific information, rather than just a text area for general comments. A survey may ask such questions as where you purchased a product, what you like or dislike about a product or service, and any other questions that the designers (or their clients) want to ask.

Checking out with a shopping-cart system

Most sophisticated commerce sites that sell products include an online shopping system, which is often called a *shopping cart* because it works like a shopping cart at a grocery store. Online shopping cart systems can be as simple as an order form that lists products and quantities and then tabulates the total purchase price or as complex as a system that lets users keep track of products as they navigate through a Web site and then pay for all the products they've chosen when they're done shopping. Although the engine that drives a shopping system is complex, the order forms and other pages are basic HTML forms that you can create in Dreamweaver.

Conversing in discussion areas and chat rooms

Online discussion areas and chat rooms enable users to post comments that others can read, creating ongoing typed "conversations" that take place on a Web site. Also called conferencing systems, *discussion areas* enable users to post comments that other users can read. These comments are archived so that users can review one another's messages and conversations can take place over time. *Chat rooms,* in contrast, let users contribute comments that are immediately posted to a Web site, enabling conversations to take place in real time. These conversations are generally not archived, so users must be logged on to the site to read comments as they are entered by other users. Creating the interface for a chat room or discussion area is easy, you use HTML form tags to create the text areas and submit buttons described in detail later in this chapter.

Finding what you need using search engines

Whenever you type a keyword into a search text field, you enter information into a simple HTML form. The text box and the search button, which is really a submit button, are both form elements that you can easily add to a Web page with Dreamweaver. When a user submits information to a search engine, a CGI script runs, which compares the information entered (usually keywords) with a collection of information, such as all the text on the rest of the Web site, and then produces a list of results that match.

Generating dynamic Web pages

Connecting a database to a Web site enables Web developers to create the most dynamic systems. Database systems serve many purposes, such as enabling salespeople in the field to search through products in a database and get up-to-the-minute pricing and availability. The most complex database systems collect information about users, such as buying habits and preferences, and then use the information to automatically create Web pages specific to each user when they visit the site.

Setting up secure commerce systems

Many shopping-cart systems link to *secure commerce systems*. By using encryption technology, secure commerce systems encode data (such as credit card numbers and customer addresses) that's entered into a form, making it difficult for anyone to steal the information as it travels over the Internet. These systems often connect to financial systems, such as Cybercash and Checkfree, that can process orders online, immediately approve or deny a credit card, and transfer funds to the appropriate bank account for the amount of the transaction. To make this easier for businesses, many ISPs now offer e-commerce solutions, designed to help you coordinate all of these requirements. Check the Web site of your service provider to find out more.

Creating HTML Forms

The basic elements of HTML forms, such as radio buttons, check boxes, and text areas, are easy to create with Dreamweaver, as I demonstrate in the sections that follow. But remember, your form won't work unless it links to a CGI script. Although Dreamweaver doesn't provide any scripts, it does make linking your HTML forms to a CGI script easy (for more on scripts, see the sidebar "Understanding how CGI scripts work"). You need to know where the script resides on the server to set this link. The name and location of the script depend on your server, but for the purposes of showing you how to link to a script with Dreamweaver, assume that the script you need to link to is called guestbook.pl (the .pl indicates that the script was written in Perl) and that the script is located in a folder on the server called cgi-bin (a common name for the folder that holds these kinds of scripts).

The following steps walk you through linking any form to this sample script. To use these steps with a different script, simply change the name of the script and the name of the directory location to reflect your system. Start with an open page — either a new page or one you want to add a form to.

1. **Choose Insert⇨Form.**

   You can also select the Form icon from the Forms Objects panel, as shown in Figure 16-1. This handy option reveals all the form elements that you may want to add as you create your form.

   A blank form in Dreamweaver shows up as a rectangle outlined by a red dotted line, like the one in Figure 16-1. This dotted line is used by Dreamweaver to indicate that an area is defined as a form in the HTML code.

2. **Click the red outline to select the form and display the form options in the Property Inspector (also shown in Figure 16-1).**

3. **Type a name in the Form Name text box.**

   You can choose any name for this field. The name is used by scripting languages, such as JavaScript or VBScript, to identify the form.

4. **Type the directory name and the name of the script in the Action text box.**

   Using the sample script I describe earlier, type **/cgi-bin/guestbook.pl** to specify the path to the Perl script in the cgi-bin directory. You can only use the folder icon in the Property Inspector to set this link if you have a copy of the script on your computer in the same relative location in which it resides on the server. Usually, you have to enter this by typing the directory and filename into the text box. Make sure that you specify the entire path (you should get this information from your system administrator or Internet Service Provider).

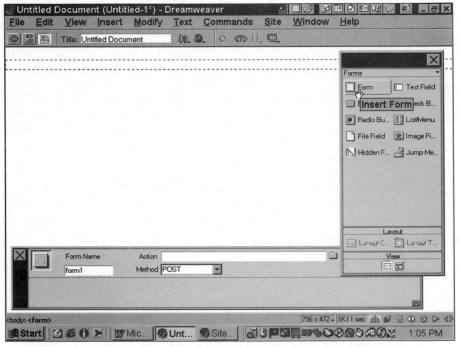

Figure 16-1:
The Objects
panel
provides
easy access
to all of the
common
form
elements.

5. **In the Property Inspector, use the Method drop-down list box to choose Default, Get, or Post.**

   The Get and Post options control how the form works. The option you use depends on the kind of CGI script that you use on your server. Get this information from your system administrator, programmer, or Internet Service Provider.

These are just the preliminary steps that you need to take to create a form. When you establish the boundaries of a form, as represented by the dotted red line that appears after Step 1, Dreamweaver creates the code that goes in the background of your form and enables it to interact with a script on your server. The rest of this chapter shows you how to add various form elements, such as text boxes, radio buttons, and drop-down list boxes.

Comparing radio buttons and check boxes

Radio buttons and check boxes make it easier for viewers of your site to fill in a form. Instead of making users type in a word, such as *yes* or *no,* you can provide radio buttons and check boxes so that the user can simply click a box or button.

What's the difference between radio buttons and check boxes? Radio buttons enable users to select only one option from a group. Thus, radio buttons are good for yes/no options or options in which you want users to make only one choice. Check boxes, on the other hand, enable users to make multiple choices, so they're good for "choose all that apply" situations when users may make multiple choices.

Creating radio buttons

To create radio buttons on a form, follow these steps:

1. **Click your form to select it.**

   If you haven't yet created a form, follow the steps in the previous section "Creating HTML Forms."

2. **Click the Radio Button icon on the Forms Objects panel.**

   You can also choose Insert⇨Form Object⇨Radio Button. Either way, a radio button appears inside the form's perimeter.

3. **Repeat Step 2 until you have the number of radio buttons that you want.**

4. **Select one of the radio buttons on the form to reveal the radio button's properties in the Property Inspector, as shown in Figure 16-2.**

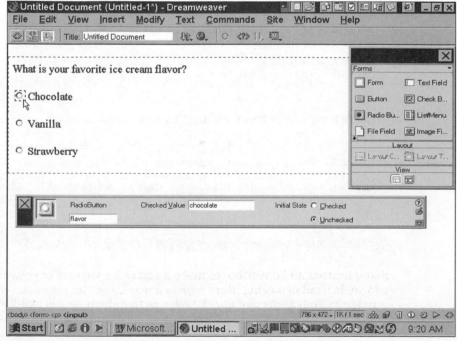

Figure 16-2: Radio buttons are best for multiple-choice options when you want to restrict users to only one choice.

5. **Type a name in the RadioButton text box.**

   All radio buttons in a group should have the same name to enable the script to identify the response and limit selections to one button.

6. **Type a name in the Checked Value text box.**

   Each radio button in a group should have a different Checked Value name so that the CGI script can distinguish them. Naming them for the thing they represent is usually best — "yes" when the choice is yes and "no" when it's no. Or, in the case of the example in Figure 16-2, each radio button is named for the ice cream flavor that the button represents. This name is usually included in the data that you get back when the form is processed and returned to you (often in an e-mail message). How the data is returned depends on the CGI script. If you're looking at the data later, it's easier to interpret if the name means something that makes sense to you.

7. **Choose Checked or Unchecked next to Initial State.**

   These two buttons determine whether the radio button on your form appears already selected when the Web page loads. Choose Checked if you want to preselect a choice. A user can always override this preselection by choosing another radio button.

8. **Select the other radio buttons one by one and repeat Steps 5 through 7 to specify the properties in the Property Inspector for each one.**

Creating check boxes

To create check boxes, follow these steps:

1. **Click your form to select it.**

   If you haven't yet created a form, follow the steps in the section "Creating HTML Forms."

2. **Click the Check Box icon on the Forms Objects panel.**

   You can also choose Insert⇨Form Object⇨Check Box.

3. **Repeat Step 2 to place as many check boxes as you want.**

4. **Select one of the check boxes on your form to reveal the check box properties in the Property Inspector, as shown in Figure 16-3.**

5. **Type a name in the CheckBox text box.**

   You can use the same name you use for other check boxes or a distinct name for each one.

6. **Type a name in the Checked Value text box.**

   Each check box in a group should have a different Checked Value name so that the CGI script can distinguish them. Naming them for the thing they represent is usually best. In Figure 16-3, you can see that I named the Rock option on the form as *Rock* in the Property Inspector. As with radio buttons, the Checked Value is usually included in the data you get back when the form is processed and returned to you. If you're looking at the data later, it's easier to interpret if the name means something that makes sense to you.

7. **Choose Checked or Unchecked next to Initial State.**

   This option determines whether the check box appears already selected when the Web page loads. Choose Checked if you want to preselect a choice. A user can always override this preselection by clicking the text box again to deselect it.

8. **Select the other check boxes one by one and repeat Steps 5 through 7 to set the properties in the Property Inspector for each one.**

Adding text fields

When you want users to enter text, such as a name, e-mail address, or comment, use a text field. To insert text fields, follow these steps:

1. **Click your form to select it.**

   If you haven't yet created a form, follow the steps in the section "Creating HTML Forms."

2. **Click the Text Field icon from the Forms Objects panel.**

   You can also choose Insert⇨Form Object⇨Text Field. A text field box appears.

3. **On your form, click to place your cursor next to the first text field and type a question or other text prompt.**

   For example, you may want to type *Address:* next to a text box where you want a user to enter an address.

4. **Select the text field on your form to reveal the text field properties in the Property Inspector, as shown in Figure 16-4.**

5. **Type a name in the TextField text box.**

   Each text area on a form should have a different text field name so that the CGI script can distinguish them. Naming them for the thing they represent is usually best. In Figure 16-4, you can see that I named the Address option *Address*. Many scripts return this name next to the contents of the text field a visitor enters at your Web site. If you're looking at the data later, it's easier to interpret if the name corresponds to the choice.

6. **In the Char Width box, type the number of characters you want users to be able to type in the field.**

   This determines the width of the text field that appears on the page. In Figure 16-4, I entered 52 to make it wide enough for a person to enter an address.

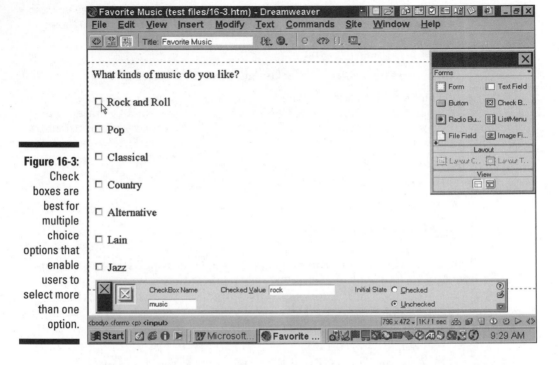

Figure 16-3:
Check
boxes are
best for
multiple
choice
options that
enable
users to
select more
than one
option.

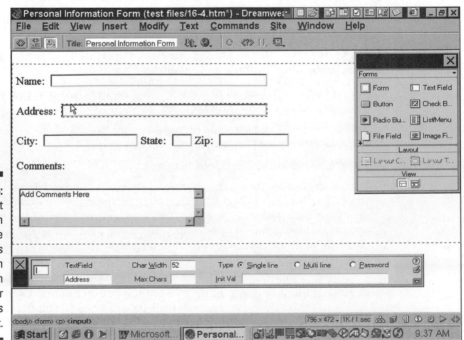

Figure 16-4:
Use the Text
Field option
to create
form fields
in which
users can
enter one or
more lines
of text.

7. Type the maximum number of characters that you want to allow in the Max Chars box.

If you leave this field blank, the user can type as many characters as they choose. I usually only limit the number of characters if I want to maintain consistency in the data. For example, I like to limit the State field to a two-character abbreviation.

You can set the Char Width to be longer or shorter than the Max Chars. You may choose to make these different if you want to maintain a certain display area because it looks better in the design but you want to enable users to add more information if they choose to. If the user typed more characters than could display in the area, the text would scroll so the user could still see the end of the text they were typing.

8. Next to Type, choose Single Line, Multi Line, and/or Password.

- Choose **Single Line** if you want to create a one-line text box, such as the kind I created for the Name and Address fields in Figure 16-4.

- Choose **Multi Line** if you want to give users space to enter text, such as the box I created for Comments in Figure 16-4. (Note that if you choose Multi Line, you also need to specify the number of lines that you want the text area to cover by typing a number in the Num Lines field, which appears as an option when you choose Multi Line.)

- Choose **Password** if this is a text line in which you ask a user to enter data that you don't want displayed on the screen. This causes entered data to appear as asterisks.

9. In the Init Val text box, type any text that you want displayed when the form loads.

For example, in Figure 16-4, the words `Add comments here` are displayed on the form in the text field under Comments. These words were typed in the Init Val field of the Property Inspector for the Comments text field. Your users can delete the Init Value text or leave it and add more text to it.

10. Select the other text areas one by one and repeat Steps 5 through 9 to set the properties in the Property Inspector for each one.

Netscape Navigator and Microsoft Internet Explorer do not support text fields in forms equally. The differences vary depending on the version of the browser, but the general result is that a text field displays larger in Navigator than in Internet Explorer. Unfortunately, there is no perfect solution to this problem, but you should test all your forms in both browsers and create designs that look okay even when the text fields display differently.

When you want to give users a multiple-choice option but don't want to take up a lot of space on the page, drop-down lists are an ideal solution. To create a drop-down list using Dreamweaver, follow these steps:

1. **Click your form to select it.**

   If you haven't yet created a form, follow the steps in the section "Creating HTML Forms."

2. **Choose the List/Menu icon from the Forms Objects panel.**

   You can also choose Insert⇨Form Object⇨List/Menu. A drop-down list field appears.

3. **Click to place your cursor next to the List and enter a question or other text prompt.**

   In Figure 16-5, I use the example *What is your favorite sport?*

4. **Select the list on your form to reveal the List/Menu properties in the Property Inspector, as shown in Figure 16-5.**

5. **Type a name in the List/Menu text box.**

   Each list or menu on a form should have a different name so that you can differentiate the lists when you sort out the data.

6. **Next to Type, choose Menu or List.**

   This determines if this form element is a drop-down menu or a scrollable list. If you choose List, you can specify the height and control how many items show at once. You can also specify if a user can select more than one item. If you choose Menu, these options aren't available.

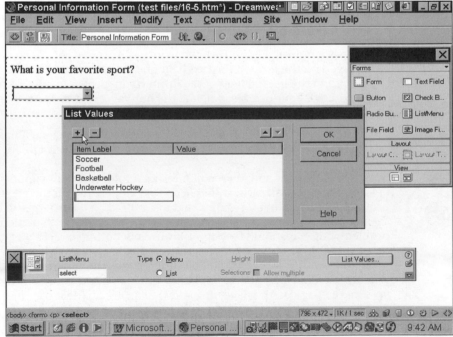

Figure 16-5:
The List/Menu option enables you to create a drop-down list of options that won't take up a lot of room on your page.

7. **Click the List Values button in the top-right corner of the Property Inspector.**

   The List Values dialog box opens (refer to Figure 16-5), and you can enter the choices that you want to make available. Click the plus sign to add an Item Label; then type the label text you want in the text box that appears in the dialog box. Item Labels are displayed in the menu or list on the Web page in the order that you enter them. Use the minus sign to delete a selected option. Use the tab key to move the cursor to the Value side of the dialog box, where you can enter a value. Values are sent to the server and provide a way of including information that you don't want displayed in the drop-down menu. For example, if you enter football as a label on the left, you may enter American as a value on the right to distinguish American football from soccer, which is often called football in other parts of the world. If you don't enter a value, the label is used as the only identifier when the data is collected.

8. **Click OK to close the dialog box.**

Finishing off your form with Submit and Clear buttons

In order for your users to send their completed forms to you, you need to create a Submit button, which, when clicked, tells the user's browser to send the form to the CGI script that processes the form. You may also want to add a Cancel or Clear button, which enable users to either not send the form at all or erase any information they've entered if they want to start over.

These buttons are easy to create in Dreamweaver. To create a button, follow these steps:

1. **Click your form to select it.**

   If you haven't yet created a form, check out the steps in the section "Creating HTML Forms." I suggest that you also enter a few fields, such as radio buttons or text fields. There's not much point in having a Submit button if you don't collect any data that needs to be submitted.

2. **Click the Button icon from the Forms Objects panel.**

   You can also choose Insert⇨Form Object⇨Button.

   A Submit button appears, and the Form Property Inspector changes to reveal button properties. You can change this to a Reset button or other kind of button by altering the attributes in the Property Inspector, as shown in the remaining steps.

3. **Select the button you just added to display the button properties in the Property Inspector, as shown in Figure 16-6.**

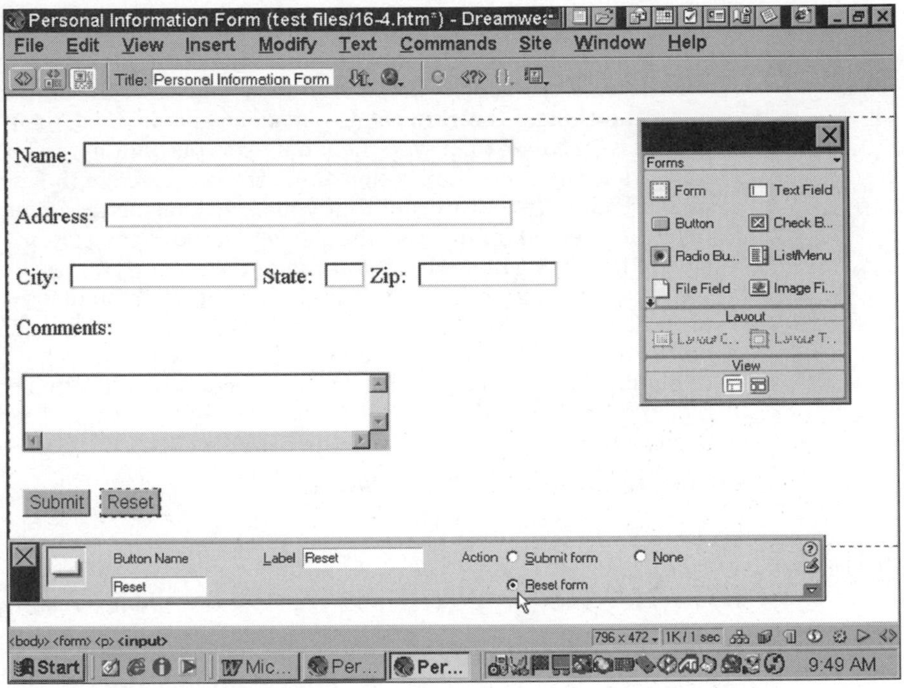

Figure 16-6:
Submit and
Reset
buttons
enable
users to
submit their
information
or clear the
form.

4. **Click either the Submit Form, Reset Form, or None button next to Action.**

   A Submit button invokes an action, such as sending the user information to an e-mail address. A Reset button clears all user input.

5. **In the Label text box, type the text you want to display on the button.**

   You can type any text you want for the label, such as Search, Go, Clear, or Delete.

So, there you have it! Now that you know how to use Dreamweaver to create the basic elements of HTML forms, you can develop more intricate forms for your Web site.

Using jump menus

Many designers use jump menus as navigational elements because they can provide a list of links in a drop-down list without taking up a lot of room on a Web page. You can also use a jump menu to launch an application or start an animation sequence.

To create a jump menu, follow these steps:

1. **Click your form to select it.**

   If you haven't yet created a form, follow the steps in the section "Creating HTML Forms." Note that you don't need a submit button to make a jump menu work.

2. **Click the Jump Menu icon from the Forms Objects panel.**

   You can also choose Insert⇨Form Object⇨Jump Menu.

   The Insert Jump Menu dialog box opens.

3. **In the Text area under Menu Items, type the name you want to display in the drop-down list.**

   Choose the plus sign (+) to add more items. As you type items in the Text field, they're displayed in the Menu Items list, as shown in Figure 16-7.

4. **Use the Browser button to locate the page you want to link to or enter the URL for the page in the When Selected, Go to URL text area.**

   You can link to a local file or enter any URL to link to a page on another Web site.

5. **Use the Open URLs In field to specify a target if you're using frames.**

   If you're not using frames, the default is Main Window. Then when the user selects an option, the new page replaces the page he is viewing.

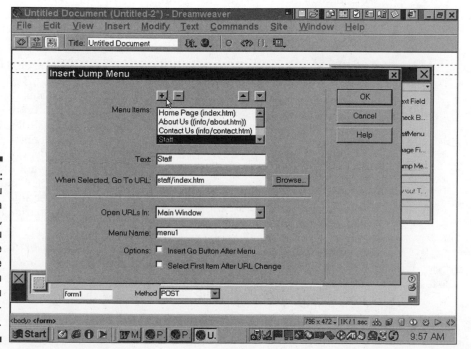

Figure 16-7:
When you create a jump list, items you type in the Text box are displayed in the Menu Items drop-down list.

6. **Use the Menu Name field if you want to enter a unique identifier for this menu.**

   This option can be useful if you have multiple jump menus on a page. You can use any name you want.

7. **Use the Insert Go Button After Menu option if you want to force users to click a button to activate the selection.**

   If you don't add a Go button, the linked page loads automatically as soon as the user makes a selection.

   If you don't use a Go button, there is no way a user can return to the same option again, even if they go back to that page or the drop-down list is still visible because it's in a frame. The Go button lets you get around this and keeps all options available.

Other form options in Dreamweaver 4

As if all of the features I describe earlier in this chapter aren't enough, Dreamweaver 4 includes a few specialized form options for facilitating inter-activity, adding images, and even hidden fields. The bulleted list here explains how you can use each of these options:

✔ **File Field icon:** Enables you to add a Browse option to a form so users can upload files from their local computers to your server. The button enables users to upload images or text files, but it works only if your server is set up to handle this kind of upload from a browser. Check with your system administrator if you're not sure.

✔ **File Field feature:** Use this feature if you want users to be able to con-tribute their own materials to your Web site. For example, *The Miami Herald* has a "Build your own Web site" system that enables readers to create their own individual sites. Many Web sites now provide this ser-vice to users. They are generally template-based systems that walk read-ers through a series of forms where they choose designs and enter text that they want to appear on their Web pages. But most people want to be able to add more than just text to their sites — they want to add their own images, such as logos and photos. That's where a File Field becomes necessary. By using this form option, you can enable readers to browse their own hard drives for a file and then automatically upload it to your server where it can be linked to their pages.

   File Field is a complex feature that requires a sophisticated CGI script and special server access to work. If you aren't a programmer, you may need assistance to use this option on your site.

✔ **Image Field icon:** Simply makes it easy to add an image to your form.

✔ **Hidden Field icon:** Inserts text that doesn't display to the user but may be used by a CGI script or other application that processes the form.

Making your forms look good

The best way to get your form fields to line up nicely is to use an HTML table. You may want to use a table to align a form by putting all your text in one row of cells and all your text fields in an adjacent row. You may also want to place all your radio buttons in the cells on the left and the text they correspond to in the cells on the right. (Chapter 9 shows you how to create HTML tables and how to use them to align information in your forms.) You can also use images and frames to make tables look better. (See Chapter 10 for information about creating frames.)

Part V
The Part of Tens

The 5th Wave   By Rich Tennant

"Give him air! Give him air! He'll be okay. He's just been exposed to some raw HTML code. It must have accidently flashed across his screen from the server."

In this part . . .

The Part of Tens features a chapter on ten Web sites that were created with Dreamweaver and do an exceptional job of showing off what Dreamweaver is capable of. These examples provide something to aspire to for all Web designers. Next, you get a chapter on ten great design and interface ideas to keep in mind as you build your Web site. Finally, you enjoy a chapter on ten timesaving tips that can make your work with Dreamweaver easier and more productive, including some great tips for getting the most out of the newest features of Dreamweaver 4.

Chapter 17

Ten Great Sites Designed with Dreamweaver

A s the popularity of Dreamweaver spreads, more and more sophisticated Web sites are built with this great tool. Checking out sites created with Dreamweaver is fun because so many of these sites take advantage of the latest Web technologies, such as Dynamic HTML, Shockwave, Flash, and more. The sites we list in this chapter provide an excellent overview of what you can do with Dreamweaver — and they're all cool Web sites. Spend time at each site and you're sure to pick up some good ideas for your own Web site.

You can connect directly to these Web sites by clicking the appropriate hyperlink in the HTML interface on the CD that accompanies this book.

CatEye

www.cateye.com

Web design company Vertical Hold designed this site for the bicycle parts and accessories company CatEye. A former Communication Arts Web Site of the Week, the site uses extensive rollovers for its navigation elements to provide a clean and easily navigable interface (see Figure 17-1). (And see Chapter 12 to find out more about working with rollovers.)

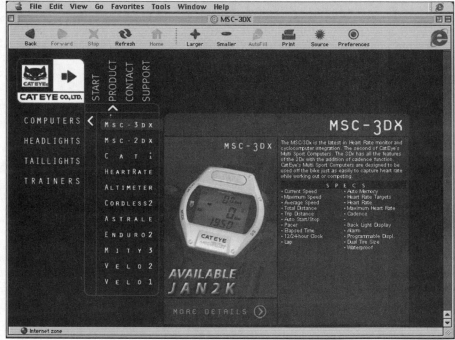

Figure 17-1:
Bicycle
products
manufac-
turer CatEye
uses
Dream-
weaver for
this award-
winning site.

Project Seven/Dreamweaver

www.projectseven.com/dreamweaver/

According to creator Al Sparber, Project Seven's Dreamweaver site (see Figure 17-2) was originally created as a Dreamweaver resource "in gratitude to the Dreamweaver community for helping me to learn how to use this most excellent tool."

And learn he did. In less than a year, Al went from Web design "newbie" to the author of a site now visited by thousands of "weavers" each week. Today, the site is one of the best Web development resources for users of both Dreamweaver and Fireworks. The Project Seven site provides detailed examples and tutorials that promote harnessing the dynamic powers of these two programs. All the covered techniques are easily duplicated using stock Dreamweaver features, along with a few select third-party extensions for extending Dreamweaver even further. The extensions, of course, are freely available. Al's own extensions are available for download at the site, and the site contains a links page listing the major Dreamweaver extension authors.

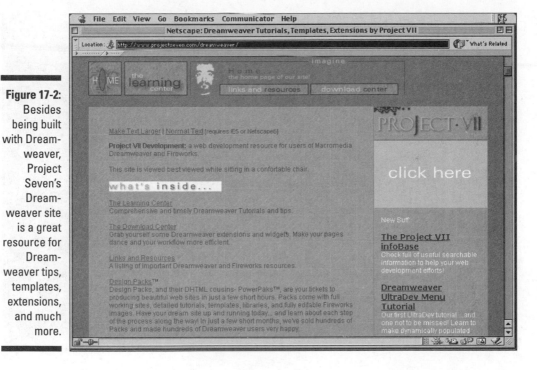

Figure 17-2:
Besides being built with Dreamweaver, Project Seven's Dreamweaver site is a great resource for Dreamweaver tips, templates, extensions, and much more.

Many of the examples and tutorials are also available for download, complete with images and style sheets. A new feature is Design Packs™, and its DHTML cousins PowerPaks™, which can be purchased on the site. These allow you to produce beautiful Web sites in just a few short hours and come with full working sites, detailed tutorials, templates, libraries, and fully editable Fireworks images.

Eighteenoz

www.18oz.com

Combining a host of technologies in Dreamweaver, Washington, D.C. designer Joel Fisher created this self-promotional site to showcase Eighteenoz's design and development services (see Figure 17-3). Showing that Dreamweaver integrates smoothly with other technologies, the site utilizes ASP, DHTML, JavaScript, Java, SQL, and Cascading Style Sheets (CSS) to help deliver its dynamic content. (For more information about DHTML, see Chapters 12 and 13. See Chapter 11 for more about Cascading Style Sheets.)

Figure 17-3:
Web designer Joel Fisher has used a lot of different tools over the years, but he finds Dreamweaver to be his top choice.

Cinemascope Photo Journey

`www.cinemascope.com/photos`

This site showcases photographer Andrew Peters's chronicle of his 1998 trip through five South American countries. Shooting with a conventional 35mm camera, Peters used a slide scanner to capture his images while combining Photoshop, ImageReady, Fireworks, and Dreamweaver to build his site. Dreamweaver was chosen because of its ease of use, templates, and style sheet features. Peters created a template for the site that allowed him to update global aspects of the interface easily while using style sheets to specify font size (see Figure 17-4). (See Chapter 6 for more on using Dreamweaver templates. Check out Chapter 11 to find out more about style sheets.)

Figure 17-4:
An amateur photographer's colorful chronicle of his trip to South America.

Axe Restaurant

www.axerestaurant.com

This small restaurant/cafe in Venice, California, utilized Dreamweaver to create a simple but effective Web site. Clean lines and pleasing colors combine to make an attractive destination (see Figure 17-5). The site utilizes layers for exact placement of overlapping images and Dreamweaver behaviors for the rollover effects. Images were created in Photoshop and sliced in Fireworks before being exporting into Dreamweaver. (See Chapter 12 for more information on positioning elements with layers.)

It's Yoga

http://www.itsyoga.com

San Francisco Web designers Biagio Azzarelli and Eliot Bates used Dreamweaver together with Allaire Homesite to create It's Yoga, a top yoga resource and promotional site for a Yoga studio (see Figure 17-6). Dreamweaver was used for initial design and mockup as well as adding JavaScript behaviors and consistently formatting forms and form objects. Later on, the designers went back and tweaked the code using HomeSite to assure the strictest W3c recommended HTML 3.2 specs.

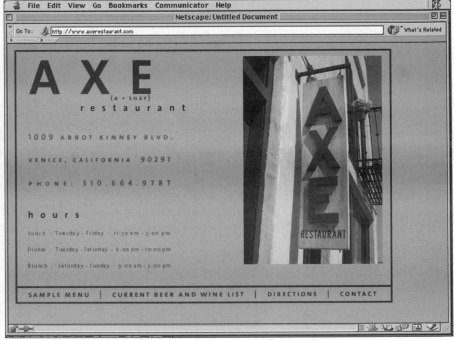

Figure 17-5:
This small
Venice, CA
restaurant/
cafe uses
Dream-
weaver and
layers to
precisely
position
page
elements.

Manipulation

www.manipulation.com

Manipulation.com is Web designer Jason Zada's personal online art space and record label, originally launched in 1995. Manipulation houses many interactive art installations as well as the record label (see Figure 17-7).

Jason Zada first designed the site in Photoshop; then the graphics were ported over to Dreamweaver, where he used layers to position the graphics perfectly. To achieve the style and type of choice, Jason used Cascading Style Sheets to control the fonts, and all the leading and kerning on the typefaces. For the dragable lemon on the home page, Jason used Dreamweaver's extensible DHTML capabilities to easily create an object that is dragable and locks into a specific position. The graphical rollovers were done using Dreamweaver behaviors, and the main point of attraction is the Flash movie in the middle which acts as a CD player, allowing users to stream MP3 quality sounds of Manipulation Records' music.

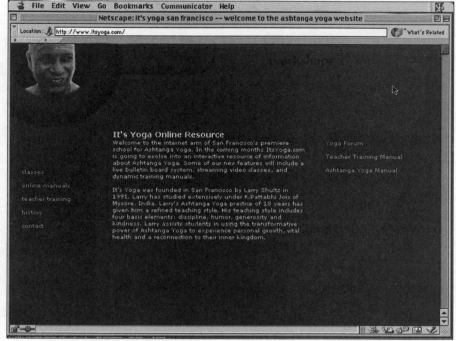

Figure 17-6:
This yoga
studio
provides
information
about its
services as
well as
general
information
for the yoga
community.

fabric8

www.fabric8.com

fabric8 has been winning awards and accolades from all over the Web with its
innovative and design-conscious clothing commerce site. Using Dreamweaver,
the site's talented creator, Olivia Ongpin, employs DHTML, Shockwave, Flash,
interactive audio, downloadable fonts, and many other cutting-edge technologies to deliver a fresh and exciting online experience. Be sure to explore
this site, and don't forget to look at its archives. Fabric8 has been developing
great stuff since 1996 (see Figure 17-8). (To find out more about Flash and
Shockwave, see Chapter 15. For more on DHTML, check out Chapters 12
and 13.)

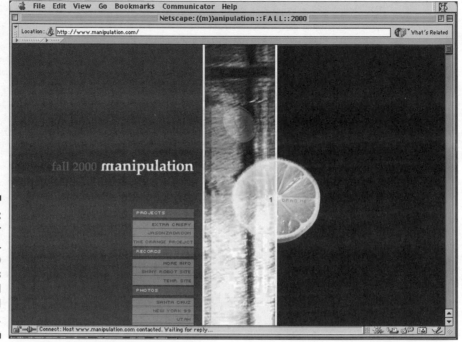

Figure 17-7:
Clever
DHTML
tricks help
make this
site original
and
compelling.

Figure 17-8:
fabric8 has
been using
Dream-
weaver
since it first
came out
and
continues
to make
creative use
of the
Dream-
weaver
multimedia
features.

Macromedia

`www.macromedia.com/software/dreamweaver`

The Macromedia Web site (see Figure 17-9) provides a rich multimedia experience that showcases the many Macromedia technologies from Shockwave and Flash to the latest Dreamweaver features. You also find a developer's section with great design and development tips and a forum where you can share information with other Dreamweaver users. (For more on multimedia and Dreamweaver, see Chapter 15.)

Dynamic HTML Zone

`www.dhtmlzone.com`

Another Macromedia site, the Dynamic HTML Zone (see Figure 17-10) is dedicated to providing articles, tutorials, discussion groups, design galleries, links, and general resources about Dynamic HTML. This is a great starting point for finding information about DHTML. (Check out Chapters 12 and 13 to learn more about DHTML.)

Figure 17-9:
The Dreamweaver section of Macromedia's Web site is a great starting point for finding out more about Dreamweaver.

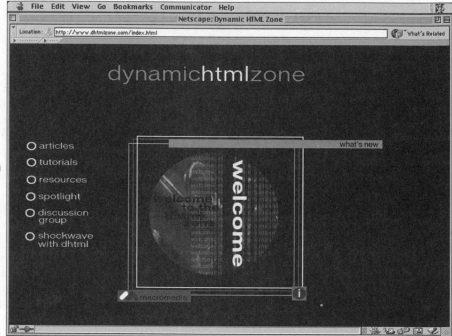

Figure 17-10:
The Macromedia Dynamic HTML Zone is the place to go to find out more about DHTML.

Chapter 18

Ten Web Site Ideas You Can Use

*A*ll good Web sites grow and evolve. If you start with a strong design and pay close attention to some basic rules about interface, navigation, and style, you have a better foundation to build on. The following design ideas can help you create a compelling Web site that grows gracefully.

Make It Easy

Creating a clear and intuitive navigational system is one of the most important elements in creating a Web site. Nothing is likely to frustrate your visitors more than not being able to find what they're looking for. Make sure that visitors can easily get to all the main sections of your site from every page in the site. You can best do this by creating a set of links to each of the main sections and placing it at the top, bottom, or side of every page. I call this set of links a *navigation row* or *navigation bar,* and it's a common feature on most well-designed sites. If the pages are very long, place these links toward the top of the page, and you may want to include them at the bottom as well. A set of graphical icons can make this navigational element an attractive part of your design. Your goal is to make sure that viewers don't have to use the Back button in their browsers to move around your site. Using the Back button wastes your users' time, and believe it or not, some browsers don't even have a Back button. You can find more tips about creating an intuitive navigation system in Chapter 5.

White Space Is Not Wasted Space

One of the best design features you can add to a page is nothing at all (also known as *white space*). Understand that white space, in this case, is not always white; it's simply space that you haven't crammed full of text or images. It can be any color, but it's usually most effective if it's the color or pattern of your background. White space gives the eye a rest, something readers need even more often when they're staring at a computer monitor. You can use white space to separate one type of information from another and to focus the viewer's attention where you want it most. Some of the most beautiful and compelling designs on the Web use only a few well-thought-out elements against lots of white space.

Design for Your Audience

No matter how technically sophisticated a Web site is or how great the writing, most people notice the design first. Make sure that you leave plenty of time and budget to develop an appropriate and attractive design for your Web site. The right design is one that best suits your audience — that may or may not mean lots of fancy graphics and animations.

Think about who you want to attract to your Web site before you develop the design. A gaming Web site geared toward teenagers should look very different from a Web site with gardening tips or an online banking site. Review other sites designed for your target market. Consider your audience's time constraints and attention span, and, most importantly, consider your audience's goals. If you design your site to provide information to busy businesspeople, you want fast-loading pages with few graphics and little or no animation. If you design your site for entertainment, your audience may be willing to wait a little longer for animation and other interactive features.

Pull It Together

As you lay out your Web page, keep related items physically close to one another. You want your viewers to instantly understand which pieces of information are related. You should give elements of similar importance the same weight on a page. Distinguish different kinds of information by their design, location, and prominence. This kind of organization makes following information visually much easier for your viewers. You can find many other design tips in Chapter 5.

Be Consistent

Make sure that all similar elements follow the same design parameters, such as type style, banner size, and page background color. If you use too many different elements on a page or within the same Web site, you quickly have a very "busy" design, and you may confuse your viewers. Defining a set of colors, shapes, or other elements that you use throughout the site is a good way to ensure a consistent style. Choose two or three fonts for your Web site and use those consistently as well. Using too many fonts makes your pages less appealing and harder to read.

Late-Breaking News

The sites on the Internet that report the most hits are those that change the most frequently, thereby keeping visitors coming back for new content. Even small changes can make a big difference, especially if viewers know to look for them. Keep your site fresh and dynamic, and let viewers know when to come back for more. If you always make changes to your site at the same time (every Friday morning, for example), viewers have a specific date to look forward to and are more likely to come back on a regular basis. Dynamic sites grow quickly, however, and generally require even more planning than static sites. In Chapter 5, you can find suggestions and strategies for building a site that can easily accommodate growth and regular updates.

Small and Fast

The biggest problem on the Internet is still speed. Making sure that your pages download quickly makes your viewers more likely to keep clicking. You may create the best design ever to grace the Web, but if it takes too long to appear on your viewers' screens, no one will wait around long enough to compliment your design talents. You can find tips about creating and linking fast-loading graphics in Chapter 8. In Chapter 15, you discover how to add Flash buttons and text — two new ways that Macromedia has integrated its vector-based image and animation program. (If you're not familiar with Flash yet, make sure you check it out. It's all the rage on the Web for a reason: Flash loads fast, looks great, and automatically resizes to fit any browser window.)

Accessible Designs

As you design your site, keep in mind that viewers come to your pages with a variety of computers, operating systems, and monitors. Ensure that your site is accessible to all your potential viewers by testing your pages on a variety of systems. If you want to attract a large audience to your site, you need to ensure that it looks good on a broad range of systems. A design that looks great in Navigator 4.0 and higher may be unreadable in Internet Explorer 3.0. And many people still use old browsers because they haven't bothered — or don't know how — to download new versions.

Accessible design on the Web also includes pages that can be read (actually, converted to synthesized speech) by special browsers used by the blind. Using the ALT attribute in your image tags is a simple way to ensure that all visitors can get the information they need. The ALT attribute specifies a text alternative that is displayed if the image doesn't appear. It's inserted into an image tag like this:

```
<IMG SRC="CAT.GIF" ALT="A picture of a black and white cat.">
```

Follow the Three Clicks Rule

The Three Clicks Rule states that no important piece of information should ever be more than three clicks away from anywhere else on your Web site. The most important information should be even closer at hand. Some information, such as contact information, should never be more than one click away. Make it easy for viewers to find information by creating a site map (as I explain in the next section) and a *navigation bar* — a set of links to all the main sections on your site.

Map It Out

As your site gets larger, providing easy access to all the information on your Web site may get harder and harder. A great solution is to provide a *site map,* which is a page that includes links to almost every other page in the site. The site map can become a busy page and usually appears best in outline form. This page should be highly functional — it doesn't matter if it looks pretty. Don't put lots of graphics on this page; it should load quickly and provide easy access to anything that your visitors need.

Chapter 19

Ten Timesaving Dreamweaver Tips

*E*ven the best programs get better when you know how to make the most of them. As I put this book together, I collected tips and tricks and gathered them into this handy list. Take a moment to check out these tips and save tons of time in developing your Web site. Most of these tips apply to both Macintosh and Windows users, but when they apply to only one or the other, I've indicated whether the tip applies to the Windows or to the Mac version.

Clearing the Clutter

Dreamweaver's many panels (called *palettes* in previous versions) provide quick access to its most popular features, but they can clutter up the design area. To get them out of your way when you want to stand back and admire your work (or tear someone else's apart), use the F4 key, a shortcut that hides all visible panels at once. To get them back, just hit the F4 key again.

To turn panels on and off individually, use the keyboard shortcut assigned to each panel. Select Window from the Menu to find a keyboard short cut listed next to each panel name. You can use these shortcuts to toggle the panels on and off individually. You can also use the Launcher bar in the bottom right hand corner of the design window to gain access to the Site panel, Assets panel, HTML Styles panel, CSS Styles panel, Behaviors panel, and History panel. For an introduction to all of the Dreamweaver panels, see Chapters 1 and 2.

Splitting the View: Working in the Code

If you like to switch back and forth between the HTML source code and the WYSIWYG (What You See Is What You Get) design view in Dreamweaver, you'll appreciate the new option in version 4 that enables you to split the window so you can view the HTML source and the WYSIWYG design area at the same time. To split the window, choose View⇔Code and Design.

You may also appreciate the enhanced features in the Dreamweaver built-in text editor, including auto-indenting and the ability to select multiple lines and indent them. You'll also discover live syntax coloring that appears as you type — you can even distinguish the colors for HTML and JavaScript. Choose Edit⇔Preferences⇔Code Colors tab to assign colors. Chapter 4 covers more on using Dreamweaver's integrated text editor, as well as using the bundled HTML Editors, BBEdit (for the Mac) and HomeSite (for Windows) with Dreamweaver.

Tabling Your Designs

HTML Tables still offer the best way to create complex Web designs (because layers still aren't supported by older browsers), and Dreamweaver 4 has made it easier than ever to create tables in its visual design area. In the new Layout View, you can "draw" tables on a page, drag them into place, and even group cells in a nested table — without ever worrying about how many rows and cells you've created. You can even use this feature to create tables that change with the window size, a great technique for ensuring your designs work on all monitors. (Did you know people are surfing the Web with Palm Pilots and Pocket PCs these days?)

Choose View⇔Table View⇔Layout View to access Dreamweaver's new table creation environment. Then just drag and drop to create any kind of table. You find cell and table layout options in the Objects panel. For more information about using Layout View, check out Chapter 9.

Designing in a Flash

Flash rocks! Macromedia's vector-based design and animation program, Flash, is one of the hottest programs on the Web today because it makes creating fast-loading images and animations that dynamically adjust to fit any screen size possible. Now that the Flash plug-in is built into most current browsers, Flash has become a standard, and Dreamweaver has made it easier than ever to add Flash buttons and text to your Web pages.

To add pre-made Flash buttons to your site, just click on the Insert Flash Button option in the Objects panel. The dialog makes it easy to choose a button design and edit the text that appears on the button, all from within Dreamweaver. You can even create your own buttons in Flash and add them to the list of available buttons.

You can add Flash Text the same way, by choosing Insert Flash Text from the Objects panel. For more on these integrated Flash features, read Chapter 15.

Converting Text

If you've gotten used to using the Paste as Text feature in Dreamweaver 3, don't be disappointed when you find that it's missing in Dreamweaver 4. Macromedia streamlined the process in its latest version. Now you simply choose File⇨Paste and formatted text from a Word processing document maintains its formatting — well, okay, it at least maintains the line spacing. Truth is, Dreamweaver is still pretty weak when it comes to converting text. You can save yourself reformatting the text in Dreamweaver if you use a word processing or spreadsheet program that includes a Save As HTML feature (Microsoft Word and many others offer this feature). Instead of copying and pasting the text into Dreamweaver, use the word processing program's File⇨Save As HTML feature, rename the file, and then open the new file in Dreamweaver. Microsoft Word and Excel even preserve table formatting, a real time-saver if you're dealing with large tables of text or numbers. Chapter 7 offers lots of tips and tricks for working with text in your Web pages.

Making Fireworks with Your Images

The Dreamweaver integration with Fireworks, Macromedia's Web image program, makes it easy to edit images while you're working in Dreamweaver. Need to change the text on a button or create a new banner? Just use the special integrated Fireworks Property Inspector to view the PNG source file from Fireworks; you can click the Edit button in the Property Inspector when an image is selected to edit it in Fireworks, and any changes you make to an image are automatically reflected in the Dreamweaver file. If you've always used another image program, such as Photoshop, this level of integration should at least get you to consider using Fireworks. It can save you a ton of time in your design work, especially when your pesky colleagues and clients are always asking for last minute changes. For more on using Fireworks and Dreamweaver in tandem, check out Chapter 14.

Finding Functional Fonts

Designers get so excited when they find out that they can use any font on a Web page. But, in reality, your viewers must still have the font on their computers for it to display. The more common the font, the more likely it is to display the way you intend. If you want to use a more unusual font, go for it — just be sure that you also include alternatives. The Dreamweaver Font List already includes collections of common fonts, and you can always create your own Font List by choosing Text⇨Font⇨Edit Font List.

And here's another tip: Windows is by far the most common operating system on the Net. To ensure the best — and fastest — results for the majority of your users, list a Windows font first.

In an effort to make text easier to read on the Web, Adobe and Microsoft have both created fonts that are especially suited to computer screens. Visit their Web sites at www.adobe.com and www.microsoft.com respectively and search for Web fonts to find out more.

Differentiating DHTML for All Browsers

If you like pushing the technical limits of what works on the Web, don't overlook one of the most valuable features of Dreamweaver: the Convert option. This feature automatically converts your complex page designs that work only in 4.0 and later browsers into alternative pages that display in 3.0 browsers. The feature converts the CSS and DHTML tags into regular HTML style tags by converting CSS formatting into HTML formatting tags and recreating layers into HTML Tables.

To convert CSS and other features on a page, choose File⇨Convert⇨3.0 Browser Compatible. Beware that HTML is not capable of the complex designs you can create using DHTML, so your converted pages may not look as much like the original as you would like; for example, there is no way to do justice to a layer that moves across the screen in a static table cell. Chapter 13 walks you through the process in detail. The conversion isn't a perfect science, but it is a relatively easy way to ensure your pages are at least presentable in older browsers.

I've heard too many good designers say that users should upgrade their browsers and that they don't care about users who are so lame they're still using an old version of AOL. Here's a word of caution: It only takes one really important viewer to get you in trouble for not doing multi-browser designs. Beware that one of the most likely people to be using an older browser is the president of the company who is travelling with his laptop that he's never upgraded the browser on because he only uses it from a hotel rooms on the road. Don't take the risk that your paying clients, your boss, or worse yet, your investors, are the ones with the old browsers. Make sure your designs work well for everyone — it's the sign of a truly high-end Web designer.

Directing Your Viewers

Creating multiple sites is the most fail-safe solution for making sure that all your viewers are happy when you use cutting-edge page designs filled with DHTML and CSS. That means you create two or more sets of pages: one that uses the latest features and one that uses older, more universally supported HTML tags. But how do you ensure that viewers get to the right pages? Use the Check Browser behavior.

The Check Browser behavior is written in JavaScript and determines the browser type used by each viewer who lands on your site. The behavior then directs users to the page design best suited to their browser version. To use this feature, choose Window⇨Behaviors to open the Behaviors panel. Then click the plus sign (+) to open the drop-down list of options. Choose Check Browser and a dialog box opens in which you can specify what browser versions should be directed to what pages on your site. When users arrive at your site, they are automatically directed to the page of your choice, based on the browser type and version that you specify.

Appreciating DHTML Differences

One of the most dramatic differences between Internet Explorer 5.0 and Netscape Navigator 4.x when it comes to DHTML has to do with style properties. In Internet Explorer 5.0, you can change style properties of elements after a page has loaded. In Navigator 4.x, you can't. That means that in Explorer you can create DHTML effects, such as making text change color (by changing the font color attribute) or change size (by changing the font size attribute). You can't do these things in Navigator. Fortunately, both browsers support changes to positioning properties, which allow animations and other tricks created by moving layers over time. For more information about working with DHTML, check out Chapters 12 and 13.

Part VI
Appendixes

The 5th Wave   By Rich Tennant

Meditations, Inc.
BOOKS • SEMINARS • TAPES

"Sales on the Web site are down. I figure the server's
chi is blocked, so we're fudgin' around the feng shui
in the computer room, and if that doesn't work,
Ronnie's got a chant that should do it."

In this part . . .

The appendixes provide some useful references. Appendix A features a wide range of Web sites that offer valuable design tips and fresh ideas to help you on your way as you create your site. And Appendix B, the CD appendix, fills you in on all the goodies — including a comprehensive glossary — offered on the CD that comes with this book.

Appendix A

Web Design Resources You Can Find Online

∙∙

*T*he best place to keep up with the latest developments in Web design is the Internet itself. Whenever I do research on new Web technologies and features, I visit a few of my favorite Web sites to see what they have to say. Visit these sites regularly to gain insight into the evolving HTML 4.0 specification and the implementation of Dynamic HTML, as well as many other aspects of Web design.

You can connect directly to these Web sites by clicking the appropriate hyperlink in the HTML interface on the CD that accompanies this book.

Adobe Systems, Inc.

www.adobe.com

Adobe is not only a great resource for graphics and other products, but its Web site features an impressive collection of design tips and strategies for creating graphics for the Web, in addition to well-designed HTML pages.

Art and the Zen of Web Sites

www.tlc-systems.com/webtips.shtml

As the name implies, this site shows you the way to simplistic yet powerful Web design.

BrowserWatch

browserwatch.internet.com

This site keeps you up-to-date on the latest in the browser wars and helps you appreciate the quantity and diversity of Web browsers used on the

Internet. If you're designing your pages for the broader Web audience, and especially if you want to use advanced features, keep an eye on this site and download a few browsers that you can use when testing your work.

CGI Overview

`www.w3.org/hypertext/WWW/CGI`

The World Wide Web Consortium offers a great guide to writing *CGI* (Common Gateway Interface) scripts. If you already have some programming experience and want to write your own scripts, this is an ideal resource. If you've never done any programming before, this site can introduce you to what CGI scripts are all about.

CNET

`www.cnet.com`

CNET gives you hot news about all aspects of the Web, as well as in-depth reports on new technologies and other news affecting Web designers. CNET also has extensive software libraries for both Windows and Macintosh platforms.

Communication Arts Interactive

`www.commarts.com`

Need some design guidance or a few tips on how to create the best graphics for your site? Point your browser in the direction of Communication Arts Interactive.

David Siegel's Site

`www.dsiegel.com`

Famous for popularizing the clear GIF trick and many other ways to "break the rules" of HTML, Siegel's site features loads of design tips.

DHTML Zone

www.dhtmlzone.com

Macromedia created this site to help developers learn about Dynamic HTML. You can find tons of information here about how to create your own DHTML features, what DHTML really is, and how to design features to work for the broadest audience.

The Directory

www.thedirectory.org/

Looking for an *ISP* (Internet Service Provider)? Look no further. The Directory is the most comprehensive guide to ISPs on the Net, featuring a searchable database of more than 10,000 ISPs worldwide.

Dreamweaver Extensions Database

www.idest.com/cgi-bin/database.cgi

A vast searchable database of Dreamweaver extensions including objects, behaviors, templates, commands, and techniques for extending Dreamweaver — all downloadable from the Web.

The HTML Writers Guild

www.hwg.org

The HTML Writers Guild is an international organization of World Wide Web designers and Internet publishing professionals. This Web site includes a variety of HTML resources, as well as Web business mailing lists, information repositories, and a chance to interact with peers.

Hungry Minds, Inc.

www.hungryminds.com

Hungry Minds, Inc., formerly IDG Books Worldwide, Inc., offers a wide range of books on Web design (including this one!) and features links to great magazines and other resources for Web designers.

ID Est

www.idest.com/dreamweaver/

This is best-selling author Joseph Lowery's (*Dreamweaver Bible*, published by IDG Books Worldwide) resource page for all things Dreamweaver. It's a great starting place for Dreamweaver online information and links.

International Data Group (IDG)

www.idg.com

IDG is the parent company of Hungry Minds (formerly IDG Books). Visit the main IDG site to find links to all its research and publication services, including magazines such as *Publish, InfoWorld, MacWorld,* and *PCWorld.*

Lynda.com

www.lynda.com

My favorite Web graphics expert, Lynda Weinman, shows off her books and insights into creating fast-loading, beautiful images. Lynda.com also carries how-to videos and offers classes on Dreamweaver, Fireworks, and many other Web and graphics programs.

Macromedia's Designers and Developers Center

www.macromedia.com/

Macromedia's official help center is filled with tutorials, samples, and other assets designed to keep developers up-to-date, especially if you use its programs, such as Dreamweaver, Freehand, and Flash.

Microsoft

www.microsoft.com

Watch the Microsoft site for updates to Internet Explorer, as well as information on how it plans to support DHTML and other advanced HTML tags.

Netscape

www.netscape.com

Keep your eye on the Netscape site for updates to Navigator, as well as the latest on how it plans to support DHTML and other advanced HTML tags.

Project Cool

www.projectcool.com

One of my all-time favorite Web sites, Project Cool is dedicated to helping anyone become a better Web designer. The creators of this site make Web design easy to understand and accessible to anyone who visits the site. They do a great job of keeping up with the latest developments, such as DHTML and Cascading Style Sheets. You can also find a great list of award-winning sites that make great examples of what works on the Web. Their newest feature, devSearch, enables you to search through Web development resources across the Web.

Search Engine Help

www.searchenginehelp.com

If you're confused about how to submit your site to search engines or you want to get better placement in the search engines where your site already appears, Search Engine Help gives you all the tips and ideas you have time for.

Weblint

www.weblint.com

Can't figure out why a site won't work properly? Run the URL through Weblint to pinpoint any errors, as well as HTML code that may not work in some browsers.

WebMonkey

www.webmonkey.com

Tune up your browser and make sure your Web site is up to snuff at HotWired's WebMonkey site. You can use its online diagnostic tools to test your browser and find out about plug-ins and other Web development tools. You can also find HTML tutorials and other Web design references.

Web Reference

`www.webreference.com`

As the name implies, you can find a long list of reference materials at this site to answer almost any question a Web designer could have.

The World Wide Web Artists Consortium

`www.wwwac.org`

Better known as the WWWAC, this nonprofit, member-supported organization of Web designers keeps you up-to-date on current Web design issues when you subscribe to its e-mail list. But as with any mailing list, make sure that you read a few weeks' worth of messages before you post one of your own. More than 1,000 people share their ideas on the WWWAC list, including some of the most respected designers on the Web.

World Wide Web Consortium

`www.w3.org`

The official source for HTML updates, the W3C sets the standards for HTML code. At this site, you find all the published HTML specifications, as well as a wide range of resources for Web developers.

ZDNET

`www.zdnet.com`

Constantly updated, this site provides a large collection of Web design resources, as well as links to more than 30 online magazines published by Ziff-Davis, such as *Yahoo! Internet Life, Inter@ctive, PC Week, MacWeek,* and many others. While you're at it, check out `www.zdtv.com`. Ziff-Davis's latest endeavor, ZDTV, is a new cable channel with programming about computers, technology, and the Internet.

Appendix B

About the CD

• •

*T*he CD-ROM that accompanies this book contains the following goodies:

- ✔ Macromedia Dreamweaver 4, a fully functional 30-day version of the program
- ✔ Macromedia Fireworks, a fully functional 30-day version of the program
- ✔ Expandable Language HTML Rename!, a filename conversion program that can save you hours of manual searching and replacing
- ✔ Lots of extra trial versions of software (see the "What You'll Find" section later in this appendix) that can help you become more efficient in many aspects of Web design
- ✔ Extra behaviors that increase Dreamweaver functionality
- ✔ Templates to make it easier to build your Web site
- ✔ Flash files for you to use when you try out the Dreamweaver plug-in features
- ✔ A few extra GIF and JPEG images for you to use while you're becoming familiar with building Web pages in Dreamweaver
- ✔ A glossary that can help you become familiar with Web design and Dreamweaver lingo

System Requirements

Make sure that your computer meets the minimum system requirements listed here. If your computer doesn't match up to most of these requirements, you may have problems using the contents of the CD.

For Microsoft Windows: An Intel Pentium 166 or equivalent processor running Windows 95 or later or Windows NT Version 4.0 or later, 32 MB of RAM (64MB recommended), a color monitor, and a CD-ROM drive.

For the Macintosh: A Power Macintosh running System 8.1 or later, 32 MB of available RAM (64MB recommended), a color monitor, and a CD-ROM drive.

If you need more information on the basics, check out *PCs For Dummies*, 7th Edition, by Dan Gookin; *Macs For Dummies*, 7th Edition, by David Pogue; and *Windows 98 For Dummies* and *Windows 95 For Dummies*, 2nd Edition, both by Andy Rathbone (all published by Hungry Minds, formerly IDG Books Worldwide, Inc.).

Using the CD with Microsoft Windows

To install the items from the CD to your hard drive, follow these steps.

1. **Insert the CD into your computer's CD-ROM drive.**

2. **Click Start⇨Run.**

3. **In the dialog box that appears, type** D:\IDG.EXE.

   Replace *D* with the proper drive letter if your CD-ROM drive uses a different letter. (If you don't know the letter, see how your CD-ROM drive is listed under My Computer.)

4. **Click OK.**

   A license agreement window appears.

5. **Read through the license agreement, nod your head, and then click the Accept button if you want to use the CD — after you click Accept, you'll never be bothered by the License Agreement window again.**

   The CD interface Welcome screen appears. The interface is a little program that shows you what's on the CD and coordinates installing the programs and running the demos. The interface basically enables you to click a button or two to make things happen.

6. **Click anywhere on the Welcome screen to enter the interface.**

   Now you are getting to the action. This next screen lists categories for the software on the CD.

7. **To view the items within a category, just click the category's name.**

   A list of programs in the category appears.

8. **For more information about a program, click the program's name.**

   Be sure to read the information that appears. Sometimes a program has its own system requirements or requires you to do a few tricks on your computer before you can install or run the program, and this screen tells you what you might need to do, if necessary.

9. **If you don't want to install the program, click the Back button to return to the previous screen.**

   You can always return to the previous screen by clicking the Back button. This feature allows you to browse the different categories and products and decide what you want to install.

10. **To install a program, click the appropriate Install button.**

    The CD interface drops to the background while the CD installs the program you chose.

11. **To install other items, repeat Steps 7–10.**

12. **When you've finished installing programs, click the Quit button to close the interface.**

    You can eject the CD now. Carefully place it back in the plastic jacket of the book for safekeeping.

In order to run some of the programs on the *Dreamweaver 4 For Dummies* CD-ROM, you may need to keep the CD inside your CD-ROM drive. This is a good thing. Otherwise, the installed program would have required you to install a very large chunk of the program to your hard drive, which may have kept you from installing other software.

Using the CD with Mac OS

To install the items from the CD to your hard drive, follow these steps.

1. **Insert the CD into your computer's CD-ROM drive.**

   In a moment, an icon representing the CD you just inserted appears on your Mac desktop. Chances are, the icon looks like a CD-ROM.

2. **Double-click the CD icon to show the CD's contents.**

3. **Double-click the License Agreement icon.**

   This is the license that you are agreeing to by using the CD. You can close this window once you've looked over the agreement.

4. **Double-click the Read Me First icon.**

   The Read Me First text file contains information about the CD's programs and any last-minute instructions you may need in order to correctly install them.

5. **To install most programs, open the program folder and double-click the icon called "Install" or "Installer."**

   Sometimes the installers are actually self extracting archives, which just means that the program files have been bundled up into an archive, and this self extractor unbundles the files and places them on your hard drive. This kind of program is often called an .sea. Double click anything with .sea in the title, and it will run just like an installer.

6. **Some programs don't come with installers. For those, just drag the program's folder from the CD window and drop it on your hard drive icon.**

After you've installed the programs you want, you can eject the CD. Carefully place it back in the plastic jacket of the book for safekeeping.

What You'll Find

Shareware programs are fully functional, free trial versions of copyrighted programs. If you like particular programs, register with their authors for a nominal fee and receive licenses, enhanced versions, and technical support. Freeware programs are free, copyrighted games, applications, and utilities. You can copy them to as many PCs as you like — free — but they have no technical support. GNU software is governed by its own license, which is included inside the folder of the GNU software. There are no restrictions on distribution of this software. See the GNU license for more details. Trial, demo, or evaluation versions are usually limited either by time or functionality (such as being unable to save projects).

Here's a summary of the software on this CD arranged by category. If you use Windows, the CD interface helps you install software easily. (If you have no idea what I'm talking about when I say "CD interface," flip back a page or two to find the section, "Using the CD with Microsoft Windows.")

If you use a Mac OS computer, you can take advantage of the easy Mac interface to quickly install the programs.

HTML converters and editors

BBEdit 5.1.1, from Bare Bones Software

For Mac. Demo version.

This demo introduces you to the power of BBEdit as an HTML text editor. The full version of Dreamweaver includes BBEdit and provides fully integrated editing so that you can move easily between the two programs. For more on BBEdit, visit www.barebones.com.

BBEdit Lite 4.6, from Bare Bones Software

For Mac. Lite version.

This lite version enables you to test out the power of BBEdit as an HTML text editor. For more on BBEdit Lite, visit www.barebones.com.

Dreamweaver 4, from Macromedia, Inc.

For Mac OS 8.1 or later and Windows 95, 98, or NT 4.0 or later. 30-day tryout version.

Macromedia's award-winning Web design program is included on the CD so that you can dive right in and start working with this program — even if you haven't decided to purchase it yet. To find out more, check out Macromedia's Web site at `www.macromedia.com`.

HomeSite 4.5, by Allaire Corp.

For Windows 95, 98, and NT. Evaluation version.

This HTML text editor for Windows enables you to work in the raw HTML code. The full version of Dreamweaver includes HomeSite and provides fully integrated editing so that you can move easily between the two programs. For more information about HomeSite, visit `www.allaire.com`.

Fireworks 4, from Macromedia, Inc.

For Mac OS 8.1 or later and Windows 95, 98, or NT (with Service Pack) or later. 30-day tryout version.

This graphics program is designed for creating images, animations, and complex design elements for the Web. The program is integrated with Dreamweaver to make it easier to edit images even after they are placed on your Web pages. Check out Macromedia's Web site at `www.macromedia.com`.

Expandable Language HTML Rename! 2.0

For Mac OS and Windows 9x/NT. 60-day shareware version.

This program started out as a simple utility and has grown beyond its creator's original vision. It's now a high-powered development tool perfect for converting Web sites from one platform to another by automating the process of renaming files without breaking links. To find out more, check out the site at `www.xlanguage.com`.

Note: When accessing the program from the CD, execute the RENAW200.exe file from the directory where the file was saved. To launch the program, click the Hrename.exe icon. If you chose Run This Program from Its Current Location during installation, Hrename.exe will be located at C:\WINDOWS\DESKTOP.

Graphics programs

Acrobat Reader 4.0, from Adobe Systems, Inc.

For Mac and Windows. Evaluation version.

This program lets you view and print Portable Document Format (PDF) files. Many programs on the Internet use the PDF format for storing documentation because it supports assorted fonts and colorful graphics.

To learn more about using Acrobat Reader, choose the Reader Online Guide from the Help menu, or view the Acrobat.pdf file installed in the same folder as the program. You can also get more information by visiting the Adobe Systems Web site at www.adobe.com.

Illustrator 8.0, from Adobe Systems, Inc.

For Mac OS and Windows 95 and 98. Tryout version.

Adobe's advanced vector-drawing program enables you to create complex images with powerful precision. To learn more, check out the Adobe Web site at www.adobe.com.

Photoshop 5.0, from Adobe Systems, Inc.

For Mac OS and Windows 95 and 98. Tryout version.

The most popular and best respected photo manipulation program available, Photoshop is a must-have for any serious graphic designer and a great tool for developing Web graphics. To learn more, check out the Adobe Web site at www.adobe.com.

Web browsers and plug-ins

Internet Explorer, from Microsoft

For Mac and Windows. Commercial product.

Microsoft Internet Explorer 5.0 provides the best support to date for Dynamic HTML and CSS. Use this program to test your work when you take advantage of the most powerful features in Dreamweaver. Keep an eye on the Microsoft Web site at www.microsoft.com. This program is updated frequently!

Communicator, from Netscape

For Mac and Windows. Commercial product.

Communicator 4.7 provides some support for Dynamic HTML and CSS. You should always test your work in this browser, as well as in Internet Explorer, to ensure that your pages look good to viewers using either program. Keep an eye on the Netscape Web site at home.netscape.com. This program is updated frequently!

Dreamweaver behaviors

Behaviors are what Dreamweaver calls scripts that let you add DHMTL features to your Web pages, such as image rollovers and animation features. You'll find many behaviors included with Dreamweaver already, and you can easily add more. The behaviors included on the CD get you started on the path to expanding Dreamweaver's functionality. Visit Macromedia's Web site at www.macromedia.com to find more behaviors to download and install.

Templates

Dreamweaver gives templates high-end functionality, such as the power to automatically update many pages at once if you change the template they were designed with. You can also control what areas of a template can be edited by designers and what areas cannot be changed — a great way to maintain quality control when you are working with a team of developers. You'll find several templates on the CD.

Flash animations

One of the most dynamic elements you can add to a Web page is a Flash animation. But inserting them on a Web page in a way that works effectively on a variety of browsers can be complicated. Dreamweaver includes several features to help you include special code so that your Flash files play well on almost any computer on the Web. You find instructions about how to insert Flash files in Chapter 15, and you get sample Flash files from Juxt Interactive on the CD that you can use as you work through the step-by-step exercises.

Glossary

Don't forget to check out the glossary on the CD. It can be your first resource when you stumble across some Web-design lingo that you're just not sure about.

If You've Got Problems (Of the CD Kind)

I tried my best to compile programs that work on most computers with the minimum system requirements. Alas, your computer may differ, and some programs may not work properly for some reason.

The two likeliest problems are that you don't have enough memory (RAM) for the programs you want to use, or you have other programs running that are affecting installation or running of a program. If you get error messages like Not enough memory or Setup cannot continue, try one or more of these methods and then try using the software again:

- **Turn off any antivirus software that you have on your computer.** Installers sometimes mimic virus activity and may make your computer incorrectly believe that it is being infected by a virus.

- **Close all running programs.** The more programs you're running, the less memory is available to other programs. Installers also typically update files and programs; if you keep other programs running, installation may not work properly.

- **In Windows, close the CD interface and run demos or installations directly from Windows Explorer.** The interface itself can tie up system memory, or even conflict with certain kinds of interactive demos. Use Windows Explorer to browse the files on the CD and launch installers or demos.

- **Have your local computer store add more RAM to your computer.** This is, admittedly, a drastic and somewhat expensive step. However, if you have a Windows 95 PC or a Mac OS computer with a PowerPC chip, adding more memory can really help the speed of your computer and enable more programs to run at the same time.

If you still have trouble installing the items from the CD, please call the Customer Care phone number: 800-762-2974 (outside the U.S.: 317-572-3993).

Index

Uniform Resource Locator
(URL). *See also* Web
sites, addresses listed
ActiveX objects and
controls, 303
associating with name, 12
browser issues, 255, 272
external link, 50–51
image links, 45
image maps, 161
jump menus, 323–324
links, 46
links, global changes, 98–99
links, setting, 46, 83
replacing hash mark (#),
249
table cells, 172
Web site, 33
UNIX
files, renaming, 84, 95
graphics links, breaking, 56
naming links, 83
Update button, 282
updating
alternative pages, 208
comments, removing, 69
documents, template, 112,
117–118
folders, creating, 96
HyperText Markup
Language (HTML), 284
images, 280
multi-version Web sites, 274
new pages, automatic, 33
styles, 21
uploading files, 52

• V •

Vander Veer , Emily A., 302
vector-based graphics
defined, 291
Flash text, 297–298
versions, 14, 25, 128
Vertical Hold, 329
video. *See* multimedia
View menu
described, 26
Tracing Image layout guide,
123
visibility, layers, 221–222,
238–240, 243–244
Visual SourceSafe, 14, 128

visual text editors
Adobe GoLive, 65
Clean Up HTML feature, 68,
70
Clean Up Word HTML
feature, 66, 68
code, viewing and editing,
23–24
cross-platform issues, 36
described, 55–56
HyperText Markup
Language (HTML) design
tools, criticism, 13
HyperText Markup
Language (HTML)
editors, miscellaneous,
66
HyperText Markup
Language (HTML) files,
57–58
importing Web sites, 59–62
Microsoft FrontPage 2000,
63–64
Microsoft Word, 65
NetObjects Fusion, 64
standards, diverging, 58

• W •

Walsh, Aaron E., 300
Web address. *See* Uniform
Resource Locator (URL)
Web Promotion, 142
Web server
access, setting up, 34–36
Common Gateway Interface
(CGI) script, 314
Design Notes, sending, 38,
125
dialing, 20
drag and drop files, 53
sites, importing, 40–41,
60–61
sites, putting online, 52–53
UNIX, 56
Web page location, 32
Web sites
creating, 31–32
defining, 21, 32–34
designing. *See* design
formatting, 43
forms, 309–317, 319,
321–325

headlines, 41
importing, 36, 39–40, 59–60
interactivity, 233, 235,
237–249, 251–257, 259,
26–264, 266–267, 269–274
managing, 37–38
multimedia, 287–307
navigation, 111
pages. *See* pages
putting online, 52–53
server, sending to, 41
style, consistent. *See*
Cascading Style Sheets
(CSS)
Web sites, addresses listed
BMW Brazil, 109
browser previews, 88
CDNOW, 109
clip art, 142
CyberSlacker, 287
design resources, 351–356
Dreamweaver Exchange,
248, 256
Dynamic HTML examples,
235
Dynamic HTML site,
Macromedia, 270
examples, 329–335, 337
File Transfer Protocol (FTP)
shareware, 53
fonts, 346
Fort Mason, 108
frames, good use, 190
image-editing programs,
144, 146
Microsoft, 128
Organic Online, 109
plug-ins, 289
PNG home page, 279
Say It Better, 156
Washington Post, 108
White House, 109
Web TV, 88
WebDAV, 14, 128
Weblint, 355
WebMonkey (HotWired), 355
Weinman, Lynda, 190, 354
white space, 340
Window menu. *See also*
Property Inspector
Behaviors, 268
described, 29
font attributes, applying,
136–137

Wiley Publishing, Inc.
End-User License Agreement

READ THIS. You should carefully read these terms and conditions before opening the software packet(s) included with this book "Book". This is a license agreement "Agreement" between you and Wiley Publishing, Inc. "WPI". By opening the accompanying software packet(s), you acknowledge that you have read and accept the following terms and conditions. If you do not agree and do not want to be bound by such terms and conditions, promptly return the Book and the unopened software packet(s) to the place you obtained them for a full refund.

1. **License Grant.** WPI grants to you (either an individual or entity) a nonexclusive license to use one copy of the enclosed software program(s) (collectively, the "Software" solely for your own personal or business purposes on a single computer (whether a standard computer or a workstation component of a multi-user network). The Software is in use on a computer when it is loaded into temporary memory (RAM) or installed into permanent memory (hard disk, CD-ROM, or other storage device). WPI reserves all rights not expressly granted herein.

2. **Ownership.** WPI is the owner of all right, title, and interest, including copyright, in and to the compilation of the Software recorded on the disk(s) or CD-ROM "Software Media". Copyright to the individual programs recorded on the Software Media is owned by the author or other authorized copyright owner of each program. Ownership of the Software and all proprietary rights relating thereto remain with WPI and its licensers.

3. **Restrictions On Use and Transfer.**

   (a) You may only (i) make one copy of the Software for backup or archival purposes, or (ii) transfer the Software to a single hard disk, provided that you keep the original for backup or archival purposes. You may not (i) rent or lease the Software, (ii) copy or reproduce the Software through a LAN or other network system or through any computer subscriber system or bulletin- board system, or (iii) modify, adapt, or create derivative works based on the Software.

   (b) You may not reverse engineer, decompile, or disassemble the Software. You may transfer the Software and user documentation on a permanent basis, provided that the transferee agrees to accept the terms and conditions of this Agreement and you retain no copies. If the Software is an update or has been updated, any transfer must include the most recent update and all prior versions.

4. **Restrictions on Use of Individual Programs.** You must follow the individual requirements and restrictions detailed for each individual program in the About the CD Appendix of this Book. These limitations are also contained in the individual license agreements recorded on the Software Media. These limitations may include a requirement that after using the program for a specified period of time, the user must pay a registration fee or discontinue use. By opening the Software packet(s), you will be agreeing to abide by the licenses and restrictions for these individual programs that are detailed in the About the CD Appendix and on the Software Media. None of the material on this Software Media or listed in this Book may ever be redistributed, in original or modified form, for commercial purposes.

5. **Limited Warranty.**

   (a) WPI warrants that the Software and Software Media are free from defects in materials and workmanship under normal use for a period of sixty (60) days from the date of purchase of this Book. If WPI receives notification within the warranty period of defects in materials or workmanship, WPI will replace the defective Software Media.

   (b) WPI AND THE AUTHOR OF THE BOOK DISCLAIM ALL OTHER WARRANTIES, EXPRESS OR IMPLIED, INCLUDING WITHOUT LIMITATION IMPLIED WARRANTIES OF MERCHANTABILITY AND FITNESS FOR A PARTICULAR PURPOSE, WITH RESPECT TO THE SOFTWARE, THE PROGRAMS, THE SOURCE CODE CONTAINED THEREIN, AND/OR THE TECHNIQUES DESCRIBED IN THIS BOOK. WPI DOES NOT WARRANT THAT THE FUNCTIONS CONTAINED IN THE SOFTWARE WILL MEET YOUR REQUIREMENTS OR THAT THE OPERATION OF THE SOFTWARE WILL BE ERROR FREE.

   (c) This limited warranty gives you specific legal rights, and you may have other rights that vary from jurisdiction to jurisdiction.

6. **Remedies.**

   (a) WPI's entire liability and your exclusive remedy for defects in materials and workmanship shall be limited to replacement of the Software Media, which may be returned to WPI with a copy of your receipt at the following address: Software Media Fulfillment Department, Attn.: *Dreamweaver 4 For Dummies,* Wiley Publishing, Inc., 10475 Crosspoint Blvd., Indianapolis, IN 46256, or call 1-800-762-2974. Please allow four to six weeks for delivery. This Limited Warranty is void if failure of the Software Media has resulted from accident, abuse, or misapplication. Any replacement Software Media will be warranted for the remainder of the original warranty period or thirty (30) days, whichever is longer.

   (b) In no event shall WPI or the author be liable for any damages whatsoever (including without limitation damages for loss of business profits, business interruption, loss of business information, or any other pecuniary loss) arising from the use of or inability to use the Book or the Software, even if WPI has been advised of the possibility of such damages.

   (c) Because some jurisdictions do not allow the exclusion or limitation of liability for consequential or incidental damages, the above limitation or exclusion may not apply to you.

7. **U.S. Government Restricted Rights.** Use, duplication, or disclosure of the Software for or on behalf of the United States of America, its agencies and/or instrumentalities "U.S. Government" is subject to restrictions as stated in paragraph (c)(1)(ii) of the Rights in Technical Data and Computer Software clause of DFARS 252.227-7013, or subparagraphs (c)(1) and (2) of the Commercial Computer Software - Restricted Rights clause at FAR 52.227-19, and in similar clauses in the NASA FAR supplement, as applicable.

8. **General.** This Agreement constitutes the entire understanding of the parties and revokes and supersedes all prior agreements, oral or written, between them and may not be modified or amended except in a writing signed by both parties hereto that specifically refers to this Agreement. This Agreement shall take precedence over any other documents that may be in conflict herewith. If any one or more provisions contained in this Agreement are held by any court or tribunal to be invalid, illegal, or otherwise unenforceable, each and every other provision shall remain in full force and effect.

Notes

Notes

Notes